EVERYONE WANTS TO BE IN THE KITCHEN.

HouseBeautiful

KITCHENS

HouseBeautiful

KITCHENS

Creating a Beautiful Kitchen of Your Own

LISA CREGAN

HEARST
books

contents

6 **INTRODUCTION**

8 **PART I: BRAVURA**

Kitchens that start with a bold vision then follow through with flair.

10 **CHAPTER 1:** Rough Luxe

The burnished, the reclaimed, and the industrial—living in peaceable harmony with the luxurious.

36 **BREAK-OUT SESSION:** Kitchen Planner

42 **OBJECT LESSON:** Chill

48 **CHAPTER 2:** Haute So Functional

Perfectly dressed kitchens that deserve a front-row seat at Fashion Week.

78 **BREAK-OUT SESSION:** A Color Consult

84 **OBJECT LESSON:** Heat

90 **CHAPTER 3:** Rebel

The unkitchen. Hidden behind cabinetry or merged into the living room, it's hard to tell you're even in the kitchen.

112 **OBJECT LESSON:** H_2O

120 **PART II: COMPOSED**

Kitchens that have balance, rhythm, and the elegance of subtle sophistication.

122 **CHAPTER 4:** Addicted to Alabaster

The all-white kitchen is an all-American classic.

148 **BREAK-OUT SESSION:** Going Green

154 **OBJECT LESSON:** Tread

160 **CHAPTER 5:** Plain Spoken

Everyday ephemera is tucked behind closed doors. All that shows is great style.

182 **OBJECT LESSON:** Splash

188 **CHAPTER 6:** Shopkeeper

Open shelves styled right down to the gravy boat. A place for everything and everything in its place.

218 **OBJECT LESSON:** Store Your Stuff

224 **PART III: REVIVAL**

Rooted in history, these kitchens hearken back to our culinary past while leaving room for innovations to come.

226 **CHAPTER 7:** Belle de Campagne

Pried from a luxurious chateau de la Loire? Shipped from a crumbling cottage in Calais? Look closer.

250 **BREAK-OUT SESSION:** Kitchen Islands

256 **OBJECT LESSON:** Chop & Roll

262 **CHAPTER 8:** New Victorian

Old-fashioned and unabashedly romantic, kitchens that recall the regal sensibility of an elegant age gone by.

286 **OBJECT LESSON:** Glow

292 **CHAPTER 9:** Scullery

Form follows function with echoes of the back-of-the-house practicality of an old-world service kitchen.

312 **OBJECT LESSON:** Take a Seat

318 **PHOTOGRAPHY CREDITS**

322 **GENERAL INDEX**

334 **INDEX OF DESIGNERS AND ARCHITECTS**

"Everyone always wants to be in the kitchen. In my next house, I'm just going to have a kitchen, a bath, and a bedroom. That's all you need."

—JONATHAN KING, CO-FOUNDER OF STONEWALL KITCHEN

Los Angeles designer Chris Barrett found the tall 1860s Czech table with beautifully turned legs, at J.F. Chen. It works perfectly in a space that was "too small for a dining table and too big to have nothing," Barrett says. The table serves as both breakfast island and buffet for dining on the terrace outside the French doors.

INTRODUCTION

We've come a long way since avocado. Liberated from old-fashioned orthodoxies like color-coordinated appliances and the sacred single work triangle, designers and homeowners today are thinking about kitchens in new and exciting ways.

As a result, the kitchens we've published in recent issues of *House Beautiful* have been nothing less than stunning. Architects and designers are pairing cutting-edge technology with a global array of materials to create kitchens custom-fitted to their clients' lives and decorating styles. Now we're able to bring them all together in one place—*Kitchens*.

From an almost invisible kitchen tucked into a contemporary dining room, to another with its traditional cabinetry stained silver and edged in shining steel, to a kitchen with a gleaming white island made entirely from crystallized glass, the range of stylish ideas has never been more inspiring.

In addition to page after page of original style, this book also offers the best advice on finding the right stove, refrigerator, flooring, lighting, even counter stools—all the things you'll need to pull together the kitchen of your dreams.

Thanks to the *House Beautiful* writers and editors who month after month knit together the lively designer and homeowner interviews featured in the magazine and excerpted here. And a special thanks to Senior Editor Samantha Emmerling, who scours the country to find the culinary confections published in each issue as our Kitchen of the Month.

Within these pages you'll find beauty, function, fun, and an explosion of creativity. Hard and fast rules? They're few and far between these days. Use our experts' advice as guidelines for making your kitchen your kitchen.

Newell Turner
Editor in Chief

bravura

*Kitchens that start with a bold vision
then follow through with flair.*

rough luxe

THE BURNISHED, THE RECLAIMED, AND THE INDUSTRIAL—LIVING IN PEACEABLE HARMONY WITH THE LUXURIOUS.

RAW INGREDIENTS

HILLARY HAYNE,
designer

Salvaged wood, lace curtains, and a farmhouse sink could easily be the makings for a treacly Cotswolds-cottage wannabe. Instead, this talented husband and wife team took those same time-tested materials and assembled them into a 21st-century dazzler.

THE BACKSTORY | "This is an authentic 1920s Mediterranean house that used to have an unfortunate 1990s kitchen. Too much polished granite for me. We hauled it all out and started over again. My husband, Robbin, is an architect, and I'm an interior designer, and we wanted to add a little romance to suit the setting. It's in Topanga Canyon. Topanga Canyon may be minutes from L.A. but it's another world—very bohemian, natural, Neil Young 1970s."

"Even when we're inside at the table, it still seems as if we're out in the garden because of all the windows. It feels like we're dining in a treehouse."

Hillary Hayne and her husband, architect Robbin Hayne, designed this modern dining table, made of 12' walnut planks, and surrounded it with midcentury chrome chairs upholstered in Brazilian cowhide for modern contrast. Unmatched vintage pendant lights and a long, reclaimed-wood china cabinet on the left—with chicken-wire doors—lend Bohemian appeal.

Retro cool meets high tech when a self-cleaning, stainless steel Kuppersbusch coffee machine is built into a reclaimed wood cabinet.

These cabinets are gorgeous!

I wanted something old and battered. Barnwood? Been there, done that. Then Tony Farmer, my cabinetmaker, said he had a source out east for wood from a tobacco shed. This is solid tobacco shed wood. Not veneers. I wanted it to be substantial, original, old—yet contemporary for today without being expected.

Are the floors reclaimed wood too?

They're actually hand-distressed walnut with a custom stain. I always like a dark floor to ground a room. It has a semigloss finish for contrast against the duller finish of the tobacco wood.

Why mismatched pendant lights?

The two that look alike are old Pasadena streetlights. Then the third light is an antique GE ship's light. I had vintage rusty heavy chains attached to all three. Most people would have put the ship's light in the center, right? I didn't because the table is 12' and we eat there every day—we sit by the windows and I use the part of the table under the ship's light for serving—so that ship's light kind of delineates the end of the table for a different purpose.

No island. How come?

I'm bored with them. I don't like a prep sink in an island, and what irks me even more is a stove top in the island. It's just not pretty. Besides, I have enough counter space and a multifunctional 12' dining table.

Tell me about this pretty lace window treatment.
I knew I couldn't get lavish there even though I love window treatments. The rod and the piece of lace were actually found on eBay. I love the rod's finials and the medallion in the middle and the way the black color picks up the black in the cowhide on the chairs.

What did you choose for the countertops?
Antique limestone from France. We were told it came out of the same quarry used to construct the Louvre, and this was the last bit left. It's natural and honest, not flashy, with subtle tones of taupe and gold and gray. Honed, not polished, and sealed with 511 Impregnator from Miracle Sealants. I don't see any stains, and I use lots of red wine and olive oil and balsamic vinegar. This is a working kitchen. We have four kids.

No wonder you need that extra-long sink.
It's a Shaws Original fireclay sink, and they've been making them by hand in the same English factory since 1897. This one is 36" long, 18" wide, and 10" deep, so you can soak big pots overnight. Just one large basin without any compartments. You don't need them, and I don't want to look at all those drains. This is pure and simple, with a clean apron front. It's the classic farmhouse sink, under the window. I have a smaller prep sink by the refrigerator.

PURE COUNTRY
The 36" farmhouse sink, made in England, available through Rohl, is the perfect glossy partner with distressed wood. The sink is flanked by two dishwasher drawers and a trash compacter—all from KitchenAid's Architect Series II—and the window has a view over the patio to a creek and a large sycamore tree.

WHAT IF...
YOU STORED YOUR FINE CHINA
BEHIND HUMBLE CHICKEN WIRE?

"I love the way the chicken wire looks against the tobacco wood and the shine of china and glass. This is a collection of candlesticks, crystal, and porcelain—it's hundreds of pieces in a cabinet that runs the length of an entire wall. I used glass shelves instead of wood so the stacks look like they're floating. And there are recessed lights in the top of the cabinet so in the evening when the light shines through the glass, it illuminates every single thing in such a pretty way."

MIRROR MIRROR

"Many years ago I bought this fabulous antique mirror, and it cracked. So I went to a mirror maker, Ginette Lemonnier, and she was able to reproduce it. Not quite the same, but pretty close. When I was thinking about the upper cabinets in this kitchen, I knew I didn't want to overuse the wood. Too heavy. Frosted glass? Too contemporary. And then I thought of the mirror and went back to Ginette, who made more for me in these lovely sepia tones. It glows in the light and adds a hint of glamour. I was trying to get away from the typical glass uppers."

CRAVING...
BOULDERS AS BACKSPLASH

"I am so bored with tile backsplashes! I think they are only meant for bathrooms. I liked the color and the scale of the sandstone so much that I decided I wanted to use it all the way up the wall, but was afraid it would be too thick and heavy. My mason, Izzy Martin, made it work."

Stone walls enhance the mood. They look rough, organic, ancient.

"I had this romantic vision of a stone nook with a range inside, and my husband, Robbin, helped me achieve it. We found this hard sandstone, quarried in Montana, that's normally used for exterior walls or fireplace cladding and we wrapped it around the stove. I need a lot of burners and two ovens because there's a rotating group of relatives living here all the time. I serve a lot of food.

Is the backsplash behind the shelf made of different stone?

Yes, it's stacked stone. I scavenged the property and saw that we had some leftover stone from another area we were renovating. I realized that little slivers of stone, one on top of each other, would be perfect there.

" When I call everyone into the kitchen for dinner they just grab a plate off the table and line up at the range. Meals are always easy and casual. It's always self-service —even at dinner parties! Opposite the stove is a long counter that I set up as a buffet for salads and sides. The system actually works really well, people mingle while they're in line!"

ROCK ON

A **V**iking 48" commercial-depth range—with six burners, two ovens, and a griddle/simmer plate—stands inside a niche made of **Castle Rock** hard sandstone. The stove is around a corner from the kitchen table in this **L** shaped kitchen, and the refrigerator is at the end of an aisle to the left of the range.

COLOR FORMS
NATURAL PLASTER BLENDS WELL WITH STONE AND WOOD.

" We sheathed the walls and the ceiling in natural plaster. The color of plaster is neutral and not too white, which is perfect when you want things to blend, not stand out. I don't ever use bright white. And these walls feel very nice and soft against the stone and the trim on the windows, which is painted a custom blend that I made with my painter— a taupe-y gray."

STALKING THE LOOK

1   2

3   4

5   6

Ditch the chandelier. (1) Find some mismatched vintage pendants to hang over your dining table. No time to scavenge junk shops? Get the look by floating a trio of these ethereal mercury glass pendants by Jamie Young Company over your table.

Feather your nest with chicken wire. (2) Fowl play! A woven wire china cabinet grille by Outwater Plastics Industries— in finishes from brass to pewter—is the ultimate rustic-chic.

Look far and wide for the prettiest battered old wood you can find and transform it into one-of-a-kind cabinets. Hayne's cabinet-maker found the source for the tobacco-shed wood she used here, but an online search might work just as well for you.

Use antiqued mirror on your cabinet fronts instead of glass. (3) The cabinets' mirrored panels look antique but are new, made by Glass Queen in L.A.

Start a collection of colorful plates, pitchers and teapots. (4) Start with Quimper Fleuri Royal through Pierre Deux.

Play fast and loose with your cabinet pulls. Hayne used a mad mix of mismatched pulls and knobs that look like flea market finds—but are actually all from Emtek Hardware in Silver Patina finish.

Install dishwasher drawers close by your table to encourage self-cleanup.

Find offbeat accessories that somehow look both ancient and modern. (5) The wobbly profile of this cast-resin Pedestal Bowl from Tina Frey Designs feels old but somehow new, too.

Banish tile. (6) Hayne used Castle Rock hard sandstone as a backsplash and took it all the way up to the ceiling for maximum impact.

DIFFERENT STROKES

ROBERT BAKES, *kitchen designer,*
and **ALEXANDRA FAZIO,** *architect*

This kitchen designer and architect team broke the culinary typecast of sleek and white with materials and methods they'd never tried before (in fact, never even seen before!)—mottled backsplashes and wood grains running in all directions resulted in a completely original kitchen that's at once mysterious, unexpected . . . and gorgeous.

THE BACKSTORY | "This is a new waterfront house in Sag Harbor owned by four brothers and their spouses. The brothers live all over the country and range in age from their mid-20s to mid-30s. Their grandparents originally owned the property and their parents live three doors down. They wanted a kitchen intimate enough for two but big enough for parties and entertaining, and they wanted it all open and casual. It's very much a family vacation spot and everyone was really engaged in the design process." —AF

Rich walnut cabinets by Robert Bakes of Bakes & Company and a 16'6" island that seats eight lend a warm, inviting atmosphere to this kitchen in a modern house designed by architect Alexandra Fazio of Cecil Baker + Partners. The backsplash is hand-troweled plaster, made to look like an old concrete wall. The white Luce di Luna marble section of the island is relief from all the dark wood. Inconspicuous drawer pulls are by Doug Mockett & Co.

"This is a very American kitchen, easy on the eye because it's not super-contemporary. All the dark wood grain is about melding some traditional style seamlessly into a house with cutting edge contemporary design." —RB

"On upper cabinets the door itself is essentially the handle. The doors are longer than the inner cabinets so you pull them open from the bottom. But the lower cabinets are more like a piece of furniture and required some hardware so we used very inconspicuous pulls." —AF

Talk about woods that are lovely, dark and deep!
RB: The cabinets are walnut, my favorite species. It's got the most beautiful grain and texture. This is actually a look I hadn't tried before. We decided we'd try running the grain in different directions.

Vertical on the top cabinets and horizontal below. It's so cool.
RB: I think it elevates this kitchen from special to extraordinary because the grains add so much interest. This house is directly on the water. A+ premium land, 30' above sea level, and you can walk out the door directly down to the beach. The dark walnut softens the impact of all the bright sunshine bouncing in off the water. If we'd put this kitchen in a dark location it would have been too dark, but this room has two huge walls of windows.

You were working for four brothers! Where did the back and forth with them lead you?
AF: The island for sure. One brother wanted it centered and furniture-like, maybe an antique or a butcher block. But the oldest brother chimed in that he wanted to see the water from wherever he was sitting at the island. So we came up with the idea of doing an *L* shape, with one long extension perpendicular to the view that looks like a marble table, and another for food prep that looks like a piece of furniture. The marble-topped counter is for casual family dining or grabbing a quick breakfast. It's huge; it easily seats six to eight people.

This is an ode to the beauty of walnut!

RB: What I can do with walnut these days would blow you away. Rift and quartered, burled, lacquered to a mirror finish.

And what treatment did you choose for the walnut here?

AF: A soft, organic, flat finish. We applied a hand-rubbed ebony stain onto the raw, unconditioned wood. That heightened the drama of all the texture. Most kitchen designers use spray-stained, preconditioned wood, and that creates a uniform, shiny effect. If we'd done that, the cabinets would have had no life.

What variety is the lighter wood that's on the island?

AF: That's also walnut, but it's unstained, treated with food oil. I wanted to create a contrast for the work surface. It looks like it's more sappy than the cabinet wood, and when there's more sap, there are more color variations. I like the way the dark cabinets look sandwiched between the lighter woods. It makes me think of a boat deck.

I love these concrete walls and backsplashes!

AF: That's actually not concrete. Poured-concrete walls get complicated and expensive. So we got an artist to mimic the texture in plaster. We could have used tile or stainless but this is so new and fresh! It has a wax finish that repels moisture.

WOOD YOU DARE?

The kitchen is a dynamic blend of rustic and industrial. Light elm floors serve as a catalyst for drama against dark wood cabinets. The Viking range, Sub-Zero refrigerator, pendant lights from Hudson Valley Lighting, and faucets from Hansgrohe are strong shots of metallic shine. On the island, the marble countertop extends from the dining portion of the L shape island, right over the walnut counter, serving as a cold surface for rolling out dough in the prep area.

WHAT IF . . .
YOUR BACKSPLASH LOOKED LIKE A WEATHERED OLD CONCRETE WALL?

. . . .

"One of the clippings the brothers showed us for inspiration was a photo of an old exterior concrete wall in Eastern Europe. We thought it was great because a house can't be all glass and white walls. We showed the photograph to an artist and said 'can you mimic this texture?' He nailed it. It's not a rough surface. If you brush against it with bare skin it's still soft but it has enough grit to play with the light beautifully." —AF

INSIDE INTEREST
DRAWERS IN THE BASE CABINETS OF THE ISLAND, FITTED TO HOLD CONDIMENTS AND VINEGARS, ARE MADE OF 100% SOLID WALNUT.

. . . .

"The solid walnut interiors are extraordinary, it's just so luxurious to pull open a drawer." —AF

CRAVING . . .
A VIEW OF SEA, SKY, TALL TALL MASTS, AND MAYBE A FEW AFTER DINNER STARS.

. . . .

"The indoor/outdoor aspect of this kitchen is why we wanted to use wood—a material that's organic, not manufactured—natural beauty outside and natural beauty inside—that's what this is about. We wanted to work with the unbelievable view—a shiny white kitchen would have grabbed too much attention." —RB

Wow. Looks like the kitchen got first call on the views!

AF: This house is all about its proximity to the water. The clients wanted the kitchen front and center, open and casual. This kitchen table is the main entertaining area. It's open to the living room where you get a great view of the garden on one side and water on the other because there's glass on both ends.

With so much glass, how did you keep it energy efficient?

AF: The vast majority of glass is positioned to the north and west. We tried to minimize the exposure from the south—because that's the direction that gets strong sun all day. This is a house that's primarily used in the summer and we made sure it wouldn't get too hot inside even with all the walls of aluminum and glass.

"This kitchen isn't huge; it doesn't overwhelm the room. We didn't need to fill the room with kitchen to have it be the heart of the home. The functionality and look draws you in, those things are much more important than the size. And the brothers were willing to take risks in this smallish space. It makes this kitchen exciting." —AF

The kitchen and dining area are one big open space with forever views of Noyack Bay. Emenco 111 Navy Chairs from Design Within Reach provide industrial punch while a farmhouse table from Restoration Hardware lends organic charm. Bakes and Fazio couldn't get enough of the hand-troweled plaster on the backsplashes so they extended it onto a wall that leads into the entry atrium.

COLOR FORMS
FAZIO KEPT THE MOOD MODERN WITH BENJAMIN MOORE ATRIUM WHITE

"I think this white has a certain modernity to it. We did the walls in a matte finish, like an eggshell, so it's not too shiny. And the smooth white walls look so beautiful when seen alongside the hand-troweled gray plaster walls—which were colored to match Benjamin Moore River Reflections."

STALKING THE LOOK

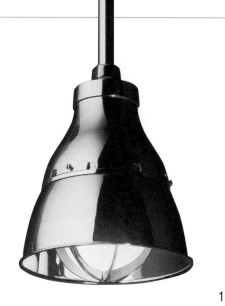

1

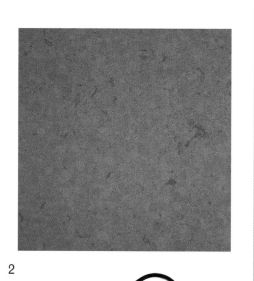

2

3

5

6

4

Don't be afraid of the dark. Bakes's dark stained walnut cabinets don't overwhelm because of the softening effect of the hand-rubbed ebony stain he used—applied directly to raw walnut.

Throw in some bright spots. (1) Lend some shine to a dark wood kitchen with the Studio Pendant Light from Urban Archeology.

Create backsplashes with concrete appeal. (2) CaesarStone in Pebble has an intriguing mottled appearance—like concrete.

Look for wood serving pieces that show off some grain. (3) This Spalted Maple Bowl from Peterman Baskets & Bowls is especially intriguing because it's crafted from one solid piece of reclaimed maple.

Lighten up. The contrast of light against dark—a pale walnut countertop on the prep island, a white marble counter on the dining section of the island and light elm floors against dark cabinets—increases the drama.

While you're at it—why not sheath the inside of your cabinets in walnut too? (4) Bakes gave the interiors of these cabinets as much attention as the exteriors, creating a sumptuous backdrop for Riedel wineglasses.

Use lanterns in place of a centerpiece. (5) The Albany Lantern from Arteriors Home adds sparkle and glow to a room.

Sink your sinks deep into the countertops so they don't distract from the sleek modernity of the cabinets.

Choose an elegant arched faucet to balance out your kitchen's straight lines. (6) Hansgrohe Interaktiv S High Arc/2 Spray Pull-out Faucet has it all: Beauty and a lifting body, so you can easily access and clean around the base and countertop.

OLD NEWS

ELEANOR CUMMINGS,
designer

Can this kitchen really be new? Ancient timbers, knotty wood cabinets, antique stone, and burnished zinc are just some of the ways Cummings made this new Houston kitchen look like a centuries-old farmhouse tucked into the Tuscan hills.

TOP: Cummings suspended an Italian window grille from iron bars and turned it into a hanging pot rack. "But when we put the pots on it, it seemed gimmicky," she says. "So we've kept it as kind of an art installation." Barstools with rush back and seats pull up to a counter made of reclaimed stone and a Viking range is tucked into an alcove sheathed in antique tile. The hanging lights look old but were actually found at Brown in Houston. "The aesthetic is rustic Italian but it's a brand-new house—just about everything in here—the wood, the stone, the furniture—is old, old, old."

BOTTOM: In the bar area, an antler chandelier and terra cotta wine racks mix with reclaimed wood cabinets that match kitchen cabinets. Simple glassware is displayed on open wood shelves. "Old wood has a patina and character that new woods will never have. The wormholes, the fading, the water damage, all give it a beauty that can't be re-created with new wood, no matter how hard you try. And I have. That sense of history and mystery—where it's been, how it was used, who walked on the floors—is really intriguing to me."

"The coolest things in this kitchen are the zinc-clad refrigerators. An incredible craftsman named James Dawson figured out how to wrap the doors so they would shut. Every time I go in there I think, 'These are the most beautiful things I've ever seen.'"

"Zinc is porous, like marble. It stains. The first night out my client got lemon on the countertops. It was inevitable. But she said, 'You know, I kind of like the way that looks.' And it does look really good. It doesn't look precious. It has patina, like all the old wood in this house."

"The walls and most of the ceilings are plaster, which has such a wonderful luminosity. We gave it what's called a diamond finish, meaning it has movement. It goes from being totally flat to having a glassy sheen, depending on the light. You can't get that with Sheetrock and paint."

ITALIAN TRIP

The warm tones of reclaimed wood and stone give this kitchen a friendly rural Italian feel. "We have a great resource here in Houston, Chateau Domingue, a huge warehouse and gardens full of reclaimed architectural materials," says Cummings. "We couldn't have done this otherwise." Cabinets are made of reclaimed poplar. "The poplar cabinets have the most lustrous chamois color, and great grain." To help sync the Viking refrigerators, the counters, and the backsplashes with all the rustic elements, Cummings had them all covered with zinc.

GARDEN PARTY

SANDY KOEPKE,
designer

The whole point of having an outdoor kitchen is to sit back, relax, and enjoy the outdoors. So to keep things worry-free, Koepke chose furniture on which nature had already done her inimitable worst. In Koepke's stylish hands, nicked, rusted, and weathered equals beautiful.

THE BACKSTORY | "This is in Manhattan Beach, California, and my clients are a young couple with a preteen daughter. When I first saw their yard it was all precast concrete, very generic and faux formal. Not 'them' at all. They love to travel to all sorts of exotic warm-weather places. So this whole thing is inspired by a town square in Mexico or Morocco, lushly planted, faded by the sun, and slightly offbeat."

"The L shape of the counters creates a bar at one end. We put some barstools there and that's the view from the kitchen, so you don't see all the metal from the inside of the house."

"Look at that old candy-store counter I found which works as an island or a bar or a place to sit and eat. It's got an iron base with a honed marble top that's very similar to the basalt we used on the countertops, so it pulls it all together."

Stainless-steel appliances and cabinetry, all from **Kalamazoo Outdoor Gourmet**, put a gleaming modern spin on sun-faded walls and crusty, weathered antique furniture from **Lucca Antiques**. From left: Beverage center, refrigerator, keg tapper, sink base, ice maker, cooktop cabinet, and **K900HT** grill make this a full-service culinary destination. **Native Trails** copper sink, a **Graff Bali Series** faucet and **Sea Ranch Sconces by Coe Studios** lend the kitchen instant age.

"I picked stainless steel because this is the beach after all. There's salt in the air, and these cabinets would sit in the sun and decay if they were in any other material. Plus with all this sleekness I could add all the rustic I wanted; it's a nice counterpoint."

This outdoor kitchen looks as if it's a part of the landscape. What's your secret?
The uneven, sun-baked-looking concrete wall we created makes this garden feel like it's been here forever. But I think the look of age always makes things easier on the eye. I like things decayed a little and I like things that weather beautifully—like this copper sink that looks better now than the day we installed it.

Contrast isn't the only thing that would play well here. Is that a beer tap?
Yes, that's the keg tapper from Kalamazoo Outdoor Gourmet. We went the whole route with Kalamazoo, not just for the appliances but also for the cabinetry, which is stainless steel inside and out. The outdoor kitchen has changed the way this family lives in their house. The doors to the patio are open all the time.

What did you use for the countertops?
Basalt. It's a stone that looks a little like lava stone—gray and black and soft. Tile or polished granite would have felt too pristine. We fabricated it to look like a big, thick slab. In reality it's only ⅝" thick, with a 3½" apron.

How does basalt hold up?
Well, you're outdoors, so everything will fade, rust, and get dirty. An outdoor kitchen is not for the fainthearted. I have this discussion with clients ahead of time. "Yes, the countertop is going to stain. Yes, the wall is going to get smoky from the grill and we're *not* going to repaint it. Relax. You're outside."

This dining area is so romantic! What do you do to light it up at night?
We wrapped the trellis arches in Christmas lights and since the chandelier is actually just an old pot hanger from a nursery, we dropped some big glass ice buckets into some of the empty rings and filled them with candles—they're like oversized votives! Then if you look closely you can see that we also welded some smaller votive holders onto the wire mesh screen at the back of the space. Parties here are magical.

What is the patio paved with? It's also got that soft, weathered look.
No fancy tile, no expensive pavers, just poured concrete. We used an aggregate mix and then powerwashed it before it set to bring out that texture. We were out there in rubber boots, flooding the patio with water, and then we flung on some Dark Walnut and Fern Green and Antique Amber acid stains from Scofield to give it that aged patina. You can't control it, so how it turns out is kind of a surprise. I also found a lot of really cool old pots and containers and filled them with succulents, intentionally overplanted, so they'd have to fight it out and fall over the side. Come back in a year when the trellis is grown out—we planted it with two different colors of bougainvillea and trumpet vine. Mother Nature will take over.

PARADISE FOUND
In order to conform to the landscape, this dining area is elevated (up six steps) from the cooking and prep area. The reclaimed old railing on the left overlooks a spa with a hot tub behind the fireplace. The two-tiered iron pot holder from Zelen Home, hanging from the iron trellis, and a zinc-topped table and chairs from Big Daddy's Antiques are elegantly aged. The vintage iron mesh screen that anchors the back of the space was found at Berbere World Imports.

WHAT IF . . .

YOUR OUTDOOR FURNITURE LOOKED LIKE SOMETHING UNEARTHED AT POMPEII?

"I really love rust and I really love old chipped paint. I used a lot of salvaged materials because it's an instant way of giving a new project some age and maturity. It can scare a client in the beginning when they see all this rusty railing showing up on the job site, but vintage pieces add character and marry the new and the natural."

WATER MUSIC
A FOUNTAIN WALL TO THE RIGHT OF THE STAINLESS-STEEL CABINETRY HIDES STEPS UP TO THE DINING AREA. IT WAS MADE FROM AN ANTIQUE FRENCH LAVABO AND AN OLD HAND-CARVED HORSE TROUGH.

"There are two huge antique spigots, one in the lavabo and one in the wall, both the size of a boot. And they're both fountains. When you turn on the one in the lavabo the water runs over the sides of the basin in rivulets into the trough and makes a pretty tinkling sound. And there's a light in the trough so at night when the light shines up through the rippling water it looks incredibly soft and pretty."

CRAVING . . .
KALAMAZOO OUTDOOR GOURMET'S K900HT, BECAUSE IT'S GOT IT ALL.

"This grill is really neat because you can cook with gas or wood or charcoal and it has a real cooktop too so you can cook anything. My client started out with a little portable grill and now he's got this Rolls-Royce."

What is the most important advice you can give someone who's doing an outdoor kitchen?
You have to acknowledge that you're going to be parking all this stainless steel in the backyard, and consider not only how it looks out there, but also how it will look from the house. We placed the long run of appliances where you don't see them head-on from the house. Instead, from the family room you face that beautiful outdoor fireplace. The smartest thing we did was to take off the whole back of the house and replace it with glass doors. Now, as soon as you walk in the front door, you see this great outdoor room, which makes the house feel so much larger. We also raised the patio to the same level as the floor, so the connection is seamless. French drains—basically a trench filled with gravel—keep the rainwater from lapping at the doors.
What a pretty fireplace!
On the top of the chimney we used an old grain bin with its bottom cut out. We needed more height there but we didn't want the fireplace to seem so massive. The bin is a great solution. The shell wreath, by Marjorie Stafford, is perfect for the beach. It pops against the fireplace, plus I think those twigs look a little like rust. And you know I love rust!

HOT SEATS
Chairs from **Casamidy** covered in **Donghia's Tamal** provide an exotic touch in the lounge area of this outdoor kitchen. The banquette on the right offers a comfortable perch and holds more people than two chairs would in the equivalent space. Koepke found an old curtain rod and hung a cushion from it—covered in Sombrero Stripe in Merengue Maroon by Donghia—for softness. The cushion's stripes feature all the colors of the pillows made of old and new fabrics from Mexico, India, and Guatemala. Behind the fireplace is a spa with a hot tub.

COLOR FORMS
KOEPKE EVOKES THE SUN-SCARRED WALLS OF MEXICO WITH DAVIS COLORS FOR CONCRETE IN PALOMINO 5447

" The walls aren't painted, there's color mixed into the concrete. This method gives the walls a wonderful unevenness and it looks hand done. I hate faux finishes where someone comes with a rag and a sponge and tries to create age. This is the real deal. The way it's done in Mexico. And the ochre color is so vibrant, it reflects light back into the house and draws you outside because it feels so warm and soft."

STALKING THE LOOK

1 2

3

4

5

6

7

Steel yourself. The stainless-steel cabinets and appliances Koepke chose are impervious to the elements.

Create a window in your outdoor wall. (1) Koepke used a semi-see-through, wood-framed iron grate from India over the sink, to break up the monolithic look of the wall and lend a feeling of expansiveness.

Look for a grill that does more than just grill. (2) Grill, smoker, cooktop, prep space, storage—Viking's C4 Outdoor Cooker on cart with side burners has many practical and innovative features for outdoor cooks.

Make an island that doubles as a table so everyone can gather around the grill master. (3) Perfect for potting plants or serving a pitcher of margaritas, this wrought-iron, zinc-topped Ornamented Utility Console from Wisteria can go inside or out.

Light your fire. Koepke planned this outdoor kitchen so the view from the family room is a cozy fireplace seating arrangement rather than a wall of stainless-steel appliances.

Go for a copper sink because it'll only get better as it weathers. (4) This is a sink you could build your whole outdoor kitchen around. The Bucket Sink from Linkasink is made of hammered, weathered copper with an inlaid turquoise drain.

Search for flowerpots with beautiful silhouettes, then place them in every nook and around every corner. (5) Turn your terrace into an English garden with hand-thrown Long Tom stoneware pots from Marston & Langinger.

Use fabrics that put you in mind of faraway lands. (6) This suzani pillow from Madeline Weinrib Atelier would add a touch of exotic fun to any outdoor décor.

Light the sink with some old-style sconces. (7) The LaGrange lamp from Troy lighting comes in a pre-aged finish.

Even the industrial-strength faucet—Parma by Danze—fits right in with the rural aesthetic of this Idaho house. Pewter outdoor lanterns by Portfolio that have an old-fashioned industrial feel are hung all around the perimeter of the work area. The window looks out over an expansive view of mountains and the Big Wood River. To the right is the refrigerator and an old glass-front cabinet Yager uses as a pantry for dry goods.

BARN RAISING

MEGAN RICE YAGER,
designer

Ahhh . . . a little place in the country. And what could be more inviting than the welcoming warmth of a rustic barn? Of course you'd have to spend years searching for that perfect barn, then months (or even years) converting it into a livable house. Or you could do what Megan Rice Yager did and create the romance of an old Idaho barn entirely from scratch. Believe it or not, this is new construction!

THE BACKSTORY | "This is my own home; our family's second home in Sun Valley. Even though we have three kids, 15, 11, and 8, I wanted a small house. The kids are outside most of the time anyway—by the river in the summer and skiing in the winter. I wanted to strip away superfluous rooms and put the dining room right in the middle of the kitchen. And I wanted it to look like an old Idaho barn, the kind of barn you see everywhere in the endless flat farmland here—kind of forlorn buildings that are also incredibly romantic."

"This is reclaimed barn wood—fir—that I sourced locally. I had the boards custom milled to a width that's not the standard. Little details like that make a project more interesting. And I wanted exposed nails on the window trim so the architecture feels more utilitarian."

"I looked at every piece of hardware in the Western Hemisphere before picking these knobs from Van Dykes Restorers—they remind me of the knobs on the stove. And I used Restoration Hardware pulls on the cabinets, centered on the top rather than on the side. The middle cabinet is actually a drawer where I keep my baking supplies but these pulls keep the look of the cabinets and the drawers uniform."

This is a cabin fantasy! How old is it?

It's brand new, but we used reclaimed wood. I wanted it to look like we had found an old barn and just retrofitted it. I hand sorted every piece of wood and had it placed on the wall exactly where I wanted it—the premier pieces with pretty silvery undertones went in the most visible spots, the not-so-prime pieces went behind the refrigerator and buffet.

It's all so wonderfully casual—the front door opens straight into the kitchen.

Come right in and sit down! The first thing you see is the stove—from La Cornue. It's so fabulous-looking that I absolutely had to have it. But to stay on budget I thought, "I'll get my sink from Ikea." This sink is great-looking and so well priced. I'm definitely not a slave to provenance.

Where did you find those old lantern sconces?

They aren't old. I saw them at Lowe's and thought they would make good task lighting—functional, yet a little different. The fact that they were only $45 apiece sealed the deal.

What's on the counters?

Two slabs of Petit Granit, a Belgian limestone. They were remnants at a stone importer. It has little fossils in it, which the kids love. I didn't have enough to go around, so I did that butcher-block insert, which turned out to be serendipitous. It's great to have that huge cutting surface.

Why did you want your dining table in the middle of the kitchen?

The kids are always underfoot, and I like having them close by. I can plop down and read a cookbook. Friends can sit down with a glass of wine. Even though I love islands, I find you end up walking around them all the time.

And no stool could ever be as comfortable as these chairs look.

They were a gift from my mother-in-law, and my husband remembers them from his childhood. They're classic Louis XVI repro chairs, and I needed to make them work in this context, so I had blue linen slipcovers made—underneath they're covered in formal damask. Now they're more kid-friendly. And I have Blue Willow china like he used to eat on at boarding school. I was trying to create some history in this house.

That's a great-looking floor. How did you do it?

The wood is from a small mill in Montana. It's larch, circle-sawn and wire brushed—using antique equipment—so it immediately looks old. Then I striped it myself with porch paint. I didn't want to create fake patina, so I just did one coat and it soon acquired a very authentic patina with the comings and goings of my three children. "Authenticity" is a big word for me. I don't like faux anything.

CABIN FERVOR

The front door, in the foreground, opens to one big room with kitchen and dining areas. French doors at the back lead to a covered porch where the family can sit and watch the elk stroll by. Matisse lithographs in silver frames line the walls and an ornate silver-leafed hanging lantern, available through meganyager.com, hangs over the table. Those formal touches work surprisingly well because they pick up the silver tones in the barn wood. A reproduction French farm table from Charles & Charles and chairs slipcovered in Pindler & Pindler's Tyrone Irish Linen are kid-friendly. The striped floor was painted by Yager herself.

WHAT IF...
YOUR FANTASY RURAL
IDAHO BARN CAME WITH A
SILVER-LEAF LANTERN.

....

" This is a new lantern but I
think it almost looks antique
Swedish with its double crown
motif. I silver leafed it to pick
up the silver tones in the barn
wood. Even though my style
is very American I like a little
bit of European like this. It's
so surprising, right? Everyone
comments on this lantern. And
it actually makes pretty patterns
on the ceiling in the evening! "

HIGH BAR
AN ANTIQUE FRENCH
NORMAN BUFFET DEUX
CORPS (A BUFFET WITH
UPPER STORAGE SHELVES
ATOP A LOWER BUFFET)
IS BEHIND THE DINING
TABLE. WHEN THE BUFFET'S
DOORS ARE OPEN, IT
DOUBLES AS A BAR.

....

" When you have an especially
fabulous piece of furniture
like this, why not use it?
I feel strongly about that.
It's from Brittany, from the
early 1800s, quite valuable
and made of an unusual type
of wild cherry, but we use it
every single day. It's where
we keep our glasses and it's
also the party bar; the place
people congregate when
we entertain. "

CRAVING...
THE CORNUFÉ 110 RANGE
BY LA CORNUE, WITH A
TRADITIONAL EUROPEAN
CENTRAL BURNER (FOR A
TOTAL OF FIVE), AND TWO
OVENS: ONE CONVECTION-
ONLY AND THE OTHER WITH
SEVEN COOKING MODES.

....

" I'm obsessed with that
stove. I just gaze at it every
morning as I make the coffee.
I actually designed the cabinets in the kitchen based on
the stove's square oven doors.
And even though you can
get it in a variety of colors,
I picked stainless steel
because I wanted the room
to look a tiny bit industrial,
more utilitarian to fit the
barn vibe. "

What's going on with that window above the sink? The windows are awning windows that cantilever out from the bottom just like in a barn. And windows are square, cabinets are square. I think it's so pleasing to the eye to see repetition, that's why I believe strongly in custom cabinetry so you can do things like that. And see how there's no kick space at the bottom of cabinets—except where you need it to stand in front of the sink? I think most kick space does nothing more than gather dust.

The room is the perfect cross between rural and elegant, and that's hard to do. I think it works because I had a story in mind. The fabulous stove stands in for the big hearth that would have been the center of the old "keeping room" in a little frontier cabin. After I had those bones in place, I let myself go with a crazy mix-up of styles—formal and casual, rural and European. My mother is an interior designer and my father is an artist. I grew up in a very visually oriented household. Somehow I know how to make it all fit together. Everything here is just the way I envisioned it.

FLOOR SHOW
The floor was painted with Farrow & Ball Hardwick White and then dry-brushed with Benjamin Moore Evening Dove—a soft navy blue that goes well with the chairs.

COUNTRY MORNING
Orange juice in a Trellis glass by Tiffany & Company and a sterling silver water goblet by Gorham are surprising trappings for a barn-inspired room.

COLOR FORMS
YAGER CREATED THE PERFECT COZY CABINETS WITH FARROW & BALL HARDWICK WHITE

"I love Farrow & Ball colors. The funny thing about this color is that it's called white but it's actually a pale gray. I tried 72 million colors because I wanted gray cabinets but the light in Sun Valley is very cold, not golden, so the gray had to be warm. It couldn't be a battleship gray with blue undertones. This gray is perfect, a little taupe-y and very natural."

STALKING THE LOOK

1 | 2

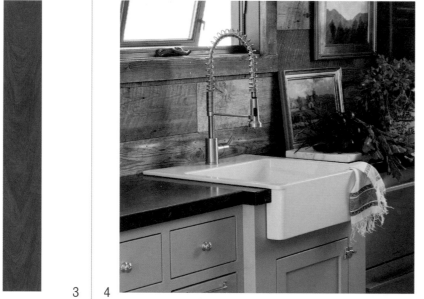

3 | 4

5 | 6

Look no further than your own backyard for inspiration. Yager put a fresh spin on the look of the humble barns that dot her home's state.

Choose a faucet that looks like it would be at home in a utilitarian barn. (1) The Arezzo Faucet from Elkay looks like an industrial sprayer but it's less tall and unwieldy, which makes it better suited to your kitchen sink.

Collect blue-and-white porcelain. Yager's collection of Chinese ginger jars and Blue Willow plates lends sophistication to her fantasy barn. (2) An antique ginger jar from John Rosselli Antiques would be an elegant standout in a rustic kitchen.

Go for yards and yards of wood grain. (3) Bioessenze stoneware tiles from Lea Ceramiche look like wood, but without the risk of moisture damage.

Remember rustic patina pairs beautifully with shiny and new. (4) Yager likes the contrast of battered old barn wood against a gleaming white farmhouse sink.

Paint your floor in pale colors. The faded look of Yager's blue and white painted floor softens the machismo of her bold walls.

Hang an exotic lantern over your table to elevate humble materials. (5) The Alhambra Lantern from Vaughan is a showstopper.

In place of built-ins, use furniture like Yager's antique cabinet that can double as storage. (6) The Lyell Tambour China Cabinet, from Martha Stewart Signature Furniture with Bernhardt, features two pullout breadboards and a silverware drawer lined in silver cloth making it a great multitasker.

KITCHEN PLANNER

THERE ARE ONLY THREE THINGS THAT MATTER WHEN IT COMES TO CULINARY REAL ESTATE: PLANNING, PLANNING, AND PLANNING.

The brainchild of architect Joeb Moore, this kitchen has the perfect layout for cooking while communing. "On one end, you have that all-glass room, which is the breakfast area and the sitting hub," explains Moore. "On the opposite end, sliding glass doors open onto a study area for the kids, so Mom can keep an eye on homework while she cooks."

Three vintage Holophane glass pendant lights from Ann-Morris Antiques are suspended from a recessed steel strip on the ceiling—task lighting is targeted where it's most needed.

Windows were integrated into the stainless-steel surround on either side of the Wolf DF606F 60" dual-fuel range.

The 14' island is topped with white Carrara marble so it feels light, like it's floating in the middle of the room.

The island countertop has a deep overhang so Shinto stools, from Lars Bolander, tuck out of the way for food prep.

ASK FOR WINDOW SEATS. Breakfast-nook diners enjoy natural light and a view while interacting with the cook. In the ceiling above the banquette, a wood lattice with lights behind it creates "a moiré effect, which helps to break up the scale of the large kitchen," says Moore.

MAKE A STUDY HALL. Sliding glass-and-steel doors close off the children's study area at the end of the kitchen opposite the banquette. They also echo the breakfast nook's wall of windows while allowing light to filter into the kitchen. File drawers have the same look and same hardware as white kitchen cabinets for continuity, and an Aeron chair stands ready at each workstation.

SPACE PROGRAMMED
"Here's how it works: To the right is the cleanup area, with a big sink and two dishwashers. To the left is command central, where all the cooking is done. There's a Wolf range, a prep sink, and the tall cabinets on either side hide the new Sub-Zero 700 series refrigerator and freezer—each just 27" inches wide, so they're easy to conceal."
—JOEB MOORE

CARVE OUT A PARTY PANTRY. A butler's pantry between the kitchen and the dining room provides storage space for all the accoutrements of entertaining— a Viking undercounter refrigerator and ice maker flank the sink, and a Sub-Zero wine cellar holds 132 bottles. The backsplash, made of bamboo suspended in polymer, is backlit for soft light during parties. Cabinets on the right, the kind used in doctors' offices to stock medical supplies, store glassware and china.

COOKBOOK AUTHOR INA GARTEN SAYS DON'T FORGET . . .

- A good set of sharp knives by Wüsthof, including a chef's knife, a paring knife, a slicing knife, and a bread knife.

- All-Clad pots—small and large sauté pans, small and large lidded pots, and a large stock pot.

- One large All-Clad roasting pan. You can make something small in a big one, but you can't make something big in a small one.

- One medium and one large Le Creuset round Dutch oven.

- A mixer. (I cannot imagine not having my KitchenAid mixer K45).

- A Cuisinart Pro Custom 11 food processor, with the slightly bigger bowl.

- A set of stainless-steel mixing bowls (try a restaurant supply house).

- Ten clear glass bowls from Williams-Sonoma.

- A big pot of wooden spoons and rubber spatulas on the counter.

- Another pot with whisks and measuring spoons.

- A Chef'sChoice electric knife sharpener.

- A John Boos butcher block cutting board.

- A meat thermometer.

- Oven mitts.

- A stack of half sheet pans. They're about 13"–18" each, with a 1" rim. I use them for roasting vegetables, baking cookies and brownies, and lots of other tasks.

1. **SEE THE SHINING SEA!**
A: Architect Wayne Good designed open shelves on open supports so the ocean view is visible from the kitchen. B: For the counters and backsplash, interior designer Mona Hajj used honed, semi-polished bluestone because it's hard to stain—and the color is reminiscent of the sea.

2. **FEELING CLOSED IN BY A U-SHAPED LAYOUT? CHOOSE A SEE-THROUGH ISLAND.**
"We tried a center island, but it looked like a behemoth. Then we found that table. It had been used by an artist and came with lots of scars, which is why no one ever has to worry about staining or cutting it."
—CHAD EISNER, DESIGNER

1A

1B

2

3

3. **HAVE A COLUMN IN THE MIDDLE OF YOUR KITCHEN? FLAUNT IT!**
"Our biggest challenge was a 4' x 4' chase—a column holding all sorts of electrical wiring and plumbing—that runs right through the room and could not be moved. So I worked around it and built it out into four areas: a cooking area with the range, a buffet for the table, a desk, and then a baking area in back where you can hide all the mess. The hood is made of galvanized metal, like an old wash bucket—patinated so it's not shiny— with copper nailheads along the seams."
—SANDRA BIRD, KITCHEN DESIGNER

4. **MAKE A HALL OF MIRRORS.**
Sheathing a long narrow kitchen and breakfast room in mirrors expands the feeling of space. "The lattice gives the room a garden feel, and the reflection brings the outdoors in."
—ALLISON CACCOMA, DESIGNER

5. **GO AHEAD. OBSESS OVER THE DETAILS.**
"I've spent so much time in French brasseries. I wanted the kitchen to look like that, with the tile and the iron and the marble, and those great blue and green chairs. The range hood is supposed to look like a fabric canopy. It's done in hand-hammered zinc. The pale chartreuse tile is the color of olive oil and the ceiling—in Cowtan & Tout wallpaper—is like a birdcage."
—JOHN OETGEN, DESIGNER

4

5

**FACING A DIMINUTIVE SPACE?
MAKE NO SMALL PLANS.**
A tiny kitchen on a tight budget
requires clever planning. A table
doubles as the island, an armoire is
made into a pantry, pots hang over
the range, and there's even storage
atop the cabinet. "The kitchen is
only about 16' x 16'. Having the table
and chairs in there is easy, because
while you're sitting you can just
reach behind you and turn the stove
off or grab something out of the
refrigerator."
—CRAIG SCHUMACHER,
     HOMEOWNER AND DESIGNER

**INVITE THE ARMOIRE
OUT FROM THE BOUDOIR.**
A HUGE ARMOIRE IS A SMART
SOLUTION IN SCHUMACHER'S
SMALL KITCHEN. FURNITURE
ALLOWS BREATHING ROOM
WHERE LARGE BUILT-IN
CABINETS MIGHT OVERWHELM.

"It's our pantry and holds
everything from tuna fish to
big bags of dog food."

INSIDER INTEL | Expert planners offer up kitchen "dos" and "don't ever" advice.

LOW CEILING HOVERING? INVITE IT ON DOWN.

" Our kitchen only had 8' ceilings, so we played that up with rough-hewn white oak beams to enhance the low effect. It feels really warm and cozy. "
—MELANIE POUNDS,
DESIGNER

" Splashes of stainless all over the place make a kitchen feel choppy and small. Stainless steel dishwashers are the worst. They attract your eye to a place you really don't want your eye to go. And be especially careful with those stainless-steel coffins—giant stainless refrigerators. They can quickly overpower a kitchen design if it's not balanced correctly. "
—MATTHEW QUINN,
DESIGN GALLERIA

"Think an island can't be too big? Wrong. Anything bigger than 8' x 4' is unnecessary. And counter space? You don't need more than 4'."
—CHRISTOPHER PEACOCK,
KITCHEN DESIGNER

" For long-term choices like cabinet finishes, tile, countertops, and flooring, live with your samples for a while before you commit. Give yourself enough time to fall out of love with them, which can happen."
—ANNIE SELKE,
OWNER PINE CONE HILL

"We're redesigning an 1850s farmhouse on Long Island and I've insisted that the kitchen flow right into the family room, unobstructed, so I can spend time with my guests. Everybody's always in the kitchen anyway—they might as well be comfortable."
—TOM COLICCHIO,
CHEF AND OWNER OF FIVE RESTAURANTS, INCLUDING CRAFT IN NEW YORK CITY

"You need a countertop around the wall ovens! Otherwise, where are you going to put the turkey when you take it out of the oven?"
—TERRY SCARBOROUGH,
KITCHENS BY DEANE

" There can be such a thing as too much storage. There's rarely a need to completely fill a room with cabinets. A good layout is a balancing act between storage, function, and aesthetics."
—BOB BAKES,
BAKES AND COMPANY

COOKS CANNOT LIVE BY BREAD ALONE. The wet bar in this St. Charles Cabinetry kitchen designed by Kim Fouquet is fully outfitted—equipped with Viking's Professional Series ice maker, a wine cellar, and blender. The screw-top counter stool in brushed steel from Design Workshop is a nice place to perch.

BE MARTINI READY. The bar area in this kitchen by Sandra Bird—open on both sides for easy access—has upholstered leather barstools and is topped with hammered copper for an authentic feel. Chrome brackets, powder-coated to look like bronze, support glass shelves. Gothic tiles from Ann Sacks in Sorrell, Otter, Champagne, Cream, and Willow are laid in a harlequin pattern with five colors, but the same colors never touch.

DESIGNER MILES REDD SAYS EVERY BAR NEEDS . . .

- Bitters

- Cocktail onions, cornichons

- Lemons and limes

- Maraschino cherries

- A bag of Kettle potato chips and a can of smoked almonds

- Mixers: soda, tonic, ginger ale, 7Up, Coke, Diet Coke, cranberry juice, Clamato juice, tomato juice, and Campbell's beef broth with the pullback tab.

- A pepper mill

- Tabasco, Worcestershire sauce

- Fresh ice, preferably chipped

- A good ice bucket: mine is glass. I find it easy to clean and I like the look of a sweating bucket.

- An ice scoop. It works much better than a spoon.

- A glass stirrer

- Two cocktail shakers: one open and one closed. A closed one is good for frothy drinks; an open one is good for stirred drinks

- A bottle opener, a corkscrew

- A strainer. Good for a poured drink.

- Cocktail napkins. I prefer cloth to paper

- A variety of glasses. A good drink is also about a good glass. If you're serving martinis, nothing tastes better than a chilled martini glass. The minimum is low ball and high ball glasses; martini glasses; wineglasses; and champagne flutes. I like to drink beer out of the bottle

- Vodka, Gin, Bourbon, Rum, Scotch, Rye, Vermouth (sweet and dry), Tequila, Triple sec, Cognac, Cointreau, Campari

- One bottle each of red wine, white wine, and champagne

CHILL

....

Choosing your refrigerator is almost as personal as picking your life partner. Your fridge will be with you a long, long time: be sure you're madly in love. First, make a list of your needs. Glass, wood, stainless? Freezer drawers or side-by-side? Counter-depth? Undercounter? Wine chiller? Ice maker? Head spinning? Never fear. After you've penned your checklist, sit down and peruse the designer ideas from the endlessly creative kitchens featured here. Your dream fridge awaits.

THE COOL CROWD

What's the difference between a counter-depth fridge, a traditional size and a built-in refrigerator?

"A counter- or cabinet-depth refrigerator is designed to fit flush with the base cabinets. They are not as deep—usually just 25–27"—as traditional sized units, which are typically 30–32" deep. Refrigerators are massive objects in a kitchen. It's especially important to me to de-mass them by using shallower refrigerators whenever possible. They feel lighter in a space but you always have to be sure the interior shelf space has room for things like serving trays and platters. Built-in units, on the other hand, are typically countertop depth (or even a little deeper) and can be fully integrated into the cabinetry. They can even be made to look like armoires or other pieces of furniture. Built-ins typically cost more but I love having the kind of flexibility they offer to customize my designs."

—MICK DE GIULIO, KITCHEN DESIGNER

When your Traulsen fridge has glass doors, do you feel compelled to keep everything neat?
"All right, I'll admit I rearrange the shelves. The beauty is you don't always have to open the door to see if what you want is in there."
—PETER FISHEL, DESIGNER

This petite pink fridge from Smeg has one big personality! Isn't it great? It's tiny—perfect for a small kitchen. The funny part is that it's English but you order it through Sears. It's not really practical, more like a dorm refrigerator. But boy, is it cute.

—**KRISTA EWART**, DESIGNER

Using a panel front to integrate your refrigerator into the cabinetry helps keep the focus on graceful millwork and painstakingly chosen color.

"It's the one thing that everybody raves about. Folly Green on all the cupboards, from a wonderful Australian company called Porter's Paints. My husband was maniacal about getting just the right shade to match a picture we had torn from a magazine. I have to say he nailed it."

—**URSULA BROOKS**, HOMEOWNER

You say you've got an entire Traulsen glass-front refrigerator that's just for vegetables?
I have four children and I buy a lot of fresh, seasonal produce. I hate to have it mashed into little drawers. You forget about the lettuce down at the bottom, wilting away. Now I throw everything into colanders and put them in the Traulsen, which has glass doors. When you can see the artichokes, you want to eat the artichokes.
—**SUSAN DOSSETTER**, DESIGNER

The Sub-Zero refrigerator has been transformed from simply utilitarian into a bling-y beauty.

"A friend jokes about my Chanel refrigerator, but that metal is probably the cheapest thing in the kitchen. It's the same diamond-patterned stainless steel you see on refrigerated trucks on the highway. Nothing custom about it."
—SUSAN DOSSETTER, DESIGNER

COLD CASES

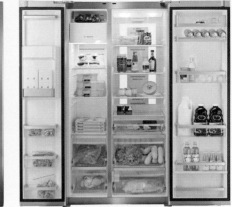

Become an efficiency expert.
Not an inch wasted! The doors of the Linea 800 from Bosch hold gallon bottles, there's kid-level storage way down low, and you don't need to empty the shelves before adjusting them.

Get wired in.
Whirlpool's refrigerator with digital picture frame is made for the wired kitchen. Its Centralpark feature can also support an Internet connection, a message center, and iPod docking station.

Leave nothing to the imagination.
You don't have to open the glass door of the PRO 48 from Sub-Zero to see if you need milk, and it's amazingly efficient—using less energy in a year than a 100-watt light bulb. The crisper drawer means produce won't wilt.

Light up your life.
Miele's Independence Series refrigerator has ClearView, halogen, and spot lighting illuminating the deepest corners.

Pick a hue.
What contemporary chic-colored glass front panels! Preference refrigerators from Dacor come in a choice of six hues that are so understated they'll work like neutrals with your other appliances. Shown: Blue Water.

Double your fabulousness.
French doors and two freezer drawers, so you can keep everyday necessities (like ice cream!) handy in the top, and meat and other staples in the lower drawer. CS 2062 from Liebherr.

Grant longer life to your lettuce.
A better crisper? Yes. BioFresh drawers maintain precise temperature and humidity to extend the life of your produce. CBS 2062 from Liebherr.

You've packed a complete kitchen into a small space, yet it doesn't feel cramped. How come? Refrigerator drawers. Échelon refrigerator and freezer drawers by U-Line. Instead of a huge, hulking refrigerator, we've got two drawers. One refrigerator and one freezer. Very compact and efficient. You can even fit tall bottles of wine on the pullout rack. It might not work for a family of five, but for two people, it's fine.

—PATRICK WADE,
DESIGNER AND HOMEOWNER

Why would someone need an undercounter fridge? I like to use undercounter refrigeration in areas close to a workspace where salads are prepared. They are great for storage of vegetables and other produce. I'll also use them to make it easier for children to access juice and milk and not interfere with the main cooking zone. And they're great in bars, of course, and even rooms other than the kitchen—like bedrooms and bathrooms.

—MICK DE GIULIO,
KITCHEN DESIGNER

Refrigerators have been able to make ice for over 40 years, why go to the trouble of installing a stand-alone ice maker? "A separate ice maker gives you a lot more capacity than the small units you find in refrigerators. They're great for entertaining—they'll typically make around 25 pounds of ice a day."

—MICK DE GIULIO,
KITCHEN DESIGNER

BOTTLE COOLERS

See eye-to-eye on wine.
This sleek modular wine storage unit keeps 18 bottles at eye level. Dimmable LEDs cast a cool glow. HWS 1800 Integrated Wine Storage Cabinet from Liebherr.

Give your vintages the VIP treatment.
The EuroCave Performance 283 Wine Cellar has 3 distinct compartments: the room-temperature compartment on top keeps red wines at their recommended serving temperature (62–66°F), the aging compartment (53–57°F) stores and ages your wine, and the serving compartment (40–44°F) chills white wines and champagne.

Wrap it up.
With its wraparound stainless-steel casing, the freestanding WS 1200 wine cabinet from Liebherr looks good from any angle.

TO CHILL OR NOT TO CHILL

Wine cellar or wine refrigerator? How do you choose? Why not just stash your whites in the fridge and stick the reds on a rack?

Most people think they should keep white wines chilled and their red wines at room temperature, but nothing could be further from the truth. Your kitchen refrigerator is too cold! The optimal condition for storing wine is between 53–57°F, and between 60–70 percent humidity. Even though it's mainly reds that age and mature, the storage temperatures apply to all wines—white, red, sparkling, or rosé.

A wine cellar has both temperature and humidity control, which is what serious collectors use. Then there are the refrigerators that maintain temperature but don't have humidity control. The real wave now is for thermoelectric units, because they're more green—they use less power, and no chemical coolants like a traditional fridge.

—**ADAM STRUM,**
   EDITOR AND PUBLISHER,
   WINE ENTHUSIAST MAGAZINE

haute so functional

PERFECTLY DRESSED KITCHENS
THAT DESERVE A FRONT-ROW SEAT
AT FASHION WEEK.

PIZZAZZ

JONATHAN ADLER,
designer

Admit it. Your kitchen
is really the only place where
the entire family likes to hang
out, so why not make it the
happiest room in the house?
Use lots of color and mad mod
trimmings like Adler did here
and you'll have a kitchen so
full of joy (and family) there'll
hardly be room for the food.

THE BACKSTORY | "This is the idyllic New York countryside, but within
a stone's throw of Manhattan. My client, Liz Lange, is a fashion designer
who more or less invented upscale maternity. She has a husband and two
children, ages 8 and 10. She's also my best friend from college—we went
to Brown together. Liz's style was always legendarily chic, but she has a
flamboyance that's totally original. She's not afraid to sparkle."

White Ikea cabinets and stainless-steel appliances—a Viking stove
and dishwasher—provide a calm and neutral backdrop for exuberant
bursts of color. Carrara marble countertops are amply stocked with
Adler's own pottery and a white vintage glass vase full of orange
mums brightens the island.

Jonathan Adler's giant
stoneware horse bowl is both
a lively focal point and a fun
way to keep fruit and healthy
snacks close to hand.

Ceiling fixtures from **Rejuvenation** take the place of recessed lights to lend a shot of vintage warmth to the space.

Walls sheathed in **Carrara** marble tile and open shelves are perfect for showing off bold blue-and-white dishes from **Villeroy & Boch**.

You're a standard-bearer for unimpeachably chic design. But you're also very playful. How do those two things exist side by side?

I think a room should be 95 percent chic. There needs to be a solid foundation of good design, functionality, and harmony. Then you have the remaining 5 percent to layer on a playful vibe. If a room is merely playful it's usually wildly unchic. Conversely, if it's too chic it's dry and off-putting. I try to strike the perfect balance of chic and cheeky—an inclusive, unsnobby sort of buoyant spirit.

A buoyant spirit—that's the perfect description for this kitchen.

It's a room you want to be in, because the outside is always close at hand—lots of green accents. We upholstered the Norman Cherner stools and chairs in this lime-green print that's sort of crisply modern yet floral and viney at the same time—perfect for the country. It's on the drum shade, too. We laminated all the fabric so it's super-duper wipe-downable. We chose marble countertops and we used Ikea cabinets because . . . why not? They're well made. I think Ikea is a treasure. You can get a kitchen that looks this fabulous and not spend squillions. To me, if things are too expensive and perhaps even too considered, it can be a bit lugubrious, which strikes me as antithetical to the spirit of a family country home.

What was the first thing you did in this kitchen?
We painted all the floors white, which is something I always love to do for instant happiness. Color is a great way to express playfulness. We used lime green, black, and white with nothing toned down. One of the nice things is that it's a light-filled house, and the colors just crank that up to the next level.

Yet the color is all tightly controlled.
Oh yes. We went with a programmatic approach— a black and white foundation infused with single punches of color. There's a purity to the colors and a purity to the nature of the design that reflects Liz's strong sense of who she is.

Does the room get a lot of use?
Absolutely! It's a sunny gathering spot with all the stuff you need for a modern family—the bells-and-whistles appliances, the big eat-in table, the island countertop and, most important of all, wireless computer reception. So it's their everything room— computers going and cookies baking and all the typical mayhem. Their meals in here range from proper breakfast or dinner at the Saarinen table to snacks in front of the computer.

Lime-green upholstered Cherner chairs from chernerstore.com, and the Eero Saarinen table by Knoll from Design Within Reach, have curvy, lighthearted appeal in the kitchen breakfast area. Doors painted glossy black further animate the cheery space. The main kitchen area is directly to the left and double doors open out to the pool so there's a seamless flow from inside to outside and through to the kitchen.

WHAT IF . . .
THE UPHOLSTERY ON YOUR CHAIRS AND STOOLS MATCHED THE LAMPSHADES?

Adler covered Norman Cherner counter stools and chairs and the trans.LUXE pendant lights in Alan Campbell's Potalla in Jungle Green.

STALKING THE LOOK

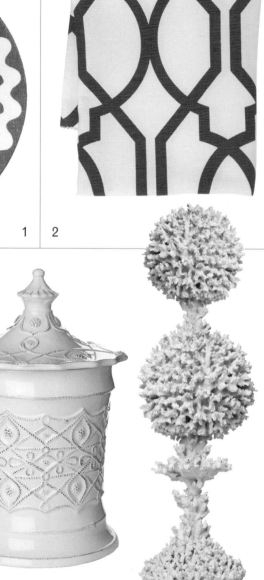

1   **2**

3   **4**

5

Choose dinnerware that pops against white shelves and cabinets. (1) With its "rickrack" border the Wave Plate from La Cafetière is a standout (and it comes in ten bright colors).

Find a fabric with graphic punch and use it on lampshades and upholstery. (2) Gazebo from Groundworks by Lee Jofa has a wide fretwork pattern that gives its bright red lines room to breathe.

Paint wood floors white for happiness. (3) "I once painted floors in this crisp, clean white—Benjamin Moore Decorators White— and the house felt much lighter and more contemporary. They'll tell you that you can just put a primer over the existing floor, but don't believe it. Sand it down first to get a better bond." —Eldon Wong, designer

Seek out accessories with unusual shapes (but stick to white so things stay calm). (4) (RIGHT) Made Goods' Monica resin topiaries add a big dose of drama and a shot of texture to sleek surfaces. (LEFT) Juliska's line of ceramic canisters—Jardins du Monde Canisters—are richly decorated and hermetically sealed, making them suitable for food or other items.

Take marble tile right up to the ceiling— sans moldings—so your backdrop for color and eye-popping accessories stays simple and neutral. Adler used the same white marble for countertops and walls.

Go for the grooviest curvy chairs and counter stools you can find to offset a simple white kitchen's straight lines.

With so much color and pattern, you can skip the curtains and let the sun shine in!

Prop a colorful tray behind your stacked dishes for visual richness. (5) This lively tray from Eduardo Garza for Formentero is made of anodized aluminum so it won't chip or fade.

BRIGHT STAR

JEFF LEWIS,
designer and star of Bravo's Flipping Out

It's big, bold, and brimming
with cutting-edge appliances—
the kind that promise delicious
food with just the press of
one exquisitely calibrated
button. That's perfect for Lewis
who doesn't cook. But he
wanted his dream kitchen to
have that *wow* factor anyway.
And boy, does it draw a crowd!

THE BACKSTORY | The editors at *House Beautiful* asked Lewis to design
the ideal kitchen for today's American family, which would be erected
right smack in the middle of Rockefeller Center for the public to enjoy one
summer. But he was unable to resist designing it for himself so Rockefeller
Center wound up hosting Lewis's very personal dream kitchen. "We all
know I'm a narcissist," he explains with a laugh.

To make a dramatic statement against pale
Antique Elm flooring by Mohawk, Lewis went
for the dark, rich tones of KraftMaid's Brockton
cabinetry. Custom hardware by Design Bath
& Hardware—glossy nickel-plated handles—is
a handsome sculptural element. The Caesar-
Stone island and countertops, both in Pure
White, pair beautifully with brushed-aluminum
counter stools from Design Within Reach.

Square 24" Kariota backsplash tiles from **Walker Zanger** offset sleekness with texture.

Jenn-Air's 36" duct-free Electric Radiant Downdraft Cooktop doesn't have knobs, it has touch controls, so the island's surface is one smooth uninterrupted plane.

You're a serial renovator, constantly buying and selling houses. Can a kitchen make or break a sale?

The kitchen is number one. It's what really sells the house. It doesn't matter how nice your living room is, or your dining room. Don't spend the money, because people are going to end up in the kitchen. I don't cook; there's absolutely no reason for people to be in my kitchen. But they're still there.

So how would you describe this dream kitchen?

It's definitely contemporary, but I wanted it to be warm, and I think we achieved that with all the wood. And I wanted a lot of seating, indoors and out, so it feels very lounge-y, very California.

No glass-fronted cabinets, I see.

Even complete minimalists have a few things in the kitchen they don't want people to see. Canned goods and stuff like that. You've got to have some closed cabinetry, and then you put in the perfect amount of open shelves to show off the pretty things. We pulled the shelves a few inches off the wall, so the recessed lights in the ceiling wash the whole wall, backlighting your accessories.

The scale of that huge island is powerful.

I wanted this humongous block of CaesarStone. Pure, clean, white, and it doesn't stain, scratch, or burn.

Very cool the way you've rested one end of the reclaimed wood table right on top of the white CaesarStone countertop. Why? It's more dramatic, less predictable this way. An artist named Jeff Soderbergh made that table out of wood salvaged from the Vanderbilt polo pony barn. I was afraid it would look a little too rustic, so we did a polished chrome X for the legs and all of a sudden this two-hundred-year-old wood looked modern. I could see a bunch of kids sitting there unable to hurt it. I think he must have put 20 coats of sealer on it.

The eye-popping stainless-steel chandelier, Licht im Raum's Dione 800 Move, is made up of three moveable rings—each ring can be turned in any direction—so the fixture can morph into different silhouettes illuminating the table in a variety of ways depending on the occasion or mood. When the chandelier is switched on in the evening, the sparkle of steel and aluminum transform this casual kitchen into an elegant place suitable for a dressy dinner for six.

MODERN MARVEL
The dining area has a "gathering table" at counter height—42" high—and leather-covered Bottega Stools from Design Within Reach that swivel 360 degrees, so diners can interact with anyone in the room. Open shelves above a beverage refrigerator by Jenn-Air keep Calvin Klein Home's elegant and modern Pulse glassware close at hand.

WHAT IF...
YOUR WINE RACK FILLED IN
FOR A WALL?

. . . .

"I needed some sort of separation
between the work area and the
living area because I don't like
to see dirty dishes. But I didn't
want to lose that feeling of
one big, open space. We took
an ordinary storage shelf and
turned it on the diagonal so it
looks more like an art piece.
You can still see through it,
but it sets off a spillover space,
a place to relax on a comfortable sofa."

RAINMAKER
WITH MULTIPLE JOINTS,
KOHLER'S KARBON FAUCET
CAN BE LOCKED INTO MANY
POSITIONS, ELIMINATING
THE NEED FOR A SEPARATE
HAND SPRAY AND KEEPING
THE BACKSPLASH LESS
CLUTTERED.

. . . .

"My eye goes right to the
faucet. You can make a
statement with a good one.
I love gadgets, and I thought
this faucet looked kind of
space-age."

CRAVING...
A MIRACULOUSLY
FAUCET-FREE PREP SINK

. . . .

"It's awesome—the Crevasse,
by Kohler. You just brush your
chopping scraps into it and
push a button and this rush of
water rinses them down the
garbage disposal."

I'm about to renovate my kitchen. Where should I put my money?

Absolutely, without a doubt, appliances. I would show everyone who comes into this kitchen the LCD screen on the Jenn-Air wall oven. I love that you can just press "Lasagna" and it shows you exactly how to cook it, with pictures. This is amazing for someone like me, who would never have made lasagna on his own.

Skipping the stove hood makes this kitchen so airy. But is it only practical for someone who never cooks?

Oh, no. This Jenn-Air Cooktop not only has a downdraft, it has this whole new technology: it's ductless, which means you don't have to vent it outside. It would be great for people in apartments. There's this unit underneath and all you have to do is change the filter periodically.

Is it always absolutely necessary to replace old cabinets when renovating a kitchen?

First ask yourself, "Do I really need new cabinets? Can we paint them or reface them?" But you should always replace outdated cabinet hardware. It's the quickest, cheapest way to update your kitchen.

The lovely (and useful!) room divider/wine rack was made by KraftMaid. Push a button and the 24" Jenn-Air microwave hiding under the island counter opens like a drawer for easy access (and its low profile keeps the lines of the island clean). Perfect for washing stemware while entertaining, the Jenn-Air TriFecta dishwasher has a top-rack-only option to save energy.

COLOR FORMS

LEWIS CREATED A STRIKING BACKDROP FOR MODERNITY WITH QUARTERSAWN CHERRY CABINETS IN KRAFTMAID'S PEPPERCORN FINISH

Rich dark-stained wood, where the grain plays a starring role, has uncommon power against sleek machine-made elements—like the hyper–modern CaesarStone island and the host of stainless-steel appliances.

STALKING THE LOOK

1

2

3

4

5

6

Everybody up! Replace your kitchen table with one at counter-height surrounded with high stools. (1) Try high dining on Lem Piston Stools from Design Within Reach.

Look for sublimely simple cabinet pulls. (2) Omnia Industies' stainless-steel cabinet pulls are the kind of hardware architects prefer—minimal and stunning.

No knobs to interrupt the clean lines of your island countertop. (3) Lewis chose a cooktop without knobs—Jenn-Air's 36" Electric Radiant Downdraft Cooktop with touch controls.

Choose counter material that's monolithic and will be forever pristine. Lewis used CaesarStone because it doesn't spot or stain.

Satisfy your inner neatnik. (4) Removable pegs in the lower cabinet drawers from KraftMaid can be adjusted to fit favorite pots and pans.

Pick upper cabinets that open like garage doors. (5) Doors on upper cabinets in Lewis's dream kitchen open up and out of the way for easier access and more interior space, by KraftMaid.

Openly display wine and water bottles. (6) Your wine may be vintage but these aluminum wine racks from Vynebar are thoroughly modern.

Find a chandelier with some major curves to balance your modern kitchen's hard edges. Lewis chose the Dione 800 Move from Licht im Raum, floating above the table like some celestial orb.

ENGLISH POP

PETER DUNHAM,
designer

Bored with your straitlaced
white kitchen? Here,
Dunham, a fabulously stylish
English expat, dishes on
how to animate those plain
vanilla bones and elevate
your kitchen from moribund
to mouthwatering.

THE BACKSTORY | "This is a very traditional 1920s house in Brentwood
Park, Los Angeles. A couple with three beautiful young daughters bought
it a few years ago and we redid it. The cabinets were fairly new so we kept
them, but we added the white marble, a new stove hood, and the pendants.
My goal was to make it super light, clean, fresh, and very fun."

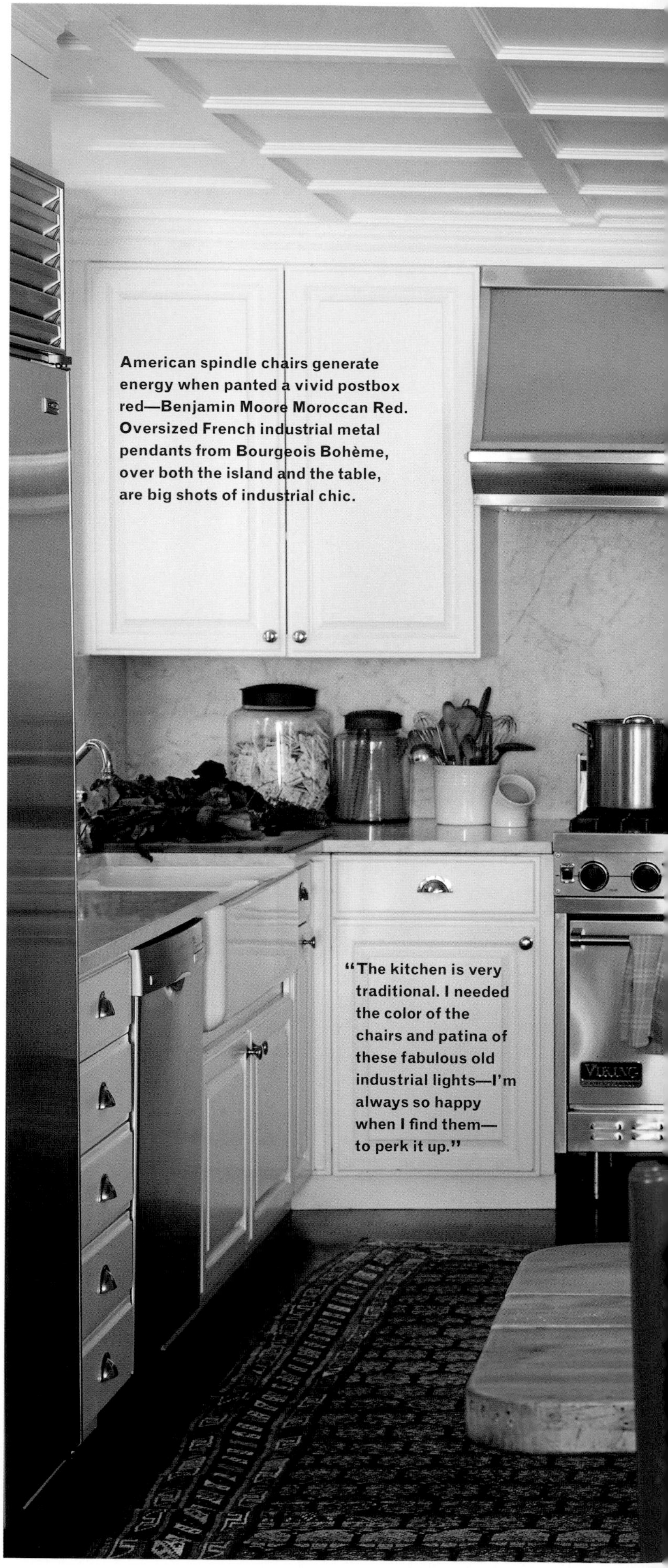

American spindle chairs generate
energy when panted a vivid postbox
red—Benjamin Moore Moroccan Red.
Oversized French industrial metal
pendants from Bourgeois Bohème,
over both the island and the table,
are big shots of industrial chic.

"The kitchen is very
traditional. I needed
the color of the
chairs and patina of
these fabulous old
industrial lights—I'm
always so happy
when I find them—
to perk it up."

A peek through an open door to the dining room's hand-painted wallpaper—copied from a paper given to legendary designer Nancy Lancaster by the King of Sweden—dazzles.

How did you transform a traditional white kitchen into something with this much drama?

I just treated white cabinets and white counters like slipcovers on a sofa. If your sofa is white anything can be built up around it, right? Well, if your kitchen is white then you're free to build in lots of really fantastic, very bold things—like these wonderful industrial light fixtures and the big green bottle on the island—for personality.

What's the one thing that adds the most personality?

A really great stove hood can make a kitchen. To me, it's like the canopy on the bed in a master bedroom. It's the one element that anchors a kitchen and gives it a strong point of view. I had this one made to resemble one of those great 1920s or 1930s hoods with contrast between brass bands and stainless steel.

What else should every kitchen have?

I always try to find a great antique table for my clients. It feels good to see age and texture among slick surfaces. And I love to use old carpets that are worn down.

But fine antiques in a kitchen?

I don't mind using antiques in a kitchen, they're very durable; but then I don't mind certain reproductions either. Like these spindle chairs. We buy them unfinished and we paint them. The pop of color is nice, but what's more, the rush seats are fantastic. They're organic and neutral, very pretty and waterproof.

CLOSE ENCOUNTERS

STEPHANIE STOKES,
designer and homeowner

To hear a kitchen described
as no bigger than a walk-in
closet is to expect the worst.
But seeing this chic little space
is to discover the best! Stokes
arranged her tight little New
York City kitchen so she could
stand at the cooktop and reach
everything she needs. Not many
square feet but miles of style.

THE BACKSTORY | "This is my own kitchen on the Upper East Side in
New York City. It's in a prewar building with 10' ceilings in what is called a
'cut-up.' It was originally part of a much larger apartment and was cut up
into smaller units during the Depression. This kitchen is 49 sq. ft. or 7' x 7',
and I wouldn't have it any other way! I approached the design like it was
a mathematical game, measuring everything I owned, even the rolls of
aluminum foil, to make sure they fit perfectly."

"I saw these hanging utensil
racks from Rösle in Italy and
thought they were the chicest
thing I'd ever seen! I hang the
small stuff over the cooktop
and the longer things over the
backsplash."

"The 5'-tall cabinets that pull
out on either side of the cooktop
are my pantries. This is where
I keep my sugar, flour, soups—
heavy stuff—so I used big
brass handles for leverage
to pull them open."

"Use every quarter inch; that's my mantra. That's why there's no trim around doors or drawers, it would have taken up too much space."

A mirrored backsplash expands the feeling of space in this tiny U-shape kitchen, where an electric cooktop doubles as a countertop. Polished Verde Guatemala marble counters and elegant cabinets, by David Benedek at BSD, lend the illusion of grandeur. Stokes designed a specific space for every pot, plate, and pepper mill.

This is a very tiny kitchen, but also very efficient. How did you manage to pull that off?
After designing so many kitchens for other people, I knew exactly what I needed and what I wanted. I entertain frequently. I can see exactly where everything is and where to put it when cleaning up. I have 14' of countertop, and the cooktop can double as a counter if necessary—it's electric because the building doesn't have gas. I also built "garages" on hydraulic lifts—custom made for me—to move small appliances into the cabinets above them when they're not needed.
Because every quarter-inch is precious, isn't it?
Absolutely. My marble countertops are only ¾" thick, rather than the usual 1¼". There are knife slots built into the counter. I even used the spaces between the studs in the walls.
You seem to have gone cabinet-crazy on top and then abandoned the whole idea on the bottom.
I have 14 sets of dishes, and I wanted them to be easy to find and reach, so I built shelves with glass doors all the way to the 10' ceiling. I counted and measured each set and designed shallow shelves to fit, without worrying about symmetry. To me, beauty is function. But I find that cabinets below are not as efficient. I prefer drawers—I can work them with my foot or my fingers. I even built drawers into the baseboards.

What's lacking in your kitchen that would probably be in a bigger one?
Well, the refrigerator is just outside the kitchen. And I have to store table linens in closets in the hallway. Then all my glasses are in the bar area in my library. But the great thing is that I put a dishwasher in my library too. And at parties I'll have both dishwashers running and no one knows because Miele dishwashers are so quiet.

No door?
If I'd used a pocket door I would have lost 4" so I installed a fabric accordion screen that pulls down from the doorjamb instead, so, when I'm entertaining, you don't see the kitchen.

This is a textbook case of "a place for everything and everything in its place." You even have a stepladder stored between the studs in the wall. What did you have to do to get it exactly right?
It took me a lot of time to draw the plans. I measured everything—my spices, my coffee tins, my bowls—to make sure they fit exactly into the drawers and cabinets and shelves. I spent a full day checking the drawings for the cabinetmaker. And then he would find another ¼" wherever he could!

The wood floor was handmade by an artisan to showcase the Stokes family crest, a way of putting a personal imprint on the kitchen design. Brass Colonial cabinet knobs and back plates from Baldwin are elegant traditional touches. Stokes stores silver trays in the baseboards, which she turned into drawers.

WHAT IF...
YOU RESEARCHED YOUR FAMILY CREST (OR JUST MADE ONE UP!) THEN HAD IT INLAID IN THE FLOOR?

"I was going to use my initials until one of my relatives said, 'It might be time to drag out the family crest!' So I researched it, discovered it was good-looking and found a Hungarian man named Josef Juhas on Long Island who has a passion for marquetry. He did such a beautiful job. And he made it so I can flip it out and take it with me if I move."

STALKING THE LOOK

1 2

3 4

5 6

Design from the inside out. Stokes says her kitchen has "inner beauty" because she thought about the insides of her cabinets and drawers before she layered on the look.

Choose a gooseneck faucet for a dash of elegance. (1) Rohl's Triflow system dispenses both hot and cold filtered water from a single elegant faucet.

Pull out all the stops. (2) Stokes's "pantry" for dry goods consists of two cabinets that slide out over the countertop. Bins for trash and recyclables similarly pull out beside the sink.

Look for the silver lining. (3) Stokes's silverware drawers are fitted with cushioned slots to hold each piece in its proper place.

Use your cooktop as counter. (4) Stokes's electric burners do the trick but Fisher & Paykel has made it possible for a cooktop with gas burners to double as counter space too. Tweak the knob of this cooktop and gas burners rise or retract to leave a smooth surface.

Make family history. You can create a custom floor crest (similar to Stokes's floor) at Imago Floors.

Use marble without fear. (5) Stokes chose thin slabs of Guatemala marble because they're "bright, light, and clean." She deals with watermarks by applying Italian Craftsman Polish every two weeks to reseal the stone.

Alphabetize! (6) Stokes says her idea of nirvana is having a drawer under her cooktop for spices that are fresh—and alphabetized.

GULF COURSE

KIM FOUQUET, *designer,*
and **NANCY BAUER,** *homeowner*

The blue-green waters of the Gulf of Mexico and the white dunes and waving grasses of Florida's Emerald Coast are the views from the windows of this remarkable kitchen. But somehow preparing dinner *inside* this beautiful vacation home feels like a day at the beach, too. Everything has a watery shimmer, even the cabinets.

THE BACKSTORY | "Nancy and Peter Bauer, and their college-age son, fell madly in love with the raw beauty of WaterSound—with its 60' dunes, freshwater lakes, and the green/blue Gulf, who wouldn't? When they decided to build a vacation house they asked my husband, Richard—who was the architect here, and me to pare our design down to the essentials. 'If it's not needed, leave it out' was their mandate. It was so refreshing! As a result everything is so wonderfully modern—not your usual beach cottage kitchen!"

The Viking Professional Series refrigerator is finished to match the St. Charles cabinetry under the windows, in Taupe. The island and upper cabinet next to the window are in St. Charles' Iridescent Blue. Custom glass- top on a satin nickel Parsons dining table, from **S&L Designs,** feels watery, and Andrew Dining Chairs in cream leather from Sunpan Imports are the color of sand. The Murano glass Spada I pendant lights in Aqua, from **CX Design,** hang over the table looking aged and beautiful. A deep inlaid sink by Elkay keeps the lines of the granite island clean.

"This is a look that appeals to a lot of people. Contemporary, but not cold—a clean, sleek design that reads as very warm—and I think that's due to the color palette. We took it straight from nature, so how can you go wrong?" —KF

"These pendant lights are so perfect—five individual pendants hang from nickel rods—the glass is emerald green, like the water, and the texture is like glass that's been blasted by the sand." —KF

"The stairs go down to the bedrooms. The living room and kitchen are upstairs to take advantage of the views of the lake, dunes, and Gulf." —KF

This looks so clean and fresh and calm, and the mood starts with those colors!

KF: We took the palette from the sand, the water, the sea oats, and the wild grasses outside. We wanted the feeling of the beach at six in the morning before everyone's out there.

How did you get such a beautiful blue watery finish on those cabinets?

NB: They're made of powder-coated stainless steel, from a company called St. Charles Cabinetry. I chose them because they look so clean. The company is now part of Viking, so you can get Viking appliances in the same colors for a very integrated look. I love that blue and taupe. If you look at the water and the sand in the sunlight, it has that same iridescent quality.

Any advantages to metal cabinets?

NB: They won't warp like wood, which makes them perfect for a beach house. And I like the fact that the steel is recyclable.

KF: All the cabinetry is made to order, so just be careful when you measure. You can shave a piece of wood but not a piece of metal. You want everything to slide right in. It helps to have a good installer.

With the dining table right there, are you worried about seeing a messy kitchen during parties?

NB: We just got the deepest, biggest sink we could find for the island. I can throw all the dirty pots in there and the kitchen looks relatively neat when we sit down at the table.

What's that wonderful misty glass on the upper cabinet doors?

NB: It's called screened glass, and I like it because everything inside doesn't have to be perfectly arranged, although it's nice when it is. The kitchen and the dining area and the living room are really one big room, so the kitchen had to be as beautiful as the rest. The upper cabinets have glass shelves and come with built-in lighting inside and underneath, which creates this lovely glow.

That island looks huge. How long is it?

KF: Ten feet. It holds a lot—the sink, the dishwasher, the trash bins, storage drawers, and a microwave that's also a convection oven.

NB: That convection microwave is fabulous. I've never had one before and I'm completely sold on it. I've got a teenage son with lots of friends and I can bake a few cookies quickly without heating up my big oven. My husband, Peter, and I both love to cook, and we wanted a big island where people could gather around and feel part of the process.

And a view of the dunes must make chopping onions a pleasure.

KF: When you're standing at the island, you see beyond the living room out through big glass windows that frame a beautiful fresh-water lake, then dunes, then the emerald-green Gulf. It's spectacular.

FULL METAL JACKET
The **Viking Professional Series** convection microwave on the working side of the island is finished in **Iridescent Blue** to match the **St. Charles** cabinetry, which—like Viking appliances—comes in 23 powder-coated colors as well as the original stainless steel. Upper cabinets in the bar area, done in pale taupe, keep the kitchen feeling airy. Fouquet chose the Venuto Bar/Prep Faucet from Brizo, with a pull-down sprayer and two settings, for both the bar sink and the island sink because of its simple lines and its versatility. A 6' x 8' walk-in pantry is behind the glass doors to the right.

WHAT IF...
YOUR KITCHEN WORE A SUIT
OF ARMOR?

....

"The Bauers really don't have to
worry about these cabinets at
all. The powder-coated finish
is virtually indestructible and
incredibly easy to clean. Plus I
love the streamlined look and
the quality of light that reflects
off the metal."

ROCK STAR
THE BACKSPLASH AND
COUNTERS ARE JURASSIC
GREEN GRANITE.

....

"Jurassic Green granite is like
looking through the water
to the bottom of the sea.
Polished, not honed, to add
to the iridescence. Granite is
so durable. I've never had a
problem with staining."
—NB

"We kept the backsplash
low because we wanted the
upper cabinets to look like
they're floating. A higher
backsplash would have
taken away from that look."
—KF

CRAVING...
POT DRAWERS! NO MORE ROOTING AROUND FOR THE OMELET PAN.

....

St. Charles drawers have magnetized wooden dowels that can be arranged in any
configuration to keep dishes or pots in place. "The drawers glide so seamlessly,"
says Fouquet. They come with full extension glides and a soft close.

How did you decide where to put the appliances?

KF: The range is the heart of the kitchen. So I centered it under a vaulted ceiling, which reminds me of the hull of a boat. Then I had to move the sink a little off-center on the island, so when Nancy's washing lettuce at the sink and Peter's cooking at the stove, they won't bump into each other. Another smart move was using drawers instead of cabinets under the counters. Much more efficient.

NB: I don't have to stoop down to see what's inside. In my other house, sometimes I'll dig into a cabinet and find things I didn't even know I had and could have used earlier.

These pulls are such a nice departure from the usual kitchen hardware.

KF: I love them. The drawer fronts feel so clean because of the built-in handles—so smooth. It's there when you need it but when you're just looking at the cabinets it's not jarring.

You matched the refrigerator and the microwave to the colors of the cabinets. Why not the stove?

NB: That Viking range is such an iconic object. I love the way it looks and decided it should be the showpiece. So I left it uncolored. That way, it relates to the stainless steel on the staircase and helps pull it all together. I wanted the kitchen to be as modern as possible, without feeling cold.

The 36" Viking Professional Series Dual Fuel Range has six burners and a convection oven—perfect for a couple who love to cook. Fouquet says that the stove's steel backsplash and large exhaust hood are strong focal points that ground the room, bringing high ceilings down to scale. Wood floors are gray-washed ash in keeping with Fouquet's "grayed out" color palette.

COLOR FORMS

FOUQUET TURNED THE VOLUME ON MUTE WITH ELMIRA WHITE AND SAIL CLOTH, BOTH BY BENJAMIN MOORE

"Benjamin Moore Elmira White is a shade deeper than Sail Cloth. We did the stove-side wall in that darker shade to lessen the contrast of stainless steel against white, which promotes a more peaceful feeling. All other walls are in Sail Cloth. I use the words 'grayed out' for the muted shades like these that I love. And then an eggshell finish was selected for all the walls for its slight reflective quality."

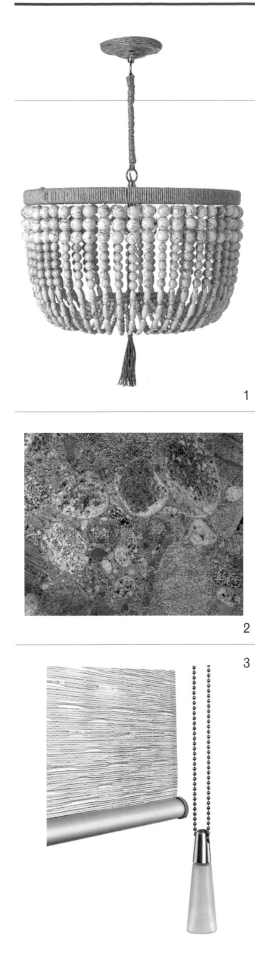

1

2

3

4

5

6

Find a chandelier with beachy appeal. (1) The natural look of the Malibu Chandelier from Serena & Lily would be just right in a beach house.

Make an upside-down house. Fouquet says, "You spend most of your time in the kitchen, so why shouldn't it be upstairs with the best view?"

Bring the landscape to your counter. (2) "This Jurassic Green granite wraps up all the colors of the landscape and all the colors of the kitchen—blue, green, and sand," says Fouquet.

Be a shade more modern. (3) A line of window shades in 17 variations from Chilewich are simple, modern, stylish, and best of all, they can be wiped clean.

Color your world. (4) The St. Charles Cabinetry frameless steel cabinets Fouquet used come in stainless steel or your pick of 23 powder-coated colors.

Bake it in color. (5) The Viking Professional Series Convection Microwave comes in 14 different color finishes—and it works as a convection, microwave, or regular oven. Available built-in or countertop.

Don't be transparent. Fouquet used screened glass on cabinet fronts so a little mild disorganization can go unnoticed.

Cover simple dining chairs in pale leather. (6) Superkidskin in Flax from J. Robert Scott wears well and improves over time. It darkens and turns waxy like a saddle.

FARM NOUVEAU

WILLIAM HEFNER,
architect and homeowner

Most travelers return from
Provence with lavender sachets
and a few bottles of olive oil.
Kazuko and William Hefner
brought back a kitchen. Or at
least the inspiration for one.
Specifically, that mix of modern
and traditional that seems to come
so easily to people from the French
countryside. Here are farmhouse
touches with contemporary lines
that are clean, clean, clean.

THE BACKSTORY | "This is a 1920s house in a traditional neighborhood of
Los Angeles, but we live in it in a modern way. My wife, Kazuko Hoshino,
is an interior designer and we have a three-year-old son, Koji. This kitchen
was actually inspired by a trip we took to Provence. The steel windows and
the semi-transparent stain on the wood are things we'd seen and admired in
contemporary renovations of old buildings in the south of France."

"At first we thought
all the light fixtures
should match, but
then we decided
a different fixture
over the breakfast
table would create
more intimacy."

The Hefners like to mix their messages. The Aspen Iron ceiling lights over the dining table on the left feel a bit more old-fashioned than the Bryant billiard fixture over the island on the right, both by Visual Comfort. And the cabinets have contemporary lines with old-fashioned drop pull handles and cottage-y tongue-and-groove detailing. The steel door to the left leads to a patio.

"We do all our prep work on the big island and then we ditch our dirty dishes in that sink at the back, which is across from a pantry. It keeps the island prep area very clean."

It's rare for a kitchen this sleek to feel so warm.
I think it's the wood. Floors are dark-stained rift oak and the cabinets are washed oak—not a veneer, but solid pieces of rift-cut white oak washed with a semitransparent gray stain.

Is that what makes the cabinets look so soft?
Yes. It tones down the grain and evens out the contrast between individual boards, kind of like a film over the whole thing.

What's a modernist like you doing with all this tongue-and-groove detailing?
I was attracted to the rhythm of that strong vertical line every four inches. You notice it before all the cuts for the drawers and cabinets. Tongue and groove is a bit rural, but the kind of wood and the finish dress it up.

The wood is great but what's really covetable is that fireplace.
Like most people, my wife and I come home at night and go in the kitchen. We cook. We eat. We usually do a little homework of some kind. Then we're asleep. The kitchen is really the only room we use during the week, so it had to have the things we wanted—a view of the yard, and a fireplace. If we're spending so much time here, let's really enjoy it.

Did you have the fireplace custom made?
Yes, without a mantel. We wanted to keep it clean. There's enough going on on that side of the room with the full-height cabinet.

**What marble did
you choose?**
Calacatta Gold—a warm
white with gray and gold
veining that coordinated
well with the wood. Being a
designer, I looked at every
stone in the world. This felt
fresh and light—good for
a room that's open to the
outdoors. And it's honed
because if it were polished
it would feel kind of fancy
and we're trying to be casual
here. The counters are 2¼"
thick with a ¼" scooped edge
detail to make it feel a little
less contemporary.

**Are there *two* refrigerators
flanking the range?**
Yes. We do all these kitchens
for clients and they go
to great pains to be sure
they've got enough storage
to accommodate plates and
platters and the million
other things they need. Then
you open the refrigerator and
things are crammed in there
with a shoehorn. Having
two refrigerators is a very
practical luxury.

**That's a serious range.
Who cooks?**
We both do. We bought a Wolf
because I was in a kitchen
appliance showroom one day,
and the salesman opened
the oven door and stood on
it. I thought, "Wow! I have to
have one of those."

**You designed your own
range hood? Why?**
I didn't think the kitchen
was modern enough for the
hood to be one long, flat piece
of stainless steel so I divided
it into three and used the
studs for detail.

FASHION-FORWARD FARMHOUSE
To balance all the wood, Hefner designed a stainless-steel cover plate for the hood, a **Calacatta Gold** marble backsplash, and a 4" wide marble frame around the range. The hardware is from **Gerber Hinge Company**, which manufactures French-style drawer pulls and knobs. Two built-in **Sub-Zero** refrigerators, flanking the range, are completely hidden behind rift-cut white oak panels.

WHAT IF . . .
YOU AND YOUR FIREPLACE
COULD SEE EYE TO EYE.

" The fireplace is elevated 30" off the floor, just a little lower than countertop height, so you can see the fire from wherever you are in the room. If you're sitting on the stools or at the table, it's easily visible. And I put the wood right underneath, because if you have to go outside to get it you're less likely to do it."

REMAKING HISTORY
KOHLER'S FARMHOUSE SINK AND PERRIN & ROWE'S BRIDGE FAUCET IN POLISHED NICKEL ADD COZY CHARM TO MODERN CABINETRY.

" This is our cleanup sink and I've found farmhouse sinks to be really durable. The porcelain apron looks so much better than the kind of panels you usually see below a regular sink, which always seem to get trashed so quickly."

CRAVING . . .
A WALL OF BLACK STEEL WINDOWS WITH A MODERN-DAY *JE NE SAIS QUOI.*

" It's like something you'd see in the south of France where someone takes an old house and blows out a wall to open it up and doesn't feel guilty about it."

The island looks like it's about the size of Corsica. It's 4' x 11'. It kind of takes up the whole room. But it needs to be that large because it's our workspace. There are no other counters, just little bits by the range and the cleanup area. We wanted windows on two sides of the room so we wouldn't feel cooped up if we were in there on a nice day—that rendered a lot of the kitchen unusable.

What's in those long cabinets next to the refrigerators?
That's where we store oils and vinegars and all the things we cook with most often and it's where we hide the microwave and small appliances. Everything is close to the prep area.

I don't think I've ever seen square recessed lights!
They're European and they come in little boxes that you install before the drywall, then you plaster all around them. There's no trim like with normal recessed lights so they're a little quieter in the ceiling.

"**The kitchen chairs are Italian from the mid-1940s. We had them restored and recovered in faux leather. The fabric feels natural but it's very tough. Believe it or not, those chairs have seen everything from cranberry juice to egg yolks!**"

Farmhouse counter stools from **West Elm** push under the island and out of the line of traffic when not needed. European downlights—the Minigrid from **Delta Light**—are set in square rather than round recesses in the ceiling, which works neatly with the coffers. Painting by **Ford Crull** is a modern touch. Chairs are covered in durable fabric, Barcelona by **Innovations**, and French doors open to the swimming pool.

COLOR FORMS
HEFNER USES PRATT & LAMBERT CHALK GRAY TO KEEP THE MOOD CASUAL

"Chalk Gray is a nice neutral, without a hint of pink or green and that's why we liked it. It works well with the natural wood and it doesn't clash with white marble. It feels casual, it's a very relaxed shade."

STALKING THE LOOK

1

3

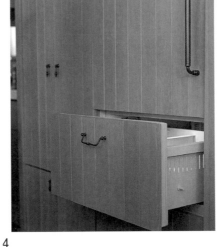

4

5

Create a mash-up of traditional and modern. Hefner's kitchen is a blend of old-fashioned faucets and contemporary light fixtures, farmhouse sinks and steel windows, and contemporary cabinets with tongue-and-groove detailing.

"X" out the French doors on the kitchen plan. Do as Hefner did, and use floor-to-ceiling steel windows and doors instead.

Install a pot filler over the stove for cleanup! (1) After cooking, Hefner puts water in the pots right away with his pot filler, by Perrin & Rowe, so they're easier to wash later.

Fill a rush basket with firewood and place it *under* **your elevated firebox.** (2) The large rectangular Rush Basket from Beach Bungalow has handles for easy transport from the woodpile.

Make a hardworking island. With no wall-facing counters, all food prep is done on Hefner's enormous island—while enjoying a garden view.

Tuck Shinto stools under your counter. (3) Earthy and graceful, this Shinto Counter Stool from Room & Board, made of Chinese hardwood, is traditional and also modern.

Play "hide the fridge." (4) In Hefner's kitchen rift-cut white oak masks a Sub-Zero 736TCI with freezer drawers.

Swap out some of the kitchen chairs for an extra-long banquette. (5) Put two 46" Ava Loveseats together, from Mitchell Gold + Bob Williams.

TRUE ORIGINAL

STEVEN GAMBREL,
designer

Talk about *Hello Gorgeous*!
This kitchen manages
to seem friendly and white-hot
hip at the same time. Gambrel
has taken familiar—dare we
say old-fashioned?—kitchen
elements and given them
a healthy dose of 21st century
cool. How does someone
make diner-style barstools
look snappy? Read on.

THE BACKSTORY | "This house is on Long Island next to the ocean, an inlet, and a lake. Everywhere around it is water, sky, reeds, grass. I tried to take what was given to me via the environment—very pale, atmospheric blues and greens, or as I sometimes say, sky into water into tree."

Gambrel used nautical latches as hardware.

"I love hardware and I love lighting—they're both jewelry for the architecture."

"We've all seen gorgeous white kitchens, and there's a place for them. I was trying to create something modern and clean. But I thought bringing in the colors of nature— silvers, grays, oysters, driftwoods, and sands—would be more appropriate."

Classic Norman Cherner plywood chairs look handsome around a vintage stone-topped table from **ABC** Carpet & Home. The 1940s rope chandelier adds a nautical note "without being hokey," says Gambrel. For casual dining at the Gascogne Blue limestone island, Gambrel covered barstools from a restaurant supply store in surprising blue leather—which picks up the blue tones of the stone.

This is such a fabulous mix! How did you do it? It's about clean and simple. I wanted everything to have a chunky, useful, casual quality to it, and a similar level of detail. I didn't want the contrast of pieces with too much intricacy. These clean-lined modern pieces mix well. I also like to use them next to things with more patina like that rustic table with a worn surface. All the light fixtures are so eye-catching. I've made a conscious decision not to rely on recessed lighting for my projects. That provides more focus on the fixtures. It's a wonderful way of bringing in something unique.

Why did you use three different kinds of fixtures? When there's no recessed lighting, you really need all of them. The flush-mounted ones have a utilitarian look and furnish good general lighting. The pendants over the island and sink add additional task lighting. The rope chandelier is more decorative and helps define the dining area as a separate space. I also think they all look really good together.

PENDANT LIGHTS from Urban Archaeology and flush-mount lights from Remains are throwbacks from another era, but because Gambrel used so many of them, and mixed them with a modern rope chandelier, they feel contemporary. Benjamin Moore Horizon on boarded walls and trim plays softly against back-splashes and counters in Gascogne Blue limestone. Floors have a natural finish. And that muted backdrop allows the upbeat pattern of window shades, in White #10 by Muriel Brandolini through Holland & Sherry, to inject a fresh pop of youth.

A COLOR CONSULT

SO YOU WANT TO BREAK AWAY FROM WHITE?

Designer Christina Rottman isn't afraid of a little turquoise. "I wanted this jolt of color to emphasize that the kitchen is the joyful heart of the house," she says. But this kind of presence isn't achieved by paint alone. Peter Boltan of Boltan Painted Finishes applied a blackened umber glaze to the cabinets, then painted over the umber with a second turquoise glaze. Buffing, stippling, and scraping gave the cabinets a timeworn look.

"It *is* intense. And I did keep it going and going once I started with the cabinets. I knew I wanted a strong statement of color."

Glass-front cabinets provide shine and depth, and keep the turquoise from completely overwhelming the room.

The taupe-y color of limestone counters is soft relief from all the strong color—white would have been too bold.

TURN UP THE LIGHT.
Turquoise cabinets
reflect beautifully off
the stainless-steel Wolf
range. Porridge-color
walls are even lighter
than pale limestone
counters, brightening
dark, turquoise tones.
Decorative artist
Peter Bolton treated
the kitchen's stove
hood with a pale, faux
limestone finish.

THE LANGUAGE OF COLOR

BY ARCHITECTURAL COLOR
EXPERT DONALD KAUFMAN

- **BRIGHTNESS:** Perceived lightness. Making a space feel full of light is different from making it light.

- **GLAZE:** A transparent paint applied over a solid background.

- **GLOSS:** The degree to which surfaces are smooth and therefore reflective. See *High-gloss.*

- **HIGH GLOSS:** Because of its expense, the most underused and underappreciated paint treatment. The only difference between a flat and glossy surface is texture.

- **INTENSITY:** A description of saturation, independent of hue or lightness. I like thinking of intensity as how much of the color is in the color.

- **LUMINOUS:** The appearance of emitting radiant energy. Because of their resemblance to burning light sources, reds, oranges, and yellows appear more luminous than cooler hues.

- **NEUTRAL:** A neutral does not have to be a shade of white, beige, or gray. It need appear neither pale nor colorless. What it does require is a balance of warm and cool tones so that it can, in context, function as a color from either end of the spectrum. It will often be as deep or light as the objects it surrounds. Like a good understudy a neutral can always take over any role.

- **TRANSITIONS:** As our vision sorts out the world, edges are more important than what they contain, so in room-to-room schemes, note where the colors change.

- **TRANSLUCENT:** The quality of partial transparency, which gives leaves and grasses great depth as light filters through them.

- **TEXTURE:** The nature of the surface, texture exerts a strong influence over color. No matter how shallow the depth, all pattern and relief will create shadows.

GUTSY ATTITUDE
"It just seemed the perfect
place for color because several
rooms spill into the kitchen,
so the blue kind of travels
throughout the house. And
the kitchen is the right scale—
you don't want strong color
in the biggest room. I always
punctuate with color. It's playful. You don't want a place to
take itself *too* seriously."
—CHRISTINA ROTTMAN

CREATE A BOLD PERSPECTIVE.
An archway in the creamy living room is a dramatic frame for the bright
turquoise kitchen beyond. "I like the way the living room's Moorish
doorway frames the cabinets, like a piece of art," says Rottman.

1

2

3

4

5

6

PLAY WITH PATTERN.
Colorful 19th-century French concrete tiles purchased at **Chateau Domingue** in **Houston**, lend this kitchen a bright attitude. Striped shirred curtains, in **Wallace Ticking** from **Carleton V**, on the interiors of the glass cabinets emphasize the green in the tile and play down all the other colors. For simplicity's sake, neutral-hued antique Italian jars are displayed.

" It's old reclaimed tile from France that was probably on the floor of some château. It was kind of a gutsy direction for me to do such a bold backsplash. But when I saw that tile—the colors—I knew I had to have it for this kitchen."
—SHANNON BOWERS, DESIGNER

**PICK ONE COLOR
AND RUN WITH IT.**
French faience on the open shelves demonstrate Bowers's design tactic— pulling only the color green from the backsplash to keep things calm. Bowers liked the look of old wood against the vibrant tiles. The big French cutting boards are both functional and pretty. Counters are concrete, an earthy material that calms all the color and pattern.

"Countertops are tricky. I don't like granite. It's too speckled and busy for me. The counters are 2" thick, thicker than normal, which makes them feel more substantial. The house is big and the ceilings are high and they had to be the right scale."

1. **TAKE GREEN GINGHAM OVER THE TOP.**
"My clients are lovers of plaids and checks. So I thought, 'Why not the ceiling?' We blew up the scale to treat the eye and painted it on canvas first. It brings extremely high ceilings down to a more comfortable place."
—GIDEON MENDELSON, DESIGNER

2. **GRANT YOUR INTERIORS LIFE.**
"Benjamin Moore South Beach 2043-50 is a really green turquoise. It reminds me of sea glass, and we used it in a beach house that was all about fresh air and fresh color. It worked well in the back of the cabinets as an accent color. And it tied in with other things we used in the kitchen."
—JASON BELL, DESIGNER

3. **SPEAK SOFTLY.**
"The name gives you the idea that it's silvery, but it's not. Christopher Peacock Paint Mercury CPP1 18 is a medium pale gray that goes really well with both traditional and contemporary and doesn't show the wear that white cabinetry does. It also looks great with stainless steel, nickel, and Carrara marble."
—PENNY DRUE BAIRD, DESIGNER

4. **COOK WITH RED.**
A restored 1950s O'Keefe and Merritt stove from Antique Stove Heaven lends new energy to an old cottage kitchen.

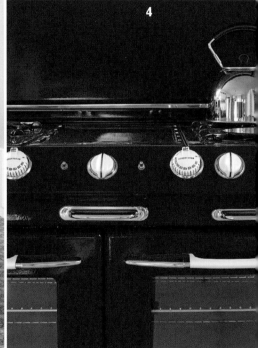

5. **HAVE A SUNNY ATTITUDE.**
"One day we decided our kitchen needed brightening. I replaced the cabinet doors with glass fronts and painted the back of the cabinet in Satsuma (from Christopher Peacock Paint) and picked the color up in the Roman shade above the sink. It totally freshened the space and lifted our moods."
—CHRISTOPHER PEACOCK, KITCHEN DESIGNER

6. **PUT A SHINE ON.**
Cabinets are lacquered in Bamboo Leaf by Fine Paints of Europe, as was the roller shade by Manhattan Shade & Glass, which hides an exhaust unit. Even the Sub-Zero is painted green in this New York City kitchen by designer Miles Redd.

GO AHEAD, GO OVER THE TOP.
The color blue is used with wild
abandon on the ceiling, but paired
only with white. That lets the ceiling
be theatrical but not busy. A Sub-
Zero drawer refrigerator means the
only obvious appliance is the stove.
Casement windows fling open,
ushering in light and greenery.

....

"Michael Duté's swirling designs
on the wall and across the barrel-
vaulted ceiling are so big, open,
and graphic. They make it airy and
dramatic. He based them on patterns
in Swedish classical rococo interiors, but it's also suggestive of blue-
and-white china, which is perfect for
a kitchen."

—ERIN MARTIN

**USE BLUE-AND-WHITE PATTERN EVERY-
WHERE AND BE ENVELOPED IN CHARM.**
The backsplash is clad in intricate blue-and-
white French tile from Country Floors—it
even runs behind the plate rack. But almost
everything else in the kitchen (aside from the
ceiling) is done in broad swathes of white or
natural wood—counters in Calacatta marble,
cabinets and shelves painted white, and an island
in chestnut—to keep the peace. Michael Duté
dressed up the Vent-A-Hood range hood
in neutral tones with a cartouche of deer in
a landscape.

....

"The tiles are an inspirational shade of blue.
They're French, but they remind me of being in
Morocco where everything is covered in colorful,
unique, handmade tile."

—ERIN MARTIN, DESIGNER

HEAT

Mankind has been cooking with heat ever since cavemen started rubbing sticks together. Of course, there's been an innovation or three since then—modern miracles like convection, induction, microwave—there are even new appliances for the purists who want to go back to burning wood. Here are some standouts from the myriad of choices, the best ways to perform what's really a very old task—applying heat to food.

HOT TOPICS

What are the practical differences between gas, induction, and electric cooktops?
"Electric cooktops are a bit slower in general. Producing even heat is their strength. Induction is electric too, but it's much faster and it's my first choice if I must go with electric. I've worked with professional chefs who actually prefer induction over any other type of cooktop for its speed (faster than gas to both heat and cool), and ease of cleanup. A big plus for gas burners is seeing the flame. Our brain has the ability to equate the size of the flame with the heat level under the cooking vessel. Gas is still the number-one choice for most people."
—**MICK DE GIULIO**, KITCHEN DESIGNER

What are dual-fuel ranges and do you like them?
Dual-fuel refers to ranges that offer electric ovens with gas cooktops. In my opinion, electric ovens offer superior performance over gas ovens, plus they have a self-cleaning feature. Gas ovens are usually not self-cleaning. I like dual-fuel for my clients—it's the best of both worlds."
—**MICK DE GIULIO**

The limestone hood above the Wolf range is the kitchen's showstopper. Walls are antique reclaimed *dale de Bourgogne* limestone and countertops are cast concrete.
"The stove hood is the focal point of the room. The pinned limestone—'pinned' means it has a soft, broken finish—gives the hood such old-world power."
—**ERIN MARTIN**, DESIGNER

You put a state-of-the-art stove in a homey beadboard niche? Isn't this BlueStar range geared to the professional cook?

"It's nice to keep the flavor of an old house! And my wife was always a good cook, but now she's a great one." —PETER FISHEL, DESIGNER

What does that huge stainless-steel box next to the range do?

"It's a salamander—a commercial-grade infrared broiler by Southbend with 40,000 BTUs. It preheats in 90 seconds. Perfect for broiling steaks. The client is a serious cook, and she also has a commercial-grade DCS range. The island was designed with open shelves on the range side so she'd have easy access to all the pots and pans."

—R. ROMAN HUDSON, DESIGNER

POWER TO BURN

How many burners are too many?

Let's be honest, who doesn't love the look of a hunky six-burner range? Add two more burners and you've got a stove as seductive as a V-8 Roadster. But before you start offering precious kitchen real estate to your new crush, ask yourself "How often do I really use multiple burners?" If your answer is "only on Thanksgiving," then four burners are more than enough. If you're a morning pancake fiend those foregone burners could be a great big griddle, or maybe a downdraft grill for those winter nights you can't shovel your way to the Weber.

Do all burners cook alike?

If you have gas you can custom calibrate your burners. You may want to set a couple that can go ultra-low for slow simmering and low-heat cooking. Then maybe designate one as your high-heat burner with a very high flame for quick searing. But whether you go with gas or electric, your stove should give you ease of control. You need to be able to simmer on low, fry on medium and sear on high. If your burners jump too quickly from low to high, or just won't go low at all, your cooking is going to suffer. Not even the Rolls Royce of ranges is worth buying if you can't get its heat under control.

This hood above the Viking range is fabulous!
"It's made out of stainless steel with polished nickel trim so you get that contrast of soft and crisp. And the rivets give a flat piece of metal some sex appeal."
—**MADELINE STUART**, DESIGNER

Who makes this amazing range?
"It's a La Cornue—they're handmade in France to your specifications. It comes with a high learning curve, but once you master it, it's fabulous. The people who sold it to us showed up with a chicken and cookie dough to give us a lesson. I love the plaque, which is this whole section on top that heats up. And it's so beautiful, almost like jewelry for the kitchen."
—**SUSAN DOSSETTER**, DESIGNER

I keep hearing about steam ovens. How do they work?
"Gaggenau makes a wall unit that does both regular and steam cooking. You pour water into it much like you would a coffee machine, and that gives you enough steam to cook for about an hour. So you can do your vegetables, or shrimp and seafood, or use it just to refresh food that has cooled down."
—**LOUIS GIOGAIA**, MANAGER, GRINGER & SONS APPLIANCES

FIREPOWER

Speak colorful Italian.
Bertazzoni breaks with tradition with burgundy and cream ranges in its Heritage Series line. Matching hoods available.

Have it your way.
Kitchen design a la carte. With CombiSets from Miele you can choose a deep fryer, a wok, a teppanyaki grill, gas or electric burners, or an induction cooktop, to create a setup that's just for you.

Save energy.
This 36" range, the Aga PRO+, was designed with energy savings in mind. It comes with a panel you can slide into the oven to partition off a smaller cooking space. Remove it to make a bigger meal.

Harness thermal energy.
Induction is fast heating, energy efficient, safe, and super-easy to clean. This freestanding Kenmore range has four induction burners, a convection oven, and a warming drawer.

Cook with sass.
Cook like a TV chef with all your burners in a row, not two by two, with this Bulthaup gas cooktop.

Get silver polish.
You can't beat the speed of induction cooking. And the mirrored silver finish on Thermador's powerful induction cooktop is one of the most elegant. Cleaning is easy thanks to the sleek ceramic surface.

Choose beauty.
The 36" dual-fuel Opera range from Smeg is so beautifully crafted, right down to those sexy knobs, that you might forget it's a kitchen appliance.

Be blue.
You won't forget to turn off the Epicure Dual-Fuel Range from Dacor—the knob glows "flame-blue" when the oven, or a burner, is on. We also like the control panel that tilts up for easier navigation.

Lose your hood.
This Miele exhaust hood knows its place: flat against the wall when not in use. Just push a button to get it moving.

What sold **Chicago** professional chef and homeowner **Joseph Decker** on the **Wolf** stove was the even heat of its convection oven, but then he also likes playing around with his wood-burning **Bistro Oven** by **Wood Stone**, built into the brick wall on the right.

"I'm executive chef and partner at the **Wildfire** restaurants and I've fallen in love with cooking in a wood oven. You get this wonderful caramelization outside and all the juices inside. You can make pizza with a nice little char on the bottom and you can really sear meats and fish."

HOT SHOTS

Make it crispier.
Thin crust, deep dish—serve it up! Kalamazoo Outdoor Gourmet's outdoor oven —Artisan Fire Pizza Oven—allows you to tailor the heat to bake your favorite style pizza with the crispiest crust.

Hurry up.
A 60-minute gourmet could do it in 4 with TurboChef's Speedcook oven. Heated air blasts through to roast, bake, even dehydrate.

Be flexible.
Steam cooking, convection, or a combination of the two—all in one wall oven by Thermador.

Pop your popcorn in a drawer.
Sharp Electronics' 24" Microwave Drawer means you can conveniently tuck it under a countertop without having to bend down to take food in and out.

Get shorty.
Two compact GE ovens in one single-wide slot: a tight 30". A 22-pound turkey has room to baste in the bottom, with convection capability.

Turn, turn, turn.
Part appliance, part eye-catching centerpiece, La Cornue's Flambergé is a built-in gas rotisserie for preparing extra-juicy meat, poultry, or fish.

Get a tutorial.
Jenn-Air ovens have 7" touch screens complete with visuals. Enter the type of food, how well-done you'd like it, and the kind of pan you're using, and the oven adjusts accordingly. Available in 27" and 30" models.

Be a control freak.
This line of electric built-in ovens from Electrolux will help you cook multiple courses all at once. The touch-screen top lets you control seven cooking modes from bake to slow cook, and ten cooking options including a "Perfect Turkey" button.

Just stick it in the drawer.
This KitchenAid warming drawer multitasks. It warms several dishes at once or keeps them moist and crisp; it slow-cooks roast beef and poultry to perfection and coaxes your bread dough to rise. Available in three sizes.

rebel

THE UNKITCHEN. HIDDEN BEHIND CABINETRY OR MERGED INTO THE LIVING ROOM, IT'S HARD TO TELL YOU'RE EVEN IN THE KITCHEN.

HIDDEN GEM

RUARD VELTMAN,
architect and homeowner

Living rooms are often
so isolated from family
life they should be stripped of
the word "living." But if you do
as architect Ruard Veltman did
and tuck an artfully disguised
kitchen into one corner,
yours could become the true
heart of the home.

THE BACKSTORY | "I'm originally from Holland and I remember gathering around these large tables for dinners that lasted three or four hours. I love that camaraderie. My wife and I will sometimes do six or seven smaller courses just so we can prolong the time at the table. We wind up sitting there for hours, even though it is just one part of a large living room."

"So many people are scared to live in their living room. They've got a formal living room and dining room in the front of the house, and they end up living in the back, in the kitchen. I dreamed of a house where you really do cook and eat and live in one room."

"The cabinets are just planks glued together with a little separation in between, to give them a bit of age and make them look more handcrafted."

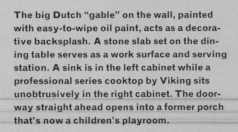

The big Dutch "gable" on the wall, painted with easy-to-wipe oil paint, acts as a decorative backsplash. A stone slab set on the dining table serves as a work surface and serving station. A sink is in the left cabinet while a professional series cooktop by Viking sits unobtrusively in the right cabinet. The doorway straight ahead opens into a former porch that's now a children's playroom.

This is one unusual layout. You've got a cooktop, a sink, and a big, long table in your living room.

Why not? It's the most beautiful space, so why would I not want to be here every day?

Did you try to make the cooktop and the sink disappear?

Not totally. I wanted them to look like two pieces of cabinetry that just happen to function as a sink and a cooktop. Both have stainless steel on top, but it's recessed. If I had wrapped them in stainless steel it would have looked too much like a kitchen.

Where's the refrigerator, and oven, and all the rest of the stuff?

In a working pantry off to the right. When this house was built back in 1949, that was the original kitchen. But it had no windows; I couldn't imagine cooking there. The table is in the original dining room, which we opened up to the living room.

So how does the cooking actually work?

You bring all your ingredients in here. I enjoy making a meal—washing the vegetables in the prep sink, chopping them on that piece of stone. You can even bring over a hot pan from the stove and serve from the stone.

So why not just open up the pantry to the living room too? Make it all one great big space?

The idea was to enjoy the things that I love to do in a kitchen—cook and chop and wash fresh fruit and vegetables—but not deal with any of the mess. The pantry is 140 sq. ft. and everything having to do with our daily routine is in there. There are two dishwashers, one on either side of the sink, fronted in simple vertical slabs of wood. The wall ovens are to the right of the sink and the washer and dryer are on the left. Sometimes the stainless prep table doubles as a laundry folding station.

What's on that wall in the pantry? Two more sinks?

Actually, four. That's a 12'-long secondhand sink that I found in this restaurant supply place, and it has four bays. Overkill, I admit, but I like those big gestures sometimes. It was also an instant countertop and I adore it. You can do anything in there and you can't hurt it—wash up kids' paints and paintbrushes, wash muddy boots, wash clothes, wash the dog . . .

What is this stunning pantry floor made of?

When I took up an old tile floor I thought the pattern of the old glue on the sub-floor looked great, really incredible. So I simply scraped, sanded, and sealed it. I think it looks like aged leather. It never looks dirty.

THE PANTRY IS COMMAND CENTRAL
If you're going to have 12' of sink you'll need extendable industrial spray faucets to clean it up. For parties, the Veltmans will sometimes place a chopping block over two of the sinks and set up this area as a bar. The sink unit, stainless-steel worktable—from Recycled Restaurant Equipment—and the stainless-steel clad Sub-Zero refrigerator (on the left) lend this utilitarian pantry some full-on industrial chic.

WHAT IF . . .

YOUR OVEN AND YOUR COOKTOP LIVED SEPARATE LIVES? MAYBE EVEN IN SEPARATE ROOMS?

. . . .

"I'm torn between two things: a very clean, modern kitchen with everything hidden, and a very utilitarian space with every-thing on open shelves—glasses, dishes, equipment, food. By having two rooms, with a prep sink and cooktop incorporated in the furnishings of one, and the ovens, storage, and cleanup out of sight in the other, I can have it both ways. After a dinner party we can quickly put every-thing to do with the meal in the pantry, turn off the light, and go on with the evening."

FALLING WATER

THE LIVING ROOM PREP-SINK FAUCET BY DORNBRACHT IS SO BEAUTIFULLY STREAM-LINED IT NEARLY DISAPPEARS.

. . . .

"I hate those two-level sinks with a tiny vegetable basin, so I designed my own, with a larger basin on one side. This is the 'clean' sink, just for vegetables and fruits. No greasy pots and pans. The faucet is very simple and the handle is within the sink, so you don't have to reach up with a wet hand and get the wall wet."

CRAVING . . .

STELLA ARTOIS ALWAYS ON TAP; IT'S ALL ABOUT HOSPITALITY.

. . . .

"Beer bottles take up a lot of room in the fridge—too much room really—and I like to always be prepared for a party. I keep three or four cases of wine on hand for the same reason. Behind this tap is the garage and that's where the kegerator lives. I can say to friends at any moment 'just come on over.' This tap is a wonderful thing."

Where did you find these beautiful light fixtures in the dining/prep area?
I designed them and had them made. The idea was for the fixture over the table to look like those lights you see strung over courtyards in Europe, draped effortlessly over a patio. They're just bulbs hung from electrical wires so you get these pretty 'V' shapes and a nice rhythm. And as with anything this simple, the result is always elegant. You can dim them down for dinner or turn them up high for cleanup and prep. Then the two sconces installed in the gable backsplash are made of hollow brass tubes, so electrical cords run right through them. It let me avoid doing an ugly sconce back plate.

" **At one point I thought of designing some sort of island to float over the table, but then I thought, 'No. Too complicated.' It should feel as if you went into your backyard and just found a piece of stone. One end is chiseled to look like it was broken off and it's propped up with two blocks of oak to raise it to counter height.** "

The dining table is 11' long and the slab of travertine (a type of limestone); makes for a beautiful and durable work surface. Veltman chose travertine not just for looks but also because "you can't hurt it and it's easy to clean." Its pitted surface is usually filled and sealed when it's used for a kitchen countertop, but Veltman likes the natural look of the unfilled crevices.

COLOR FORMS

VELTMAN CREATES TRANQUILITY WITH BENJAMIN MOORE WHITE DOWN 970.

" It's the warmest white and it's always soothing, never too bright. You know how some movie stars' teeth look way too bright and you think 'what is wrong with them?' This white is never like that. It can be a little loose or it can be formal and it's a great backdrop for art, flowers, vegetables, whatever—nothing competes with it. "

1

2

3

4   5

Go for very unkitchen-y task lighting. Veltman designed surprisingly elegant sconces for over the sink and stove. (1) Place 420650 from Fine Arts Lamps over your workstation and suddenly food prep becomes gloriously swank.

Design cabinets that jibe with your decor. The "gable" backsplash and built-ins in Veltman's kitchen have a simple Dutch farmhouse feel that's in perfect harmony with the rest of the room. The sink and cooktop hide ever-so-discreetly in plain sight.

Choose an unobtrusive range. The Viking Professional Series Cooktop works in the Veltmans' kitchen because knobs are on top, rather than arrayed across an apron, so the stove stays undercover.

Pick a durable splash-ready dining table so you can site a food prep station right on top. Veltman's Verellen farm table is made of reclaimed teak. (2) The elegant Mayan Teak Rusa Dining Table, from HOM Escape in Style by Cisco Brothers, will gussy up your kitchen even though it's tough enough to use outdoors.

Seek out dinnerware that multitasks— casual enough for everyday, fancy enough for entertaining. (3) (LEFT) Ballard Designs' Siena Goblet hits just the right note; pretty not prissy. (RIGHT) Metallic glazed stoneware, Pewter Stoneware from Juliska, looks antique but it's actually freezer, microwave, oven, and dishwasher safe.

Be brave. Choose sophisticated seating that might not feel like it belongs in a kitchen. (4) The Classic Cove Settee by Barbara Barry is living-room-chic but it's also perfectly scaled for breakfast rooms and kitchens.

And for something completely unexpected: candlelight in your pantry. Veltman hung an ornate antique candle sconce next to his beer tap—talk about mixing high and low. (5) You could use Tuvalu Home's Vintage Flowers Bouquet Wall Sconce in your bedroom but think of the impression it would make in your pantry next to the breadbox.

Use an industrial sprayer as sculpture. Sink sprayers by Fisher lend maximum impact to Veltman's pantry, and oh, they're practical too.

An opulent silver-leaf Napoleon III mirror hangs over the FiveStar stove. The chandelier was fashioned from a pair of large antique bronze sconces.

GRAND MANNER

MARK LESLIE AND RICHARD NORRIS,
designers and homeowners

Is this a glamorous dining room or a hardworking kitchen? The sink sits in a chest of drawers, the 9'-long oval island resembles a dining table, the stove is freestanding and backed with an elegant mirror. With quietly confident choices like these, two clever homeowners transformed their kitchen into the dreamiest, dressiest room in their house.

THE BACKSTORY | "In 2000, the lady who owned this house, built around 1915, passed away one month shy of her 100th birthday. We weren't looking for a house, but one day we wandered in: they were having an estate sale," says Norris. "Then I called up her niece, the executrix of her estate, and we hit it off. We told stories, had a great time. After two hours on the phone, the house was ours."

> "When we bought the house, our kitchen was the dining room. So we got the idea to make our kitchen *look* like a beautiful dining room."
> —RN

> "It became a sort of game to make every part of our new kitchen correspond to a piece of dining room furniture. The little old lady who owned the house before us had a huge oval table in the middle of it. So the elliptical marble island is like her table. The sink is like a buffet. The refrigerator is like a china cabinet—we actually had an armoire made to put it in. And the stove is like a sideboard. Don't dining rooms always have big mirrors over the sideboard?"
> —RN

Is cooking in front of a silver-leaf Napoleon III mirror even remotely practical?

RN: Absolutely! People always ask, "Aren't you going to ruin that precious thing? Doesn't it get spattered?" Well, you take out the Windex. It couldn't be easier. Besides, I love a good contrast. Always have.

What's reflected in the mirror?

RN: Opposite the stove there's a big bay window overlooking the garden, that's why we came up with the idea of putting that enormous pier mirror over the stove and turning it into a window. You can look up while you're cooking and see all the greenery behind you, or talk to people via the mirror.

Truthfully, do you really cook every day in this over-the-top space?

ML: Actually, I've just finished writing an Italian cookbook, *Beyond the Pasta; Recipes, Language and Life with an Italian Family!* And it was wonderful to have the island—a big, beautiful sheet of marble, about 6'-long and 5'-wide—without a sink or anything breaking it up. It's a counter, a table, a display, and a work surface where I can easily roll out pasta for 20. I'm a practical Midwesterner and I like things to work. I prepared and tested all the recipes in my book right here.

It's not often you see bat prints over a sink.

RN: The sink was designed to have a set of five framed prints over it—the marble backsplash behind the faucet acts as the sixth print. Mark and I love Halloween, and one October we were vacationing in Siena. We walked into this print shop and Mark asked the owner in very broken Italian if he had any bat prints. What ensued was a lot of arm flapping and squeaking. The guy finally shouted, *"Pipistrelli!"* And he pulled out these. We actually have several sets of prints and switch them out. The seaweed prints come out for summer, and we have some green grapes that we usually put up around Lent.

Why did you choose white marble for the counters?

RN: We went with local marble, Alabama White marble. This house was built around 1915 and it probably had Alabama White marble in it originally. We looked for a clear white color with gray veining. It's honed so it has a dull finish, not polished because we didn't want it to be shiny. And even though Mark cooks a lot we haven't had many stains. If something spills, we just wipe it up right away.

ML: Plus this white marble works so well as a serving surface for a buffet. Dark surfaces, like dark plates, make food look dull but everything looks great on white marble!

BATTY
McAlpine Tankersley Architecture, the firm where **N**orris works as the business manager, designed the island and lower cabinets to resemble elegant dining room furniture. The sink is undermounted to be unobtrusive and the **KWC** faucet has a wing-like silhouette—echoing the surrounding bat prints.

WHAT IF...
YOU USED YOUR
FAVORITE FRAMED ART
FOR A BACKSPLASH?

....

"**We never considered a
traditional backsplash.
And this way we can
switch out the prints and
change the feeling of the
room without having to
repaint! Tile or quilted
stainless steel would have
been so utilitarian, this
makes the room a place
you want to spend time
in. And glass is the best
material for a backsplash,
no grout to worry about,
it doesn't scratch, and
we just Windex,
Windex, Windex.**"
—ML

CRAVING...
TASK LIGHTING THAT'S
A GLORIOUS RIFF ON
OLD-WORLD GLITZ.

....

"**This chandelier is actually
made from two big sconces
that were in an antiques
shop for years. We couldn't
figure out how to use them.
One day we were in the shop
with a friend, and he put
the two ends, the backs of
the sconces, together. We
said, 'That's it!' They're held
together by two screws.**"
—RN

Did you install this gorgeous wall of windows? "That's actually the original dining room's bay window. The windows bring in incredible light and those doors make it so easy to just go out and eat on the back patio, which we do all the time. And when we're entertaining we can set up a buffet on the island and let the party flow out into the garden. Even in winter I can cook a beautiful meal while experiencing the beauty of nature!" —ML

The island extends into the kitchen's light-filled bay window, which opens onto a patio overlooking a parterre garden filled with herbs and fruit trees. Leslie and Norris often bring in stools and pull them up to the island to enjoy a meal and a view.

COLOR FORMS

LESLIE AND NORRIS EXPAND THE FEELING OF SPACE WITH MARTIN-SENOUR PAINTS SOAPSTONE FOR WALLS, BELGIAN ENDIVE FOR TRIM, AND SPARTAN STONE FOR CABINETS.

" This kitchen isn't terribly large—maybe only 10' x 15'—and it's got these big thick old moldings and built-in cabinets; there's a lot going on. So we thought we'd keep the color palette simple: beige and gray so that the kitchen feels bigger, lighter, and brighter for Mark, who's recipe testing in there all day long." —RN

1

2

3

4

5

6

Go big, be bold. The mirror in Leslie and Norris's kitchen is not just ornate; it's enormous, almost too large for the space, adding to its window-like appeal. (1) The oversized St. Germain mirror from Ralph Lauren Home is 40" x 60". It'll turn a blank wall into a picture window.

Choose a range that brings along its own backsplash. (2) Leslie and Norris's FiveStar Range has a stainless back guard that protects the antique mirror from burns and spills.

Design your cabinetry to look like freestanding dining room furniture— right down to the smallest details. (3) In Leslie and Norris's kitchen even the drawer pulls, from Brass Hardware Alabama, look like something that came off an old antique buffet.

Invest in copper pots—so pretty you'll leave them out on the stove rather than hide them away. (4) Copper Cookware, a five-piece set handcrafted in France by Mauviel, is so attractive you'll display it like your best china, available through Williams-Sonoma.

Keep it meaningful. Hang a collection of prints with themes you love over the sink and change them out when the spirit moves. Leslie and Norris always have something interesting to look at (bats, for instance!) while washing the dishes.

Install a chandelier over the kitchen island to cast a dining room glow on your culinary arts. (5) The Sharp Leaf Chandelier from Rose Tarlow Melrose House provides a robust shot of burnished iron panache.

Use plain white dinnerware to take the formality of posh accents down a notch. Leslie and Norris use plates from Crate & Barrel. (6) Eternity Fine Bone China from Wedgwood is sublimely simple, and so strong it comes with a ten-year guarantee.

DOUBLE TAKE

BETSY BROWN
designer

Think formal dining rooms
are about as hip as tomato
aspic? Then follow designer
Betsy Brown's lead and
eliminate the dining room all
together. With Brown's stealthy
strategies you can create
a kitchen sophisticated enough
for a sit-down dinner but not
too posh for pizza.

TOP: Painted white and mounted without visible brackets, the floating shelves melt into the walls. An elegant **Dornbracht** faucet extends straight out of the wall for ultra-chic appeal. A dark **Blanco America** double sink is undermounted to make the counter's lines appear uninterrupted. Even the **Baldwin Brass** cabinet hardware is unobtrusive.

BOTTOM: Open shelves holding inconspicuous restaurant-supply dinnerware and serving pieces are conveniently located by sink and dishwasher to make cleanup quick and effortless.

Limed oak cabinets and Carrara counters are elegant and simple. They don't grab the limelight, keeping kitchen-y elements in the background and dining room furnishings, like the astonishing oak table, at the forefront. The showstopping painting by Guido Maus adds a note of posh sophistication, lending this functional space an aura of grandeur.

"This kitchen is service-able, and looks really elegant with very little effort. It's divided into a preparation and a cleanup area, with open shelving for plates, glasses, and serving pieces. Meals are fun because they're about preparing and eating together."

"The house wanted a big kitchen to be its symmetrical core but that meant losing the dining room, so the kitchen had to be both."

"The table is 16'-long, made from two old oak planks by Tim Bell, a furniture maker in North Carolina."

FANTASY FOLLOWS FUNCTION

KEN PURSLEY,
architect and designer

With walls sheathed
in antique paneling under
a soaring ceiling, this kitchen
is more like a drawing room
in an oh-so-proper English
Country house (one with a
faucet, that is). Pursley created
this "non-kitchen" from a
former back porch—cleverly
hiding it behind a façade
that's as polished as a
Sheraton sideboard.

THE BACKSTORY | "This house was built in the 1930s. It was renovated over the years but not in a good way! It had English Tudor bones and so we tried to restore that feel. The homeowners have three teenagers and what's interesting is that this is a rather sophisticated look for a young family but it works well for them. They're very arts oriented. That's why the artwork is so prominent."

"We added the vaulted ceiling because there were two big concrete beams that we had to deal with, and vaulting was a way to make it more interesting."

"That lovely sofa is actually a space-saving device. Since you can slide in and out of it we could put it right up against the island. So often, beauty and function are at odds. What this kitchen proves is that they don't have to be."

Reclaimed walnut paneling from Antique Building Products is applied to walls in a graceful grid pattern, creating a rhythmic and harmonious backdrop. The floor is covered with Pennsylvania bluestone set in a random ashlar pattern that extends onto a terrace. The antiqued texture of the rug from Brocade Home adds to the room's settled air.

This looks more like a cozy English living room than a kitchen. Was that the idea?

In a sense. For a long time, the trend has been to make the kitchen as big and important as possible. What I love about this room is that it's almost a non-kitchen. It's a beautiful space that happens to function as a kitchen.

But where is everything? I don't see a single cabinet.

They're hidden behind touch-latch doors in the paneling. The entire section to the right of the stove alcove opens up. It holds cookware on shelves and in a series of sliding drawers. Lower cabinets to the left and right hold more utensils. The island holds trash, recycling, the dishwasher, a big deep indestructible farm sink, and another bank of drawers.

Wait. Where's the refrigerator?

In the adjacent pantry, which is like the backstage component. That's where you'll find the cleanup sink, the dishes, the dry storage.

So you converted an old porch into this extraordinary space?

Yes. The original kitchen was off in a cul-de-sac, but kitchens shouldn't be dead-end spaces. They should have at least two doorways, so they're part of the circular flow of the house. These old center-hall houses often present this problem—living room, dining room, cramped kitchen, and no room for the family. So we converted an exterior porch into this kitchen, to make it part of the circle.

How did you make this island feel so substantial?
The marble on the island is actually two slabs, each with an ogee edge, glued together back-to-back. And the marble alcove around the range is made with big slabs. It wouldn't have looked so calm if we had tiled it.

The white marble adds a nice contrast. What is it?
Calcutta Gold. It's warmer than Carrara because the veining is more brown and cream, which ties in with our palette. And it provides a nice bright relief from all the dark wood paneling.

How is it this room is so luminous when you've used materials that sponge up light like leather and wood?
The natural tendency is to push the cabinetry and sink up against a window, so you can look out. But we put it on an interior wall and saved the other for French doors so we could have even more light. You need it with the antique walnut paneling. We wanted the warmth of an English pub, but not the darkness.

OLD WORLD, NEW TRICKS
A 17th-century Italian wall sconce above the Viking stainless-steel range adds a touch of the antique to modern appliances.

CRAVING...

A STONE SHELF BEHIND THE STOVE TO MAKE PLATING FASTER AND EASIER.

"That ledge in back was inspired by Waffle House. I was in there eating and noticed they had something similar behind their range, deep enough to hold plates. It certainly increases the odds of a warm dinner and adds more usable space next to the stove."

WHAT IF...

YOUR FAVORITE PAINTING WAS MADE INTO A CABINET DOOR THAT OPENED TO REVEAL KITCHEN SHELVES?

"We hid shelves behind the oil paintings to get more immediate storage for things you use every day. But the client found she already had plenty, so she uses it for the silver she pulls out on special occasions."

This pantry expresses a whole other idiom, doesn't it?

It's intended to be a departure from the kitchen. It holds the bulk of the storage and everything's out on open shelves. On the wall opposite the sink the shelves are filled with boxes of cereal and other dry goods. So the room is intentionally not formal. It's more like a backstage component, not high style, spare, and minimal. It's about 7' x 14', functional and tight.

Why the switch to limestone counters in the pantry?

Well, it's always aesthetics first for us, and we really liked the color of the Lagos Azul limestone. It is a little more durable than the marble but it will stain. However this particular limestone is somewhat mottled so the spotting often blends naturally into the stone.

In the pantry, a chalky gray palette, open shelves, and farmhouse-style cabinetry impart a very different mood. The undermounted stainless-steel sink by Franke is set into a Lagos Azul limestone countertop, and the wall-mounted faucet, with a separate sprayer, has a vintage farmhouse look.

COLOR FORMS

PURSLEY ENVELOPED THE PANTRY IN SOOTHING GRAY WITH FARROW & BALL PIGEON.

"In a small contained space I like to introduce a muted color like this. Here we were inspired by the bluish gray tones in the bluestone floor. This kitchen is like a great brown jacket and the pantry is its colorful lining. You might not always see the lining, but when you do it's a great experience."

STALKING THE LOOK

Use touch-latches with complete and utter abandon. Press lightly on almost any wall in this kitchen and it will magically spring open to reveal things, like pots! Be creative. Stealth storage can be anywhere.

Tuck a freestanding banquette under one side of your table. Pursley had a sofa custom-made for his clients, with low arms that make it easy to slide in from either side. (1) The Finley banquette by Mitchell Gold + Bob Williams is a great way to break up the ubiquitous landscape of chairs around a kitchen table.

Stick with time-honored materials that lend a sense of age, like marble. (2) The muted tones of the brown and cream veining in Calcutta Gold marble, which Pursley used for the counters and alcove here, work well with deep walnut paneling.

Choose simple chocolate-brown leather kitchen chairs; they look handsome against wood paneling. (3) The Capri faux-leather side chair by Arhaus feels like a modern version of an English leather desk chair. Plus, it's indestructible.

Cover the floor in bluestone and let it run out onto an adjacent terrace. (4) Pursley used large rectangular blocks of bluestone laid in a random fashion, a style that works well inside and outside.

Warm stone floors with a rug that intensifies the aura of history. Pursley chose a new rug with a faux-worn patina. (5) Hand-tufted of wool and silk, the Memento rug from Tai Ping is designed to have a gently sun-faded look.

Be on the lookout for white crockery for your pantry; it contrasts beautifully with chalky gray walls. (6) The curvy lines of the Sydenharn Shape Ironstone Pitcher from Bridgehampton Florist look great inside a grid of open shelves.

Use reclaimed antique wood for paneling. Pursley says despite all the ornate trim, this kitchen feels pleasantly opulent rather than ostentatious because the walnut's graceful aging offsets the newness of the detail.

READ ALL ABOUT IT

WINDSOR SMITH,
designer

When Smith rehabbed her 1980s-era house she did away with the dining room and conceived a new kitchen that would reference a traditional library—albeit one where the librarians do a lot of entertaining. Lessons gleaned from Smith's kitchen will help you create a room so dazzling your guests won't notice they're seated next to the stove.

"The room is painted Benjamin Moore Polo Blue. I started out with navy but that felt too nautical, and I kept going darker until I got to this color that you can't quite define."

Midnight-blue paint covers walls, molding, and even window mullions lending this kitchen an aura of drama and mystery. Yet the room doesn't feel heavy because it's set off with a white tin ceiling and a Thassos marble tile floor from TriStone. The table and chairs are strong dark European antiques that might as readily be topped with leather-bound tomes as with wine glasses and plates.

"For a dinner party, the chandeliers are lit very low, and all the silver sparkles." The pot rack is illuminated by two hanging chandeliers from Baker Signature Lighting.

"Is it an industrial kitchen or an elegant library? I really wanted that back-and-forth."

"I didn't want a formal dining room that we'd use once a year, so I decided to put the dining room in the kitchen. It can get very interactive, with the food moving right off the stove onto the table."

BOOKISH
Airy open shelves and a Putnam rolling ladder are nods to the look of an English library. That feel is furthered by a pair of wingback chairs from Smith's own line. Smith has not just one, but two Grand ranges by Thermador (with blue knobs that jibe with walls). Shelves in front of the windows leading out to the garden hold glassware and a collection of hotel silver.

H_2O: two parts hydrogen, one part oxygen. Simple, right? Sure, except there are endless ways that water enters your life, most of them piped through your kitchen. Let's start with the basics: faucets and sinks. Today there are dozens of elegant fixtures for filling a pot and washing up after. Which brings us to dishwashers. Do you take one or two? Shining in steel or disguised as a cabinet? If you're worried about jumping in, here's your life jacket.

GO WITH THE FLOW

With so many, many choices, any tips for finding the right faucet? First, focus on function. Do you want a single- or double-handle configuration? A wall-mount or a deck-mount? For smaller kitchens, a wall-mount faucet can free up precious counter space so you can have a larger sink. You also need to make sure the faucet's arc and swivel have an adequate reach for the sink basin and its compartments. Note the faucet's water trajectory—where the water will hit the sink. It's all about making sure you have a perfect proportionate pairing. Remember that although a faucet is functional, it's also an opportunity to add beauty. Whether you're looking for something traditional, or sleek and contemporary, you can find a faucet and finish to match your décor. Keep in mind though, if you have two sinks in your kitchen you should choose both faucets from the same collection for a cohesive look.

—**DIANA SCHRAGE,** SENIOR INTERIOR DESIGNER, KOHLER CO.

So you paired a new faucet, Perrin & Row's Bridge faucet, with this pantry's original 100-year-old German silver sink? And somehow it's perfect!
When we started renovation my clients had two rules. Number one: keep it functional. Number two: they didn't want to know new from old.

—**R. ROMAN HUDSON,** DESIGNER

Ann Sacks's Zeus sink with an antique copper patina, and Kohler's Vinnata faucet in Vibrant Brazen Bronze, looks incredibly pretty with this Velvet Taupe Antique Limestone counter. But down to brass tacks, what about practicality?

"This sink is part of a major cooking triangle, with the refrigerator on its right and the range on its left. I always make sure there's at least 30" of counter space between the refrigerator and sink—so there's a place to put things down—and another 42" of prep area beside the sink."

—SANDRA BIRD, DESIGNER

ADVICE THAT HOLDS H$_2$O

What are some important things to consider when choosing a sink?
We're all pretty hard on our kitchen sinks—think of everything you toss, drop, and soak in it! It has to be durable and deep enough to accommodate those large cookie sheets and bulky roasting pans. If you long for a sleek look to complement your solid surface counters select an undermount sink. Self-rimming models offer quick and easy installation. More and more homeowners are choosing apron-front sinks in traditional and modern spaces alike, and Kohler actually has models that don't require any modifications to the cabinetry below which makes installation much easier. Materials are another thing to think about. Stainless-steel sinks have come a long way with new angles and curves—they're stunning from a design perspective. And then there are our premium cast iron sinks. Some of them are available in as many as 16 different colors!

—DIANA SCHRAGE,
SENIOR INTERIOR DESIGNER,
KOHLER CO.

The apron-front sink and contemporary counter-mounted faucet, both from Franke, have such clean lines they almost seem modern! And I love the way the sink is set off by the slightly darker cabinets painted Farrow & Ball Skylight.

"We are modernists but we wanted some traditional elements. I like mixing it up."

—ELDON WONG, DESIGNER
AND HOMEOWNER

The island, inset with a **Waterworks** copper sink and faucet, was inspired by an **Edwin Lutyens** design, and the Carrara marble sink with a factory style industrial sprayer has a European appeal as well.

"Architect Bob White designed the thick marble apron on the sink by the window. The idea is that it's a modernized Italian farmhouse kitchen."
—MICHAEL SMITH, DESIGNER

WATERFALLS

Be more flexible.
Water flows in any direction with the Karbon articulating spigot from Kohler. Aim the spray head and let fly.

Tap your tap.
Have your hands full? Turn the water on (and off) by tapping your wrist or forearm to the neck of the Venuto Single Handle Pull-Down with SmartTouch from Brizo.

Get polish.
Michael Berman's Single-Lever Single-Hole Faucet with Sidespray available through Rohl recalls the best of Streamline Modernism. In four finishes, shown in Polished Chrome.

Fill 'er up.
A pot faucet from the White Haus collection fits seamlessly into the stove backsplash created from blue diamond-shaped Macuba tiles mixed with hexagonal Carrara tiles by Waterworks.

Have brass.
You'll never have to polish Harrington Brass Works' Victorian Faucet in Perma-brass finish. With a convenient swivel spout.

Fit in.
Even the tallest pasta pot fits beneath Kohler's HiRise faucet, and sink inserts like Kohler's drying rack and cutting board make prep and cleanup a breeze.

Filter it out.
This three-way faucet with a built-in filter delivers hot, cold, or filtered water all from the same tap. Perrin & Rowe Country TriFlow 2-Lever Kitchen Faucet from Rohl is shown in polished chrome with side spray.

Elkay undermounted stainless sinks and gooseneck faucets by **Dornbracht**, plus **Absolute Black** granite counters equal elegance.

"The house was originally done by architect William Wurster—he was a great modernist who knew how to use traditional details but kept things pared down. We wanted our new kitchen to look like something Wurster might have done."

—**PETER FISHEL**, DESIGNER

"I am loving my new Dornbracht kitchen faucet—the Elio Single-level mixer in brushed nickel. It looks like a beautiful sculpture, as if modern geometric design had somehow converged with a swan's neck. What I love most: the way it adds so much style to an otherwise not-very-interesting place in my apartment."

—**PHILIP GORRIVAN**, DESIGNER

AQUEOUS VESSELS

Choose a sink that's not just a sink.
Elkay's Cascade Sink by Fu-Tung is a 6' workstation and centerpiece for the kitchen. It includes two wire racks and drain board, sliding colander, and cutting board for multiple workspaces.

Be proud of your curves.
Originally made in Germany in the 1880s, this sink from the German Silver Sink Company, with its friendly S-curve, is not really silver, but a soft, lustrous alloy of copper, nickel, and zinc.

Get organized.
Make over your sink into an all-purpose workstation with a built-in soap dispenser, utensil holders, even a knife block with the Worktop Kitchen Sink from Julien.

Think small.
The Kohler Iron Tones Trough Sink, in cast-iron, comes in a space-saving trough design and takes up only a 22" x 12" area. In Vapor Blue here, it's available in 25 colors.

Think classy glass.
A glass-topped sink!? No worries here—this Franke sink is made of tempered safety glass and the basin is stainless steel. Even better: glass is easy to clean and nonporous, so it won't absorb odors. Available in Seafoam (shown) or Black.

Be artistic.
Tiny stainless-steel tiles are laid by hand to create a true mosaic and a stunning sink from Linkasink.

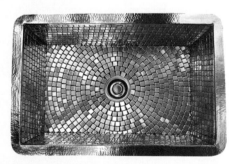

Get it together.
It's a countertop. It's a cutting board. It's even a colander. It's the Mythos modular sink, as fashionable as it is functional.

Stay high and dry
That high lip on the Country Kitchen Sink means the counter and walls stay dry. And check out the built-in soap dish on the Amarilis Heritage Faucet, both from American Standard.

People so often disguise their dishwashers, but you're actually showing off these single-drawer numbers from Fisher & Paykel!
This is a conversation I have a lot with my clients. I say "Listen, this is a kitchen. It is what it is. So don't hide anything." And to me, stainless is gorgeous. I love it.

—**EILEEN SEGALMAN**, DESIGNER

Why are there two Excella dishwashers by Miele on either side of the main sink?
There are two dishwashers because a family always has one running and one filling.

—**MADELINE STUART**, DESIGNER

"If I'm being really honest, I'd have to say my Bosch dishwasher is the thing in my home that makes me the happiest. I have two kids and they're usually eating, and their friends are here eating, and my husband and I are constantly having friends for dinner. The dishwasher is always full, always running. Better it than me, you know? My only regret is that I don't have two."

—**SHARONE EINHORN,**
CO-OWNER OF RUBY BEETS

CLEANING SOLUTIONS

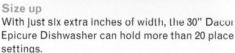

Dispense judiciously.
The GE Profile Dishwasher with SmartDispense will hold an entire 45 fluid-ounce bottle of detergent and dispense the right amount, based on water hardness, soil level, and cycle.

Size up
With just six extra inches of width, the 30" Dacor Epicure Dishwasher can hold more than 20 place settings.

Top drawer.
Quick! Throw those glasses in before the guests arrive. The Double Drawer Dishwasher from KitchenAid easily handles large or small loads.

Be gentler.
Jenn-Air's SteamClean dishwasher offers a steam-cleaning cycle that's extra gentle for china and crystal. No more hand-washing the wineglasses.

Set a shining example.
A stainless Viking dishwasher isn't paneled to match the cabinets so its shimmer echoes the silvery gleam of the crystal chandelier. And practically speaking, the dishwasher's proximity to table and sink makes cleanup quick and easy.

"The three most important dishwasher features are performance, quietness, and energy efficiency.

- Most home hot-water heaters are set at 131 degrees but the minimum temperature for best cleaning is 140 degrees, so all upscale dishwashers offer a heating feature to boost water temperature to an optimal level.

- As for noise, today's dishwashers are far quieter than they used to be. A unit that's as loud as boiling water is what's currently acceptable as 'quiet' today, and there are brands you'd have to place your ear against to hear running.

- Longer wash times use less energy, so wash times have lengthened tremendously over the past ten years to where a normal cycle today is 1½ to 2 hours. Most manufacturers have eliminated heated drying to be more energy efficient as well, so you should use a rinse agent for best drying results."

—**STEPHEN WEINER,**
STORE MANAGER,
ABT ELECTRONICS

composed

*Kitchens that have balance, rhythm,
and the elegance of subtle sophistication.*

addicted to alabaster

THE ALL-WHITE KITCHEN IS AN ALL-AMERICAN CLASSIC.

TICKLING THE IVORIES

CAROLE LALLI,
designer, homeowner, and food writer

What style really lasts? The quintessential white kitchen for one. Food writer Carole Lalli's version comes with the rusticated pleasures of a wood-burning oven and fireplace grill. It's the country kitchen of our dreams. Here's how Lalli went from an initial strategy that was simply "white" to an endgame that's a foodie's heaven.

THE BACKSTORY | Lalli is a revered food writer; she was also editor in chief of *Food & Wine* magazine and she's been editing cookbooks authored by fabulous chefs for decades. She lives in **New York City** most of the week and this is the kitchen she designed for her new country house in **Lakeville, Connecticut,** where she spends weekends and holidays with her husband, two grown daughters, and two grandsons. "We like to be together," says Lalli, "so we made the kitchen the biggest room in the house."

"I like glass-front cabinets because they help me find things, but also because they make the room feel more open. I tend to be neat with my glasses and plates so the shelves always look semi-organized."

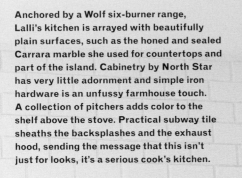

Anchored by a **Wolf** six-burner range, Lalli's kitchen is arrayed with beautifully plain surfaces, such as the honed and sealed Carrara marble she used for countertops and part of the island. Cabinetry by **North Star** has very little adornment and simple iron hardware is an unfussy farmhouse touch. A collection of pitchers adds color to the shelf above the stove. Practical subway tile sheaths the backsplashes and the exhaust hood, sending the message that this isn't just for looks, it's a serious cook's kitchen.

"We found four of the ceramic painted masks in Italy—traditional representations of winter, spring, summer, and fall—and the one in the middle was done by one of my daughters."

"I tried to keep all the spatulas in one pot and wooden spoons in another but in the end it became about size. Organizing cooking utensils by size seems to make it easier to find what I need. Then I keep really large things like tongs and skewers in the drawer to the right of the stove."

You've studied every extraordinary kitchen on the planet. Why did you settle on a clean, classic white kitchen for your family's new country home?

I've seen kitchens with fantastic displays of tile. I've seen marvelous faux-French kitchens. But in the end, I didn't want to get caught up in something trendy. I was drawn back to simplicity, classicism, and my own craving for everything to be open, clean, airy, and light. Also, I resisted the urge to be original. I needed to have a white kitchen, even if it's what everybody else likes.

Why did you cover the exhaust hood with white tile?

I wanted this kitchen to be up-to-date but not sleek, and I thought that a stainless hood might look too cold. Plus, I can clean it so easily. I just wipe it down. I think tile is such a great material, if I could do this kitchen over I would do everything from floor to ceiling in tile!

Do you have any advice for cooks who are designing kitchens for themselves?

In general I think after you do the base plan you should then figure it out as you go along. I really didn't plan out the details of this kitchen ahead of time. Once you get into a space you can see how you'll want to use it and things will just fall into place.

You've made the white kitchen your own in a marvelous way—the primitive romance of an Italian wood-burning oven and then, right next to it, a fireplace fitted with a Tuscan grill. What a foodie heaven!

Cooking is a huge passion. The wood-burning oven has pieces of terra-cotta fitted together to form the wall, ceiling, and floor. It gets to be 800 or 900 degrees. The most delicious food comes out of it—roasted meats, roasted vegetables, au gratins. One of our favorite activities is to gather a lot of toppings and stand around making pizzas.

How did you first learn about wood-burning ovens?

Driving through the Italian countryside, my husband, Frank, and I noticed that many people had these ovens standing alone outside the houses with smoke curling up. Then we visited Giuliano Bugialli, a cookbook author and food authority, who has a house in Chianti. When I told him we were obsessed with the ovens Giuliano said, "I'll send you one!" At the time, they cost about $500.

Was it troublesome to install?

Indoors you need a chimney. We put the fireplace/grill next to it because they share the same chimney. And our contractor, Richard McCue, found this wonderful mason who really, really loved doing all the stonework.

TUSCAN FANTASY
A leg off the main room contains the heart of the kitchen, a fireplace inset with a Tuscan grill and a wood-burning oven. Firewood is stored under the oven. A large pendant light from The Demolition Depot & Irreplaceable Artifacts adds a shot of age to new construction. An old Roman clay pot, a Southwestern twig basket, and a statue of St. Francis are some of the things Lalli displays on her mantel. "My theory is that if you don't get clouded by trends and you buy things you love, they will all look good together," she explains.

WHAT IF...
YOUR ROMANTIC KITCHEN FIREPLACE COULD ALSO GRILL A SUCKLING PIG?

Lalli ordered two Tuscan grills from a catalog and had them welded together to fit the two-foot-wide opening in her kitchen fireplace. The grill is spacious enough for two butter-flied legs of lamb or twelve ears of corn. Lalli uses it 12 months a year and cooks only on hardwood charcoal.

CRAVING...
THAT PERFECT, WOOD-SMOKED CHAR—WITHOUT GOING OUTSIDE!

Lalli uses the Italian wood-fired oven next to her fireplace (they share the chimney) to roast meats and vegetables and to make inspired pizzas.

PERFECT FIT

"I love the way the hutch from my mother fit exactly in the space between the door and window. And the way the 18th-century French cherry farm table we bought thirty years ago was just perfect for that end of the room. I think people should try to keep their things, the things they have real affection for. My girls have eaten at this table forever."

Why such an enormous island?

The really large island is because my daughters cook with me when they visit, and my husband is America's best prep cook. **And the island is part marble and part butcher block?**

It's about one-third marble. One reason is to roll pastry. The other is because I wanted that very pretty hammered nickel sink there for washing hands or doing flowers. I've noticed over the years that if you have a sink set in wood it gets funky around the edges, and I hate that. **Why do you have those cutting boards by the refrigerator when you have a butcher block counter to chop on?**

I cut most things on the counter but if I'm chopping something potent like onions or garlic I pull out a cutting board so strong flavors don't affect the other things I'm preparing on the island. And of course, if I'm chopping meat I use a cutting board so that I can properly sanitize. **Are these pretty pendants the only light in the whole kitchen?**

Oh no, we have lots of recessed lights. I think they are inevitable if you do a lot of cooking. I get anxious if there's not a lot of light. We also have under-cabinet lights. But when we're eating at the table we turn off the recessed lights and use only the pendants, it's a nice glow.

Brass pendants from O'Lampia illuminate the island where Lalli makes bread and pastry dough. The round hammered nickel sink and faucet, both from **Waterworks**, are used for food prep plus flower arranging and hand washing before cooking. Lalli keeps kitchen knives organized and at hand on a magnetic strip beside the refrigerator. There are two **Bosch** dishwashers, one in the island opposite the stove, and one near the main sink.

COLOR FORMS
LALLI KEEPS THINGS "LIGHT AND REFRESHING" WITH WALLS IN BENJAMIN MOORE DECORATORS WHITE.

"I did not want to match the white of the cabinets. I wanted this kitchen to have many shades of white. There's the marble, the tile, the cabinets, and the walls, all slightly different. This way it doesn't feel dull, it's interesting but still a very soft palette."

STALKING THE LOOK

1

2

3

4

5

Stick with the classics. (1) Lalli used tried and true 3" x 6" ceramic white tile from Lanka through Nemo Tile Company and a traditional farmhouse sink from Waterworks.

Make home cooking where the hearth is. (2) A Tuscan grill from The Gardener fitted inside your fireplace means no more mad dashing between patio grill and kitchen.

Set a pristine stage. Paint the walls and cabinets white and sheath everything else in white tile (even the stove's exhaust hood). White makes everything feel crisp, light and clean.

Show off your cooking brio—keep cutting boards, coffee grinders, and mixers in full view. It'll simplify prep and add personality at the same time.

Get milk (glass). (3) A simple white opaque pendant like Lalli used over her fireplace is a graceful old-fashioned touch. The FADO pendant light from Ikea is retro cool.

Floor them. (4) Lalli's reclaimed, antique French terra-cotta floor tiles from Michael Trapp are her home's showstopper.

Plant a chic indoor garden. (5) At six inches tall, this petite terra-cotta pot from Seibert & Rice is the perfect size for a windowsill herb garden.

WHITE NOISE

AMY NEUNSINGER,
designer, homeowner, and photographer

This is an extraordinary
mash-up of old and new,
urban and provincial, functional
and feminine. Photographer
Neunsinger melded her
love of hard-edged industrial
elements—even exposed air
ducts!—with her passion for
the achingly beautiful light
of the south of France.

THE BACKSTORY | "When we bought it, it was just a 1400 square foot
rectangle that looked like an underfunded schoolhouse. It had good bones
but bad doors and bad windows. Lots of ivy covering everything. And it
was pink—on the inside and out. We needed more space and more function.
I wanted that 'old with new' look because I love the feeling you get when
you use old materials. And I love mingling indoors and outdoors."

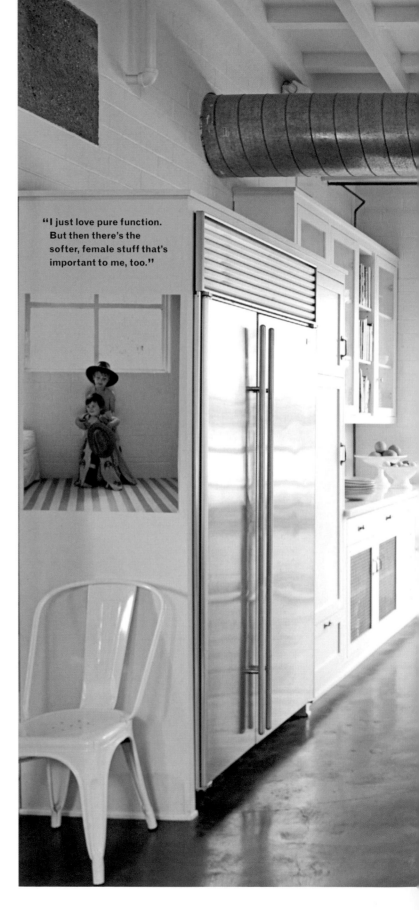

"I just love pure function.
But then there's the
softer, female stuff that's
important to me, too."

Industrial elements like exposed air ducts, polished concrete floors, and stainless-steel appliances are warmed by open shelving and vintage accessories and hardware. The wall near the Sub-Zero refrigerator "needed some life" so Neunsinger hung a photograph of her sons, Jackson, six, and August, three. Walls are painted Dunn-Edwards Van de Cane.

"When the doors are open the fragrance of roses fills the place."

This kitchen literally glows!
The house was actually designed around getting great light. That was one of the most important factors. I'm a photographer, and the whole house had to double as a photography studio, so it was designed to follow the sun's arc.
You use the whole house as a studio?
Everywhere. I've shot ads in my kitchen, outside, inside. I have celebrities here for shoots, huge diamonds, tons of food, animals, toys, toothbrushes, everything.
This black and white palette is so appealing.
I like high contrast. I love black and white; that's how I decompress when I come home. Having been art-directed all day, I want to come home to a lot less color.

A LARGE INDUSTRIAL SPRAY FAUCET at the end of the island illustrates Neunsinger's love for warehouse-style detail. And the farmhouse sink in the island, by Michael S Smith for Kallista, shows her passion for French provincial details. The area under the island sink was left open and sheathed in gleaming white marble tile while vintage industrial French pendants from Obsolete hang from a coffered ceiling; both furthering this farmhouse meets factory vibe. The island's black soapstone counter echoes the color of dark concrete floors. Cooking oils and dried herbs are contained in a vintage stainless-steel tray beside the Viking range.

How did you create the romantic look of an ancient concrete wall?

When the workers were chipping the tile off the master bathroom—which is now the kitchen's dining area—Juan-Felipe Goldstein, the architect, called me and said, "Amy, we cannot touch that wall anymore!" So we left it like that, unfinished. That is my real South-of-France moment.

How so?

I wanted that "old with new" here. I love that feeling where you get those old materials and that mingling of the indoor and the outdoor. At night it feels so cavernous and cozy when you've got candles lit and they pick up the texture of the wall. Then, during the day, it takes on a completely different look. It can be everything from austere to decadent.

This whole indoor-outdoor vibe is so quintessentially L.A.

As a family, we're constantly outside, having a meal at one of the outside tables.

Even your kitchen table feels as if it's outside, with those huge glass doors.

I wanted the house to be the kind of place where food and family would reign, so it made sense to put the table right in the middle of it. Do you remember *Moonstruck*, how the whole family would gather in that kitchen with the table? I saw it when I was young and I thought I had to have that.

ROUGH TERRAIN
When turning a former master bath into the kitchen's dining area, workers chipped away tiles to reveal a raw concrete wall, inadvertently creating what Neunsinger calls "the ultimate old-world design moment." Simple Pottery Barn chairs are intriguing partners with a crystal festooned Lily Juliana Chandelier by Rachel Ashwell.

STALKING THE LOOK

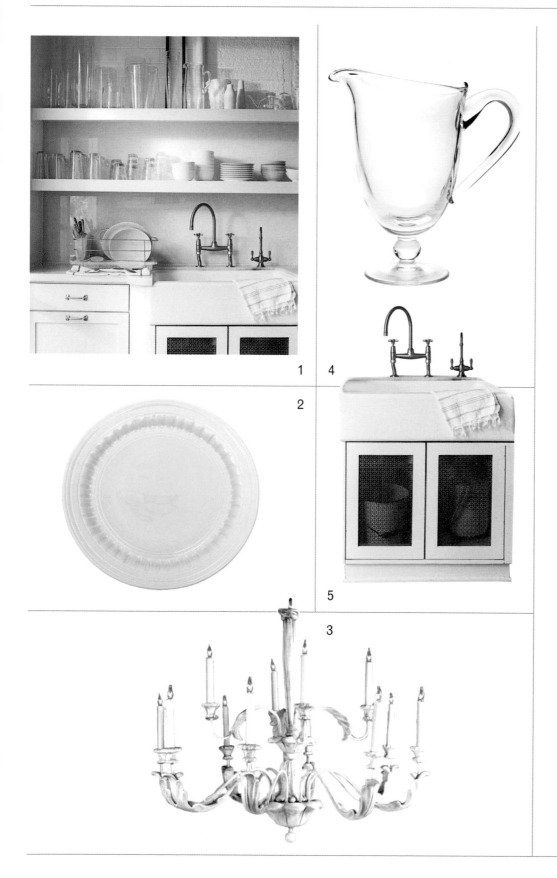

1 2 3 4 5

Make a sparkling wall of tile.
(TOP LEFT) In Neunsinger's kitchen, white Thassos marble tile, from Walker Zanger, extends up behind open shelves from a white Thassos marble countertop.

Display everyday tableware On extra-long open shelves like you might see in a warehouse or laboratory.

Don't forget to add farmhouse touchstones to warm things up.
(1) (TOP LEFT) Neunsinger's farmhouse sink and faucet, both from Waterworks, break with the industrial look of exposed air ducts and concrete floors to add homey charm.

Provide only subtle shots of color.
(2) Hand-pressed china from Frances Palmer Pottery, in the prettiest shade of robin's egg blue, softens a hard white landscape with a wisp of color.

Contrast rugged walls with a ladylike chandelier. (3) A soft, sheer Parisian white finish gives the Saint Germain Chandelier by Niermann Weeks its graceful aura.

Keep glassware simple. (4) This handblown crystal pitcher—the Esmeraldo Pitcher from Belongings—lends classy elegance to open shelves.

Use industrial mesh screens in place of lower cabinet fronts. (5) Black mesh plays up the industrial theme in Neunsinger's kitchen and contrasts beautifully against white.

Treat an industrial sprayer like a thing of beauty: silhouette it against your prettiest view.

Like Radin's kitchen design in the movie, this **Los Angeles kitchen** opens up to a major living area. Radin chose black **Windsor chairs** for contrast—"like a punctuation mark"—in the creamy room, painted **White Dove by Benjamin Moore**. Tiles, sinks, and faucets by **Waterworks** have farmhouse appeal. Stove and wall oven, warming drawer, microwave, and hood, all **Viking**, are clad in unpretentious stainless steel. And a seagrass rug atop hand-planed, slightly distressed floors adds another low-key casual touch.

For convenience, everyday plates are stacked on open shelves on either side of the sink, just above a pair of **Miele** dishwashers.

SET PIECE

JAMES RADIN,
designer

Quick quiz: what's the most covetable movie-set kitchen of all time? If you answered Diane Keaton's Hamptons kitchen in *Something's Gotta Give* you've got plenty of company. This kitchen was designed by the interior designer that director Nancy Meyers consulted during the movie's filming. It's got star power.

THE BACKSTORY | "My clients wanted the same casual, warm feeling as the *Something's Gotta Give* kitchen. They have three girls, ages one to six, and they wanted a house that was livable. Nothing is too precious."

Elegantly sleek pendant lights from Ann-Morris Antiques play up Radin's "traditional minimalist" style.

You've designed houses in two hit movies by director Nancy Meyers: *Something's Gotta Give* **and** *The Holiday.* **Are you a set designer or an interior designer?**

I'm an interior designer. I designed Nancy's own house, and she asked me to help the production design team with Diane Keaton's house in the movie. She wanted it to look professionally decorated, like Diane's character would have had.

How would you describe your style?

Traditional, in a light way. I like interiors to be calm, restful—that's what underscores my work. I think that's what people responded to in the movie. You can imagine yourself in those rooms—you want to be there. That's a lot of the appeal, just being pretty.

I see lots of similarities between this kitchen and one in the film—the room that made us all swoon.

There are similarities—the sense of it being airy and open with lots of light. The clients wanted the look of an old-fashioned country kitchen, so we used old-style lights, beadboard on the ceiling, and elaborate crown molding. I've done this kind of kitchen 50 times, and one day I asked myself, "What is it that makes it work?" And I think it's about the underlying quality—the nickel faucets, the Carrara marble, and so forth. It's also about the simplicity. It's what I'd call traditional minimalism.

SIMPLY SPOTLESS

JUDITH BARRETT,
designer, homeowner, and cookbook author

Ever seen a kitchen as
remarkably organized and
clutter-free as this one? Leave
it to a cookbook writer to know
what to edit away. Barrett
created a professional chef's
kitchen with an aesthetic as
clean and pristine as a fresh
sheet of paper—it just happens
to be gorgeous too.

THE BACKSTORY | "My husband and I have two grown daughters in their thirties. Both are really good cooks! Our house in Cambridge is old, from 1846, and it's been added on to many times, including our redo of the kitchen. I've written six cookbooks and I wanted a lot of counter space here so I could work with an assistant while recipe testing. And because the kitchen is very narrow we chose to have no upper cabinets to maximize the sense of space."

"This is everything I wanted in a kitchen. I can have eighteen people standing in here, having wine and hors d'oeuvres, with four of us cooking, cutting, and chopping. Big kids and little kids. It's so much fun."

"This particular limestone, from Ireland, is very durable with a soft grayish hue and various discolorations, which mask our dog's muddy paw prints."

Suspended from the kitchen's double-height ceiling, five new American Holophane pendant lamps, from Ann-Morris Antiques, provide ample lighting. Gleaming white subway tiles from Urban Archeology clad the lower walls—and the upper ceiling is painted a sunny yellow. Floors in Iscan Blue Limestone tile from Paris Ceramics are a soft natural counterpoint to all the industrial stainless steel.

"The jars are filled with dry beans: cooking with beans was the topic of my last book!"

You needed—and got—a kitchen that's super high-functioning. Yet you also wanted a big, warm, beautiful gathering spot for family and friends. Did you have a guiding vision?
I once saw a picture of an enormous kitchen in a grand old house in—I forget which—England or Newport. I tried to capture that feeling of a place where a lot of work gets done, yet also has a domestic kind of elegance.
How big is your kitchen and who designed it?
It's 27½' long and 16' wide. It was a collaboration involving several architects and one very opinionated client—me.
What did you ask for?
I needed a lot of work space and I wanted it very clean, no clutter. So my microwave, toaster oven, second refrigerator, and second dishwasher are in pantries just behind the kitchen. I have a KitchenAid mixer that's stored in the island on a roll-out shelf. I have three food processors in one of the cupboards. Everything is behind brushed-stainless-steel doors or white cabinets.
What else makes it feel so open and airy?
There are no upper cabinets in the kitchen. It's like an old villa. To me, upper cabinets seem like a 20th-century thing, and though I needed a modern kitchen, I wanted it to feel old. And of course there's the fact that it's two stories tall. We get natural light on all sides and from the skylights. Even on gray days, I never turn the lights on.

What do you think is the room's most striking element?

The central 10' marble island. It has tremendous scale and sleekness. It's a single slab of Carrara marble, two inches thick, honed instead of polished—I wanted it to look worn and used. A lot of islands have stoves, sinks, and other things built in, but mine is an open, uninterrupted work space.

What do you store in the island?

All my pots and pans are stored in deep drawers; smaller drawers have knives, silverware, place mats, and miscellaneous tools like a food mill, ricer, steamer. Also in the stainless cabinets are my pressure cookers, pasta machine, and water bottles. And lots of stuff I don't use often like the mandoline.

Why did you choose this particular Wolf range?

I chose the range because it's a commercial range with maximum flame heat. I also have two electric wall ovens.

Which features make you wonder how you ever lived without them?

I love my sinks. Both are by Franke—they're very deep, rectangular sinks, one 16" wide and the other 32" wide. The large one can accommodate the biggest roasting pan I have. I also have a heavy-duty, pre-rinse sprayer typical of restaurant kitchens—great for rinsing baked-on greasy pots and pans before they go in the dishwasher.

TASTEMAKER

In the range niche, a stainless-steel exhaust hood mounted directly onto white subway tile furthers the no-fuss, no-nonsense appeal of this kitchen. And installed over a stainless-steel **Wolf Challenger** professional series range is a **Pot Filler Faucet** by **T&S Brass**.

WHAT IF . . .

YOUR CEILING INSPIRED AWE
LIKE A MEDIEVAL CATHEDRAL?

. . . .

"The double height ceiling
was actually inherited from
the previous owner. It makes
a dramatic and wonderfully
light space with windows on
all four sides!"

PRACTICAL MAGIC
The extra-deep, extra-durable stainless sink, Franke's model **PSX 110-30-12**, can accommodate a big
pile of dirty pots and pans, no problem. And it's undermounted so the lines of the thick **C**arrara marble
counter are unbroken, in keeping with Barrett's strict streamlined aesthetic. The forceful spray from a
Pre-Rinse sprayer by **T&S** Brass makes cleaning up fast and easy. Above the sink a pair of **Boathouse
Wallmount Sconces** from **Urban Archeology** are a chic industrial note.

CRAVING . . .
A PLACE FOR EVERYTHING
AND EVERYTHING IN ITS
PLACE—EVEN THAT ELUSIVE
MELON BALLER.

. . . .

"Once the drawers were in
place, I had them section
each one. Now I have a knife
drawer with all the short
paring knives in one section,
the bread and carving knives
in another, and the chefs'
knives in a third. I have six
different vegetable peelers
shaped to do different tasks—
they're all in one place."

The pantry flooring is American Olean 1 white unglazed hexagonal tile—a gracefully old-fashioned choice. All the cabinetry in the pantry and kitchen is by Heritage Custom Cabinetry and all the hardware is by Siro—both are practical and utilitarian, their simplicity imparts elegance. The Barber Wilsons Faucet has streamlined appeal and the Meile dishwasher on the right is covered with a painted panel.

"I think this pantry's look is totally in keeping with the aesthetic of the kitchen; a mix of traditional and professional."

There's not a curtain or shade covering any of these windows.
I don't like curtains or shades. There are no curtains or shades on any of the windows on the ground floor. We like a lot of light and also find the windows very beautiful on their own. They are original windows.
So, you have three separate pantries here?
Yes, there are two other smaller pantries. One has dry food items like cereal, flour, baking stuff, canned tomatoes, pasta, rice, tuna, etc., plus a shelf for the microwave and the toaster oven. The other one has a second refrigerator—our older Sub-Zero from our previous kitchen (before the renovation). It has cleaning supplies, and less-used cooking equipment (ice cream maker, heavy cast-iron pans, copper bowls).
What do you use this pantry for?
We use it primarily for making coffee in the morning. And when we have big dinner parties, we use it for cleaning plates (there's a garbage disposal in the sink). We gave it a marble backsplash because we didn't want to introduce another material, and marble is neutral and white.

COLOR FORMS
BARRETT BRIGHTENED UPPER KITCHEN WALLS WITH A DKC-3 FLAT LATEX PAINT, A BUTTERY YELLOW FULL-SPECTRUM HUE BY DONALD KAUFMAN.

"We wanted a color to contrast all the white in the kitchen, but subtly. And then we went for a subtle gray in the pantry."

STALKING THE LOOK

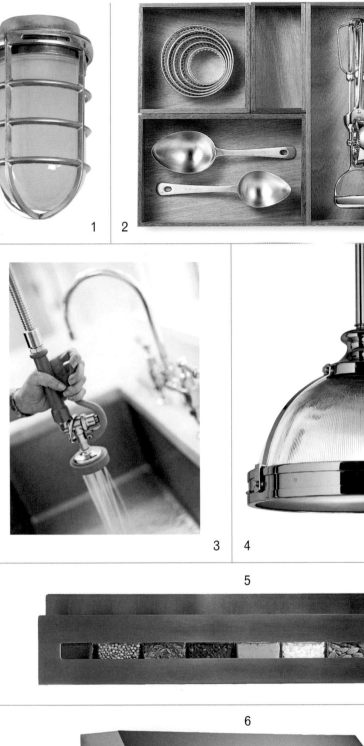

1

2

3

4

5

6

Open up! Why not make your task light natural light? Place windows so you have light streaming in from everywhere—even the ceiling. Barrett doesn't have to flip a light switch all day.

Bottle up your sconces. (1) Originally made to keep volatile fumes away from hot bulbs, these airtight Industrial Wall Lights from PW Vintage Lighting will add even more sparkle and gleam to a white tile wall.

Customize your drawers. (2) Modular Drawer Organizers from Williams Sonoma, made of lacquered mahogany, will keep your measuring spoons from getting frisky with your zesters.

Spray your cares away. (3) A strong shot of water from Barrett's Pre-Rinse unit by T&S Brass and grease is history.

Consider, if one pendant light is good, five must be better. (4) Buying antique Holophane lights en masse could be pricey but Restoration Hardware's Clemson Pendant lends the look without breaking the bank.

Go to the big island—no stools, no prep sink, no microwave allowed—just lots of real estate. You'll get a sleek look that's nonpareil and you'll love having the space to spread out.

Display ingredients as artwork like Barrett's stacked containers of colorful beans. (5) Cloves, cardamom, cayenne—it's kitchen art! Spice up your walls with the Aperture Spice Rack from Desu Design.

Embrace exhaustion. (6) A serious chef needs a serious exhaust hood. Broan's Elite 64000 Hood keeps the home chef happy, with professional-style features like infrared food-warming lamps.

BALANCING ACT

LINDSEY BOND,
designer

Easygoing and modern
was Bond's mantra, but
getting there took old-fashioned
hard work. To overhaul this
1950s Birmingham cottage
kitchen Bond employed strict
symmetry, precise balance,
and miles and miles of white.
The reward? A *so-so* kitchen
became *oh-so-sleek.*

The designer is a stickler for symmetry and balance. She had the window moved four inches so that it would be directly opposite **GE**'s **C**afé range and **P**rofile hood, and directly above the **GE C**afé dishwasher. It's centered between two perfectly square **B**lanco stainless sinks (one for prepping and one for cleaning up) that are undermounted to keep the lines of the **C**arrara marble counters sleek. **S**chon **403** Gooseneck Faucets have a single control lever for a streamlined look, and open shelves have no brackets or hardware interfering with their floating-on-air appeal.

Dinnerware and glasses are organized neatly on shelves. "I kept my plates and serving pieces to natural colors; the kind of stone colors you can find in restaurant supply stores," says Bond. "And there are tons of huge oaks out these windows, so I have some natural wood plates and bowls to reference that. Sticking with simple dinnerware in natural colors like this makes it easy for everything to look good together."

For tranquility, a sheetrock-clad stove hood and wood cabinets—both designed by Bond—were painted the same color as the walls, Benjamin Moore Super White. Stainless pulls match the stove and dishwasher material. The Danze Melrose Pot Filler is perfectly centered on the stove's Carrara marble backsplash.

"This kitchen is simple, utilitarian. I mostly wanted it to look clean. And white feels clean to me."

"I style the shelves every day but it's all very functional. Cookbooks go to the left of the stove and plates are stacked on the right for easy grabbing. It's not hard to style open shelves in a kitchen. A stack of plates looks so pretty, it almost looks styled to begin with."

"This is a starter house, our first house, so the kitchen needed to be improved without too much expense."

CARTE BLANCHE

MICK DE GIULIO,
kitchen designer

Snowy white, alabaster white, blinding white—this kitchen takes white-on-white-on-white to a level that's beyond chic. De Giulio kept building on his all-white theme— over the stoves, under the shelves, across counters and cabinetry—until white was wrapped around this kitchen like a cool, crisp sheet.

"They keep newspapers, magazines, and a computer in the cabinets on either side of the stools in the island so they can grab something to read or to look at while sitting there."

THE BACKSTORY | "These are 'family' people. They have two young daughters. He's in a family business and their whole extended family gathers here in Glencoe, Illinois, on the weekends where they can all be together. It was the wife's idea to have an all-white kitchen, it was her dream, and I thought it would be fantastic, ethereal, to do everything, even the ceiling, in shades of white."

This kitchen is essentially an extension of the family room. The island is topped with an extra-thick slab of **Calacatta Gold** marble, and for dramatic contrast back counters on either side of the stove are topped with **Pietra Cardosa**: a dark, slatelike stone. The ceiling is clad in beadboard, which helps this soaring space feel cozy. White subway tile on the backsplash, by **Waterworks**, adds a shot of texture. Polished nickel hardware from **Mick de Giulio** is all about elegance. **Mig & Tig** barstools are exceptionally simple and windows are left bare.

"There is a large limestone fireplace on the wall opposite the stove hood so I kept the hood design simple, because I never like to have two hearths in a room. I did it in beadboard with just some small brackets on the bottom: a simple decorative touch."

This simple white kitchen feels so elegant. How did you do that?

Well the 13' cathedral ceiling really helps. When the owner called me, the house was under construction and the kitchen was going to be in a totally different place. This was the family room. But when I walked through and saw the ceiling being roughed out, I said, "You've got to put the kitchen here, too. This is where you're going to live." It's got all this great space, and light, and a fireplace where she sits and reads to her kids. It just underscores the idea that the living space of a kitchen is every bit as important as the working space.

Some people think islands are getting too big, but yours feels right.

It's all about proportion. If you had a small island under this huge ceiling, it would have looked ridiculous. This is 14' x 4', much longer than it is wide, and that makes it seem slender. Everything is about proportion and relationships. The marble edge is 2¼" thick—1" thicker than normal. One inch can make a big difference. It feels chunkier and stronger. But then the countertop on the back wall is thinner. I like to vary it, for more interest.

And you varied the color. Why?

Just to mix materials and add a little contrast. If it had been white, too, you wouldn't even have noticed it.

CONTINENTAL DRIFT
The breakfast area is just to the right of the island. De Giulio gave the plate rack a vintage European look, designing it in polished nickel with brass trim and slatted oak shelves. Antique English ladderback chairs surrounding a French farmhouse table add another layer of continental appeal. The counter behind the breakfast table adds a secondary work area for making coffee or serving drinks; it's equipped with a Waterworks sink, a Sub-Zero refrigerator, and a wine cooler.

The plate rack is so eye-catching. Is it French?

It looks very Paris flea market, but I just drew it out of nowhere. I didn't go around saying, "Well, they would have done it this way in France." I always say "every kitchen needs a hook" and here that hook is this dish rack. There's a French farmhouse table and English armchairs and a vaguely Swedish chandelier. To me, the room is a mix—it feels a little New England and a bit beach house with some Scandinavia thrown in. The only theme was fresh and crisp and clean.

Why did you bring the tile behind the plate rack up to the ceiling?

The tile brings the kitchen over to this area, it connects the two areas and then when you put the nickel right over the tile like this they sparkle together.

What's in those little niches on either side of the counter below the rack?

Those niches hold things like the toaster, the coffee machine—all the things that play into everyday life that you don't necessarily want to look at all the time. Appliances can be plugged in and pulled out as needed.

What does all this play of dark against light do for a room?

I think it grounds it. That's the beauty of a dark wood floor. It makes the line where it meets the white walls very crisp, and that makes the whole room feel cool and clean. Yet at the same time, the dark wood is warm. It's nice to have some counterpoint. There's something so serene about white, but you don't want it to get boring. If you have a honed finish on the marble, do gloss on the tiles. Have different textures that play against each other.

WHAT IF...

YOUR DISHES, YOUR GROCERIES, EVEN YOUR FRIDGE, WERE TUCKED INSIDE TALL WHITE TOWERS?

" The height gives these armoires such elegance and they provide so much more storage than upper and lower cabinets would, which would be interrupted by a counter and backsplash. The armoire to the left of the door is 12" deep and the pantry next to the range is 24" deep—but the pantry is recessed into the wall so it looks narrower. I'm always trying to move things away from *kitchen* and reinforce *room*."

WHITING DESK
A comfy chair and a built-in desk, with a **Pietra Cardosa** stone top, is at one end of the kitchen. The window looks out onto an outdoor walkway—so the wife can sit and work and watch for her daughters to arrive home from school.

CRAVING...
CELESTIAL LIGHT FROM A HIGH WINDOW AND A CRYSTAL CHANDELIER TO REFLECT IT.

The **Leiden Chandelier** by **David Iatesta**, "is very transparent so it doesn't block the view to the ceiling or the window, and it's whitewashed which gives it a relaxed kind of elegance," says de Giulio.

There's no excess decoration. The tile wall and the cabinets are so plain they almost disappear.

That's what I like. What's not there is just as important as what is. I could easily have done glass-fronted cabinets on either side of the range, but I didn't want upper cabinets. They give it away as a kitchen and I wanted it to feel more like a room. So I did those tall cabinets, like armoires.

What's inside?

The one to the left of the door holds dishes and glassware. Then there's a pantry to the left of the range and a refrigerator on the right. If you look at the depth of the window, you can see how we built out the wall so we could recess the refrigerator. And it's 6" back from the counter, so everything doesn't meet in one straight line. More natural, less built-in.

What else should we keep in mind?

Simplicity. That's the real story.

And simplicity equals elegance?

Exactly. But it's hard to get people to trust in simplicity. A kitchen like this doesn't look very exciting on paper. Where's the design? Where's the drama? Where's the decoration? But if you have the courage to do something this simple, it can really sing.

The wide-plank heart pine floor from **Carlisle**, stained a dark chocolate brown, conveys a feeling of age and keeps an all-white kitchen from floating away. The **Waterworks** under-mount sink has a sliding cutting board for food prep. **Viking**'s 60 dual-fuel range in stainless steel is the only visible surface, everything else is sheathed in shades of white. The mud-room beyond extends the all-white theme.

COLOR FORMS

PURE WHITE PAINT ON THE WALLS AND CEILING— BENJAMIN MOORE SUPER WHITE WITH SIMPLY WHITE TRIM—HAS THE LOOK OF FRESHLY FALLEN SNOW.

" Because it's all white, you see colors in the white depending on where the shadows are. Things go from warm taupe to gray in varying degrees during the day. And any color you bring in just explodes, even a bowl of fruit looks vibrant."

STALKING THE LOOK

1

2

3

4

5

Get touchy-feely. An all-embracing all-white palette is most dramatic when filled with texture. Differently textured materials like honed white marble against white-painted tongue and groove paneling, and matte white china against glossy white tile, lend depth and interest to a restricted color palette.

Embrace *chiaroscuro*. It's an artistic trick that dates back to the Renaissance, using distinct areas of dark and light to create drama. Place your pretty white cabinets on a dark, dark floor and they'll look even prettier.

Hang a posh chandelier from a humble beadboard ceiling. (1) The Large Bead and Tassel Chandelier, from Visual Comfort through Circa Lighting, makes a splash in a simple white kitchen.

Stock your shelves with pewter jugs and white ceramic plates. It's a classic combination that pairs beautifully with nickel hardware. (2) Pewter and white ceramic come together in the Convivio Caffe Canister with Scoop by Match.

Embellish your white cabinetry with gleaming polished nickel. (3) The Channel Pull from Martha Stewart Living at Home Depot is the perfect pristine choice.

Find a table and chairs with dark good looks. (4) This dark dining chair, the Klismos Dining Chair from Ralph Lauren's Beverly Canyon collection, has the kind of rich texture and sculptural interest that's heightened by a backdrop of white.

Make your refrigerator disappear into the walls. Why let a massive fridge be your kitchen's focal point? De Giulio recessed the refrigerator into a wall, then covered it with a panel; it looks like one more beautiful cabinet.

A vase of simple white flowers. (5) In a white kitchen, in a clear glass vase, like the PS vase from Ikea, convey pure tranquility.

BREAK-OUT SESSION
GOING GREEN

BIG KITCHENS CAN HAVE SMALL CARBON FOOTPRINTS

Two clever eco-experts, Mary Richardson Kennedy and Robin Wilson, renovated Kennedy's kitchen incorporating lots of cool, environmentally responsible ideas—here they share the joys of sustainability. Kennedy, who has six children and many friends, says "This kitchen is more like a community center." The large island, big enough to serve a buffet dinner, is equipped with a microwave, two dishwashers, and a warming drawer—all energy efficient—all Electrolux.

The walls are painted with Benjamin Moore low-VOC Aura in Hancock Green.

Marvin windows are double-paned and made of Low E 366 glass, for energy efficiency.

A reclaimed church pew anchors one end of the room.

CHOOSE A TILE THAT GIVES BACK. Rittenhouse Square subway tiles in Arctic White are by Daltile. The company tries to minimize waste by recycling scrap tile back into the manufacturing process.

- **GEOTHERMAL PUMP**
"A geothermal heat pump can cool as well as heat your house. It's incredibly efficient compared with the usual cooling and heating systems—at least 25 percent more efficient, and often much more. That could mean substantial savings on utilities. Because all the hardware for a unit is underground and inside the house, it's not susceptible to corrosion from weather. So while a typical air conditioner or heater may need replacement after 15 to 20 years, a geothermal pump can last 30 years, and usually requires less maintenance." —Lew Pratsch, Zero Energy Homes Project Manager for the U.S. Department of Energy.

- **ENERGY STAR**
The EPA awards the Energy Star logo (a blue and white sticker) to appliances that generally use 20–30 percent less energy than required by the federal government.

- **LOW VOC PAINT**
Some paints contain high levels of VOCs (volatile organic compounds) that produce a toxic gas when applied. VOCs diminish air quality and may be detrimental to your health. Today alternative manufacturing techniques have allowed the development of low- and no-VOC paints that release no, or minimal VOC pollutants, and are virtually odor free.

- **LED AND CFL BULBS**
Light bulbs that have revolutionized energy-efficient lighting. Unlike incandescent bulbs, LEDs (light-emitting diodes) contain no toxic mercury and they can last up to 50 times longer than incandescents. The average rated life of a CFL (compact fluorescent light) is between 8 and 15 times that of an incandescent and, on average, use 50–80 percent less energy.

- **PHOTOVOLTAICS**
Roof panels that convert the sun's rays into energy. Some photovoltaic shingles actually blend with conventional asphalt and slate roofing for a seamless effect.

DOUBLE VISION

"On the left side, you've got the classic work triangle with sink, cooktop, a full-size refrigerator on one end, and a full-size freezer on the other. On the right, those square doors above the counter fold back into the cabinetry, and there's your appliance garage."

—ROBIN WILSON

"We worked with Green Demolitions in Greenwich Connecticut to salvage anything we could. We used recycled sheetrock and reclaimed brick."

—MARY RICHARDSON KENNEDY

WASTE NOT.
The island is 6' x 17' and Kennedy says she had one end fitted with six recycling bins, "I'm militant about waste, and my children are very well-trained."

1

2

1. **COOL OFF.**
The handsome 365+Brasa pendant from Ikea and the cabinets are fitted with energy-saving **LED** lights by Oznium that generate less heat and last for years.

2. **SAVE A TREE (OR LOTS OF THEM).**
RW: Holiday Kitchens made all the cabinets. They use recycled wood, formaldehyde-free glues, and low-**VOC** paints and stains. People tend to equate eco-friendly design with plain and ugly, but this is no longer the case. They've got over 100 different door styles.

3. **DO BAMBOO.**
Carbonized Strand bamboo flooring from Dragonfly Bamboo has an anti-scratch **UV** coating to prevent fading. "This kitchen gets a lot of traffic, and a lot of boys. Everything had to be extremely durable— and healthy," says Kennedy.

4. **APPARENTLY DIM BULBS CAN BE SMART.**
The Electrolux Icon convection double wall oven has a control panel that lights up when you need it and dims when you don't. Electrolux has been included in the global Dow Jones Sustainability Index, which includes the 10 percent best-in-class economic, environmental, and social performers of the world's 2,500 largest companies.

3

4

5

6

5. **BE EARTH-FRIENDLY AND TOUGH, TOO.**
Eco in Black Forest by Cosentino is a durable quartz-like surface made of 75 percent recycled content bonded together by an eco-friendly corn-oil resin. "The amazing counter material looks like granite but isn't. It's made of all this stuff that would normally go into a landfill— porcelain tubs, sinks, glass, mirror. It's all mushed together, and then with a great amount of pressure and corn resin it's turned into a countertop," says Wilson.

6. **UNEARTH THE POWER.**
"We switched to geothermal, solar, and solar thermal energy to get off fossil fuels," says Kennedy. A geothermal pump in the basement supplies radiant heat to the floor.

STRETCH YOUR LIQUIDITY.
The **Kohler HiRise Bridge Faucet** in polished stainless steel is equipped with an aerator to reduce water consumption while maintaining a steady flow. It's paired with a **Kohler Undertone** sink. The blue tumblers, made from reclaimed wine bottles, and **Umbra's Frosine** stemware—reclaimed wineglasses that have been sandblasted—are from **Green Depot**.

DON'T THINK COMPOST CAN'T BE GLAMOROUS.
THIS STAINLESS-STEEL COUNTER-TOP BIN FROM CRATE & BARREL HAS A CHARCOAL FILTER IN THE LID TO CONTROL ODORS.

"**Our chickens, falcons, peacocks, and crows are fed bits from the compost pail, and the vegetarian compost is put aside for the garden.**"

INSIDER INTEL | Ways to be eco-friendly in the kitchen (while avoiding the dread crunchy-granola vibe).

IT'S HIP TO BE OLD

" Everything is old in my kitchen, except for the cabinets and the appliances. I couldn't have done this kitchen without the Internet. It enabled me to search all these salvage yards from here to California. I found the marble countertops at www.omegasalvage.com—they're from the library at the University of California, Berkeley. I went to www.pioneermillworks.com for the flooring—from a barn in upstate New York, and www.recyclingthepast.com for the subway tile—from a house in Bucks County, Pennsylvania."
—BRENDA KELLY KRAMER

" I've given up using precious woods in my design, something I really love. In my latest commercial project I've incorporated bamboo floors and recycled aluminum tiles."
—VICENTE WOLF

"I install Lutron's whole-home dimming system in every house I design. It saves energy, and also makes it so easy to set the right lighting for a gorgeous meal at home with friends."
—ERINN VALENCICH

"If you're environmentally conscious, compact fluorescents are now the bulbs of choice. The quality of light can be icy cold and blue, although I've found one I like that almost exactly replicates the yellow light of an incandescent bulb—the Westinghouse 14-watt Mini-Twist in soft white."
—MARSHALL WATSON

"I'm using less-toxic paints, those with lower VOCs. I like Benjamin's Moore's Aura collection. My two favorite colors are Solitude, for walls, and Constellation, for trim. Together they create a Gustavian look, a room that is as cool and crisp in summer as it is elegant and dramatic in winter. I also like Armstrong's Lock & Fold laminate flooring. It's pre-finished, so you don't need chemicals to glue it down or seal it."
—ERIC COHLER

"Trade just one incandescent for a compact fluorescent (CFL) and prevent the emission of over 400 pounds of greenhouse gases."
—KATHERINE TIDDENS,
FOUNDER OF THE GREEN BOUTIQUE, TERRA VERDE

ECO PICKS

1. **Get Milk.**
   Designer Kevin Ritter uses traditional milk paint finishes. The process of making milk paint has been the same for hundreds of years. You mix milk protein, lime, clay, and pigment. It's a more earthy, organic material, all natural, biodegradable.

2. **Cook "green" eggs and ham.**
   Worthy of the organic eggs and artisanal cheese in your omelets—Cuisinart has set out to save the planet one pan at a time with its GreenGourmet line of nonstick cookware. The water-based coating contains no harmful PTFE or PFOA substances.

3. **Make a sweeping change.**
   Brooms from Sweep Dreams come in seven unexpected colors and are handmade in Thailand using sorghum grass, bamboo, and eco-friendly dyes.

4. **Deposit your bottles on the counter.**
   Bio-Glass countertops from Coverings Etc are made from recycled glass. The 3/4" top comes in green, white (shown), or brown.

5. **Paint with cleanable "green."**
   Olympic Premium Interior Latex Flat Enamel is nontoxic and dries to a flat finish that's even scrubable. In Asparagus, or 1,200 other colors, from Lowe's.

6. **Keep recyclables from taking over your kitchen.**
   Operated by a foot pedal, Ecopod crushes plastic or aluminum and stores up to 50 containers. Two other "pods" hold newspapers, glass bottles, or other recyclables. Ecopod Recycling System; through Williams-Sonoma.

7. **Be beautiful while you save energy.**
   The Plumen is an 11W designer compact fluorescent bulb that's so imaginatively designed, you might want to leave it exposed. It uses about a fifth of the energy of a typical incandescent and lasts up to eight times longer.

TREAD

Talk about overworked and underappreciated. Your kitchen floor takes a bigger beating than any other surface in your house. Too often it's an afterthought when planning a kitchen. But flooring can make or break the look, not to mention your aching feet. So, if you're the type who thinks choosing a kitchen floor isn't sexy, you'll think again after perusing the stones, tiles, hardwoods—and even linoleum—this section lays at your feet.

TILE TALK

What's the best way to take care of tile floors?
Use a cleaner that has "neutral pH" on the label. Or you can mix baking soda and water as a homemade cleaner. Pour half a cup of baking soda into two gallons of water and mix very well. Then apply the liquid with a string or sponge mop. You don't want to put harsh chemicals on tile, not even the chemicals that are in steel wool pads—there's always a risk that you will affect the color or etch the polish. There might be fading or staining that you don't notice that seeps in over time.

Are there sealants I can put on to prevent that kind of damage?
That's a really tricky area. I don't want to bad-mouth the stores, but the sealants that a homeowner can buy are poor quality—they won't work and might even damage the floor. Have a sealant applied by a professional who is experienced with your specific tile.

—MARTY HOFFMAN,
HOFFMAN BROTHERS FLOORS

Not only is a tile floor durable—spills are a cinch to mop up—it also offers an opportunity to unleash creativity by creating a distinctive pattern underfoot. This kitchen by designer Jason Bell is defined by its large scale black-and-white checkerboard floor.

Did you know that terra-cotta's ability to retain heat makes it an excellent choice if you're installing radiant heat beneath your kitchen floor? And since terra-cotta tiles are made of fired clay (sealed for durability) no two tiles are alike. With their intriguing irregularity, earthy colors, and conductive properties, terra-cotta tiles are particularly good at bringing warmth of all kinds to a kitchen—like this one by designer David Mitchell.

"If someone drops a cast-iron skillet that creates a dent a ¼" deep in a wood floor, then sands a ¼" off the whole floor to smooth it out, that will greatly shorten the floor's lifespan. A few sandings like that and your wood floors will become veneer."

—JAMES BOORSTEIN,
INTERIOR RESTORATION
EXPERT, TRADITIONAL LINE

What do you love most about the kitchen floor in this new house?
"The floors are wide-board pine, very soft and worn-looking, although they're new. Pine is a soft wood and marks easily, quickly imparting the look of age. This is important in a new house."
—JACQUELINE DERREY SEGURA,
DESIGNER

Limestone is a natural material that formed in ancient seas under the relentless accumulation of shells. As you might expect, it's also a millenniums-old flooring material (think sphinxes and pyramids). Properly treated and sealed to prevent stains, limestone floors will last a lifetime. It comes in a variety of soft creamy neutrals like the pale-toned tiles designer Peter Fishel chose for his own kitchen. "Limestone makes sense for us since we're constantly coming in and out from the yard," Fishel says. "And we got rid of the old bulky radiators and went with radiant heat under the floor."

KILLER UNDER TOES

Try Technicolor.
Why confine color to your walls? A floor this vibrant would wake up your kitchen faster than the morning sun. Stained ash is available in six colors through Model Hardwood.

Use the Right Side of Your Brain.
Here's how to create a beautiful floor: pull out a few Tribeca Hexagon Field Tiles—stone tiles in Classic White and Basic Black from Walker Zanger—from the prearranged strips and get creative.

Be Romantic.
Ah, remember Paris. Remember Casablanca. Promenade Fleurette Concrete Tile through Waterworks combines the durability of concrete with the romance of high heels clicking down exotic corridors.

Cover Up.
Stylish and 100 percent synthetic, the Greek Key & Medallion rug (5' by 8') from Lane Venture is the perfect foil for muddy paws, tipsy guests, even the bright sun (it's fade-proof). And all you need to clean it is a hose.

Preserve the Forest.
The Bioessenze Collection of porcelain tiles from Lea Ceramiche looks like wood (the grain even varies from tile to tile) but it's resistant to warping and scratches.

Pull a Mat Up to the Sink.
So many color combinations—and you'll be thrilled by how little these sink mats from Ikea cost! Try walking away without buying several of them (2' x 2'11").

Be Spill-Proof.
Spills at the sink won't harm indoor/outdoor Rain or Shine Rugs from Dash & Albert Rug Company (small throws to room size), made of a machine-washable synthetic that looks (and feels) like cotton.

Is this a reclaimed brick floor?
"They're old bricks from France. I liked the warmth and the variation. And it's really forgiving, easy on the feet. We use this kitchen hard. You can make a mess here and it doesn't show."
—DAN RUHLAND, DESIGNER

Are certain sizes or finishes of tile more practical for a heavily trafficked floor?
The size is an aesthetic question—it's all about the look you want. Small tiles have a busier look, but make a small room look larger. The finish is up to you, too. Matte tiles tend to be less slippery, but a professional can give any finish more grip.

Does each kind of tile require a different kind of grout?
In general, you want high grout lines. Low grout collects dirt. If it's a heavily trafficked area, you might ask for acid-resistant grout—it's what we use in commercial applications. It won't discolor the tiles, and it won't react with anything else spilled on it.

What about colored grout?
Use whatever color you like. Just be sure it's properly sealed and maintained— maybe a darker color in a very heavily trafficked area.
—MARTY HOFFMAN,
HOFFMAN BROTHERS FLOORS

SLATE COMES IN A VARIETY OF DEEP RICH SHADES— BROWNS, PURPLES, GREENS, GRAYS, AND HAS A KIND OF MYSTERIOUS DEPTH THAT EVOKES PEACE.
It's also nonporous, which means it's highly resistant to staining, and its texture makes slate less slippery than most other kinds of stone. *House Beautiful*'s editor in chief, Newell Turner, chose Brazilian Slate tile for his own kitchen floor and echoed the slate's deep, dark color with CaesarStone countertops in Raven.

A glossy white painted ceiling is a bright counterpoint to matte dark wood floors in designer Jean-Louis Deniot's Bridgehampton house.

Would you recommend any particular stains and finishes for wood floors? For stains, we use aniline dyes or pigmented stains. Minwax and Dura Seal both make good stains—there's not much difference in quality between the brands. For finishes, urethanes can be tricky. If they're not applied well they can have a cheap, tacky, glossy look, and if you reapply one over an existing coat, it won't readily stick to itself. We tend to use boat varnishes, floor paint that's been varnished, or a super-strong sealant from Glitsa that holds up for decades, even in public lobbies.

Is there any maintenance I can easily do myself? Whatever the finish, damp-mop once a week with a mild soap like Murphy Oil Soap. Mineral oil will hide some scratches, and a rag dipped in alcohol can draw out moisture if you have a patch of cloudiness on your floors, what we call a blush or haze.

—**JAMES BOORSTEIN**, INTERIOR RESTORATION EXPERT, TRADITIONAL LINE.

Linoleum is "in" all over again. Did you know it's actually an eco-friendly material? Linoleum is made from all-natural materials like linseed oil, flour, limestone, and recycled wood. It's also antibacterial, biodegradable, and infinitely versatile—not to mention affordable. In designer Michael Berman's Palm Springs house he did a quick and easy kitchen rehab by simply laying down linoleum over the original floor and staining his original cabinets the color of black tea—one of the speckled shades in his newly laid floor.

plain spoken

EVERYDAY EPHEMERA IS TUCKED BEHIND CLOSED DOORS. ALL THAT SHOWS IS GREAT STYLE.

SHIP SHAPE

SANDI HOLLAND, *designer,* and **RAY POHL,** *architect*

Like a well-loved old sailboat, this kitchen will maintain its shine for a long, long time. Holland and Pohl's sublimely simple plan along with a classic earthy brown-and-white palette keeps the kitchen grounded, while brass accents and a vaulted wood ceiling conjure up Nantucket's seafaring past.

THE BACKSTORY | "I've known this family for 22 years. I renovated this 150-year-old house when they first bought it. I was brought in again now that their children are grown and they're using the house in a whole new way. It has fantastic views of Nantucket harbor." —RP

Navajo White paint on the walls has a hint of brown in it, which relates to the Tudor Brown on the cabinets; both paints by Benjamin Moore. Brass hardware, from Nantucket Housefitters feels very appropriate for a boating family. Holland, chose black for the 48 dual-fuel Viking range so that everything below the counters would stay dark. Provenance Woven Wood Rustica Shades from Hunter Douglas echo the texture of the owner's collection of Nantucket lightship baskets.

"This is one of my favorite Nantucket kitchens. It has all the charm of an old house and all the light of a new house." —SH

"The woven wood blinds are clean yet warm, because they have some texture to them." —SH

"The sink is 10" deep and then you get an extra inch or two because it's undermounted. I prefer stainless-steel sinks to porcelain because they're more forgiving. If you drop a heavy pot, it can hit the porcelain and chip it. But stainless steel kind of bounces back." —RP

This kitchen seems as plain and simple as one of those old Nantucket baskets on the shelves.

SH: That's the essence of Nantucket—simplicity. This is an old house, recently renovated and I wanted to see the architecture without a lot of accessories getting in the way. The baskets are made of oak staves, very tightly woven and unusually strong.

The play of light and dark is so dramatic!

SH: Everything above the countertop is light and everything below is dark. The cabinetry has that quiet Quaker austerity. But the dark color is brown not black, which means it's still warm. We needed that dense chocolate brown to ground the room and balance the vaulted ceiling.

What's on the countertops?

RP: Calacatta Gold marble, which has beautiful veining. We wanted something glorious because there's so much countertop. The run of cabinets under the window is a place for phone books and keys and recipe files. If you don't allow for that desk function in a kitchen, it will just happen where you don't want it.

SH: It's a place to put down the groceries or arrange the flowers, and it's a great staging area when the owner has a big party.

What's up above?

RP: The catwalk links the master bedroom wing with the rest of the second floor. It's nice, when you've got a space like this, to be able to look down on it.

SAIL RACK
Vintage pond yachts, collected by the owner, sit high on a shelf specially designed by Botticelli & Pohl Architects. The backsplash tiles from The Tile Room, handcrafted in Mexico, have some variation in the surface, which suits an older house. 14" Holophane lights in Statuary Bronze from Ann-Morris Antiques have nautical appeal. An Elkay Gourmet sink and the Ashford Faucet by Grohe in Satin Nickel are directly across from the stove and dishwasher. Floors are reclaimed Pumpkin Pine that match the Pumpkin Pine in the 150-year-old rooms in the house.

The curve of the wooden ceiling makes me feel like I'm on a ship. How did you get that height in an old house?

RP: We got rid of a rabbit warren of bedrooms on the second floor, which the clients didn't need. Parts of the house dates back to the early 1800s and the ceilings were low. We wanted some relief, so we put in a cathedral ceiling, faced in V-groove, which is a variation on beadboard but with a simpler cut. Wood walls are a long-standing Nantucket tradition. You don't want drywall in all this humidity—it soaks up moisture and gets moldy. Imagine taking a rowboat and laying it upside down, and you're inside looking up at the hull. That's what this room feels like.

Counter space is definitely not a problem. The island is huge.

SH: I'm a great believer in big islands. To have that large surface with lots of storage underneath is fantastic. You can have three or four things going on at once. The mistake people often make is putting the island and the counters too far apart. All you need is room for two people to pass.

RP: This kitchen is the hub of the house. There are doors on three sides. You want to create an easy flow. The island is the resting spot in the middle. Half of it is devoted to seating, and the working part of the kitchen is all on the other half where you have the classic triangle of stove, sink, and refrigerator.

STALKING THE LOOK

1 2

3 4

5 6

Lead the eye upward by sheathing a soaring curvilinear ceiling in glossy white planks.

Lift your room higher by keeping to dark colors on lower cabinets and light colors on uppers. (1) Paint only lower cabinets Benjamin Moore Tudor Brown to ground your kitchen in a rich chocolate-brown shade.

The black 5-burner Double-Oven range (2) by Cluny through Lacanche blends beautifully into dark cabinets.

Chain, chain, chain. Hang your pendant lights from the kind of dark chains that always seem to be scattered around boatyards.

Weave a tangled web. Use woven window shades, straw baskets, and rush place mats to add texture to your shipshape theme. (3) (RIGHT) A rush place mat from Mimi's Mercantile lends organic texture to a table setting. (LEFT, OPPOSITE) Handmade field baskets by Alice Ogden have a Nantucket-style feel.

Finish the look with green glass accessories that look like they might have been in the hold of the Mayflower. (4) This goblet from The Green Glass Company (made from reclaimed wine bottles) has old harborside pub appeal.

Add a little Nantucket. (5) Place a bouquet of blue hydrangeas in an unpretentious pitcher for a dash of ageless "Cape and Islands" charm.

Be brassy. Sparkling brass pulls are great nautical touches. (6) Classic polished brass pulls from Nantucket Housefitters look handsome against chocolate brown drawers.

WABI-SABI

MARGUERITE RODGERS,
designer

Why do some people have
all the style? Short answer:
they're fearless. Imagine
having the temerity to create
handcrafted cabinets inspired
by traditional Japanese
tansus—storage chests fitted
with drawers and sliding
doors—for a place at the
Jersey shore! This is a kitchen
that's more old Kyoto than
modern Garden State.

THE BACKSTORY | "This kitchen is part of the total rehab of a small '70s bungalow in Loveladies, New Jersey. I began planning it as a weekend house for a single gentleman who lives in Philadelphia, but by the time it was finished he'd married! She's very happy with the design because it's an easy kitchen for two and there's a great flow out to the pool deck and the bay. They have guests and entertain here frequently, year round."

Cabinetry designed by Marguerite Rodgers has horizontal detailing typically found on sliding doors on tansus in Japanese kitchens. Compact and efficient: A slim pull-out pantry for dry goods is just to the right of the refrigerator. Pine Valley granite on counters and backsplashes has a watery feel. Iron hardware from Hida Tool & Hardware has an ancient Japanese look while the Altar hanging light with electrified candles from Holly Hunt lends modern day zen to the room.

"The inside extends to the outside here. The walnut floors blend into the mahogany pool deck; the granite is the color of grass. There's no beginning and no end. We even painted the outside of the house gray so it would recede into the sandy landscape."

"We covered the exhaust hood in cabinet panels so it would blend."

"I like pull-outs in lower cabinets, but that doesn't mean you have to do them all as drawers. Here I installed pull-out shelves in the island behind sliding doors."

A Japanese-style kitchen for a beach house in New Jersey? Please explain.
When you arrive, you open a gate and walk through a courtyard to get to this very compact one-story house, where all the rooms flow into each other. The spirit of the place reminded me of a Japanese teahouse. I've studied woodworking, and when we started this project, I suggested that we look at Nakashima furniture. My client and I bought that walnut table and chairs at auction and chose walnut for the cabinetry. A space feels calmer when you don't have a million different woods.
Cooking, dining, and living all happen in one big room. How did that affect the design?
I didn't want it to scream, "Kitchen!" So the island and the cabinets look more like furniture. We modeled them on a Japanese tansu—a storage chest that often has slatted doors. They slide open, as opposed to swinging out, which allows you to have larger openings and works really well in a small kitchen.
No seats at the island?
No. Too kitchen-y, and if people are sitting around the island, it really limits the chef when he's trying to work. He can't spread out. Instead, we put a slim counter against the window where you could sit and have a cup of coffee and look out at the bay. And it's another strong horizontal, which is very typical of Japanese architecture and makes the space feel wider than it actually is.

What's that pretty stone on the counters and backsplash?

A watery granite that's the color of the sea grass outside, and the bay on a cloudy day, polished to bring out all the greens and grays and even a tick of terra-cotta that picks up on the walnut. It would have looked a little dull if it were honed. Another great finish for granite is to sandblast it and acid-wash it, which we do with black granite all the time. It gives it a little texture and nothing seems to show on it.

You set up the furniture concept and then you put a big stainless-steel top on the island. How come?

To be modern. It looks so pure and simple when the counter and the sink are molded out of one piece of stainless steel, and it's actually easier to clean—no crevices to collect dirt. If I'm not doing a custom sink, I'll often use a brand called BLANCO. They make a sink with the kind of perfectly square corners I like.

Why did you want the steel on the island to look so thick?

I wanted the wood part of the island to be the same height as the Nakashima dining table, for a consistent line, and then the stainless steel brings it up to a better height for chopping. In some way, for me, the stainless steel just disappears—it's almost like glass or a mirror. You look right through it.

YIN AND YANG

The artisan **George Nakashima**, who made the table and chairs, was famous for highlighting the unrivaled beauty of nature. Rodgers tried to echo his ideals in her design by celebrating the splendor of natural wood, even covering the refrigerator in walnut panels. The cool stainless-steel island contrasts with the warmth of the wood. "It's the yin and the yang," says Rodgers. Kitchen tools are arrayed on the granite backsplash in a straightforward manner on a hanging system from **Rösle**. A living area and a large courtyard are to the right of the island.

WHAT IF...
THE ONLY HINT YOU OWNED
A DISHWASHER WAS THREE
INNOCUOUS LITTLE BUTTONS.

....

"It's all about keeping the island
looking like a piece of furniture.
And this dishwasher is only a
single drawer. It's a Fisher &
Paykel dishwasher drawer with
a walnut panel and iron hardware so it looks appropriate
within the context of the rest of
the kitchen."

BAY WATCH
THE BREAKFAST BAR'S
PINE VALLEY GRANITE
FROM DOYLE GERLACH
BRINGS THE COLORS OF
NATURE INTO THE ROOM.

....

"I looked for granite in a color
that felt like the landscape.
When you sit at the window
and look out at the pool, the
seagrass, and the bay it's
very soothing and calming.
It almost feels like an extension of the room."

CRAVING...
CABINET DOORS THAT SLIDE
AWAY LIKE A TEAHOUSE'S
SHOJI SCREENS.

....

"This is a very clean look and
so practical in a small kitchen.
If two people are cooking, one
doesn't have to move out of
the way every time the other
opens a cupboard."

What's the best way to care for this stainless-steel island and sink?

Wipe down the sink after using it so you don't get that drippy, drainy look, and buy one of those cleaners made specifically for stainless steel by 3M or Miele or Mrs. Meyer's. But you have to accept how it's going to patina. I look at that Nakashima table and see all the age and character in the wood, but if you can't stand any imperfection certain materials may not be for you.

Did you choose this faucet for its wonderful curve?

It does look sculptural but also we wanted a faucet with controls and a spray all in one to keep the counter uncluttered. And this is a very large faucet. If it were smaller it would be out of proportion to the length and width of the stainless-steel island, it would look puny.

Where else did scale come into play?

Everywhere. This whole house is only 2000 square feet. So we used smaller appliances: a dishwasher drawer instead of a dishwasher and a 27" wide refrigerator rather than 36". But since the island is large it can service other areas as well as the kitchen table. It's a staging place for appetizers when they're grilling outside on the deck or for sandwiches if there's a crowd in the pool.

Rodgers had the long stainless-steel sink and countertop fabricated by Barry's Commercial Installations to make a seamless transition. Even the satin nickel Mythos Faucet by Franke seems to simply rise up from the island's surface. Sliding Brazilian cherry cutting boards by Old World Butcher Block are infinitely useful for prep work and they echo the sliding action of the cabinet doors.

COLOR FORMS
NATURAL UNSTAINED WALNUT LENDS THIS KITCHEN UNCOMMON WARMTH AND TEXTURE.

"I personally love the look of unstained walnut when it is simply treated with a satin varnish. That brings out the luster, the cocoa browns, and the honey tones in the walnut and here, it helped the cabinets feel cohesive with the Nakashima furniture."

1

2

3

4

5

6

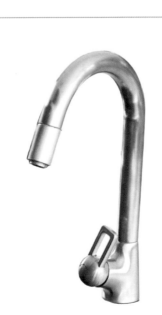

Embellish your cabinets with details as carefully calibrated as a Japanese tea ceremony.

Look for furniture so finely crafted it doesn't need nails. (1) One of George Nakashima's signatures is the butterfly joint, as seen on this kitchen's dining table. He was a master of traditional Japanese woodworking techniques and was also influenced by American Shaker furniture.

Enter the new iron age. (2) (TOP) The Roji iron teapot is a classic Japanese Tetsubin pot, an icon of refined simplicity. (3) The iron Moon Pull from Hida Tool & Hardware has an antique Japanese feel.

Pay homage to Master Nakashima. (4) Originally designed by George Nakashima in 1948, the Nakashima Straight Backed Chair reissued by Knoll for Design Within Reach is made of solid walnut with hickory spindles.

Serve on plates as handcrafted as your cabinets. (5) Rodgers set her client's table with handmade ceramic plates by Alice Goldsmith, through Barneys.

Fold in a faucet as graceful as an origami swan. (6) The Mythos Faucet by Franke has elegant pared-down appeal.

RHAPSODY IN BLUE

KATHRYN FEE, *architect,*
and **LISA MCCARTHY,** *homeowner*

This kitchen offers up
a major hit of blue—and
not just any blue—this is a
regally confident shade
that's paired with bright white
marble and tile. It's a big
bold statement, but the real
genius of Fee and McCarthy's
design is that they've made
this intense blue hue feel
friendly and approachable.

THE BACKSTORY | "The McCarthys purchased this newer shingle-style house in Bridgehampton around eighteen years ago as a refuge from Manhattan where they live with their two teens. Recently they decided to redo the kitchen but they weren't looking for a modern kitchen—they wanted a traditional look with a just a bit of detail, not too plain but not too formal either. The blue adds just the right punch." —KF

"This kitchen has a bit of formality but the blue gives it a country feeling that's appropriate for a country house."—KF

Luscious deep blue cabinets are set off by white Carrara marble countertops, finished with a traditional ogee edge. Even the ceiling molding and the Sub-Zero 642 refrigerator's panel are painted to match cabinets. A 36" dual-fuel Viking range and hood is complemented by a Viking wall oven—their reflective stainless-steel facades take on a bluish cast, helping them to blend into the scene. The amount of stainless is carefully calibrated though: the cabinet door just above the oven hides the microwave.

"The island is 5' x 6' with a deep overhang to accommodate stools."
—KF

"The kitchen opens up to a dining area and a bay window and everything has a view out to the pool, the yard, and a split rail fence with horses and paddocks beyond."
—KF

You could dive right into that blue. How did you choose it?

KF: I can't take credit for that. My clients, Lisa and Brian McCarthy, did not want the typical white kitchen, and their interior designer, Barbara Uzielli, picked the shade of blue. I was the architect. We gutted the original kitchen and added 400 square feet to open it up to the view. Now there's a breakfast area just beyond the island with a big table, and windows on three sides.

LM: We look out on an agricultural preserve and there's so much light that the color never gets too dark, even on a gloomy day. It's a deep cobalt blue that we pulled out of a piece of Chinese porcelain. I love the combination of blue and white. It always looks crisp and clean.

KF: The bold color adds a bit of an edge to a traditional kitchen. The cabinets are classic, with an inset panel and applied moldings. The knobs and hinges were going to be chrome, but I convinced Lisa to do satin nickel. I think it looks richer, and it's a better match for the stainless-steel appliances. It also goes nicely with the gray in the Carrara marble.

I notice you have glass doors in the storage cabinet, but not anywhere else. How come?

KF: The stove generates a lot of grease. If you've got glass doors nearby, they get dirty. Solid doors don't show it and you don't have to worry about how everything looks inside—although Lisa is very organized. When we built the storage cabinet, she knew exactly what she wanted to keep in each drawer, and we sized them to fit.

LM: It's a good idea to figure all that out beforehand. Think about how you're going to use every fixture.

The Carrara marble looks so pretty against all this blue.

KF: Carrara immediately feels familiar, as if you've walked into a wonderful old country kitchen, and it's one of those materials that never goes out of style. We had it honed, because polished marble looks too glitzy to me. The subway tiles are another classic, and they're a little more reflective, which really makes the blue pop. We used the 4" x 8" size rather than the usual 3" x 6" to get more scale.

What's Carrara marble like to work on?

LM: It's very high-maintenance. Even though it's sealed, I'm constantly wiping it off, and I still have to bring somebody in once a year to take out all the marks. But I wouldn't have done it any other way. Granite would have been too dark.

THE WHITE STUFF
In a storage cabinet, white ginger jars from **Two's Company** visually pop from cobalt blue cabinets. Table linens are stored in the drawers below. "When we're giving a party, I'll often set up that little area as a self-service bar, with a tray of liquor and an ice bucket," McCarthy says. Two prints by **Beth Weintrab** are propped casually against the **Carrara** marble backplash.

WHAT IF...

YOU PULLED YOUR KITCHEN'S COLORS FROM A FAVORITE OBJECT?

"I knew that Lisa collected Chinese porcelain because she asked for display space for her collections. But I thought what a great idea to match the blue from her collection for cabinets! It's a beautiful color; all-white would have been too stark."
—KF

CLASSICS REDEFINED

When you take the classic building blocks of a traditional kitchen—stately raised-panel cabinetry, subway tile backsplashes, Carrara marble counters—then give that combination a full-on dose of deep color like this cobalt blue, drama can't help but ensue. Taking dark blue (or chocolate brown, brick red or charcoal gray) all the way up over the crown moldings creates contrast that makes the combination of white tiles and counters richly distinctive.

CRAVING...

THE 24" DUAL-ZONE VIKING WINE CELLAR BECAUSE IT KNOWS WHAT YOUR WINE NEEDS, EVEN IF YOU DON'T.

"It holds up to 44 bottles on six horizontal shelves in this kitchen's island. "I like my Viking wine cooler because you can set two different temperatures, one for white and one for red." —LM

Were there any special sink requirements?

LM: I knew I wanted a sink that would be deep enough to accommodate my lobster pot, so I took my pot with me when we went shopping. The faucet looks good and it's also practical with a separate spray. That's all you need. I think it's ridiculous to buy all these gadgets you don't know how to work.

Any advice for would-be kitchen rehabbers?

LM: My kitchen is pretty simple. I don't like a lot of stuff. But I believe in buying the best appliances. I've got a Sub-Zero refrigerator and two Sub-Zero refrigerator drawers in the island, which I keep filled with sodas and water for the kids. And I've got a Miele dishwasher and a Viking stove with six burners, which is very helpful. I only have one wall oven and I wish I had done two, but we'll live. The kitchen really works, and that's because Kathryn really listened, and the contractor, Declan Murray, was a dream.

" The sink is undermounted, which also adds another inch or so of depth and functions much more efficiently. You can just take a sponge and—whoosh—wipe everything off the counter right into the sink. I can't even remember the last time I did an overmounted sink.**"**
—KF

An Elkay stainless-steel sink and Dornbracht's Madison Flair Faucet pair nicely with the gray veining in the Carrara marble. And the white counter, with its traditional stepped-down carved ogee edge, sets off the raised panels in the cabinets.

COLOR FORMS

FEE SAYS BENJAMIN MOORE CHAMPION COBALT LENDS DAZZLING WARMTH.

" I think this color makes you feel so good. But then it also adds a lot of drama because the contrast that happens between the marble, the tile, and this blue is absolutely beautiful.**"** —KF

STALKING THE LOOK

1

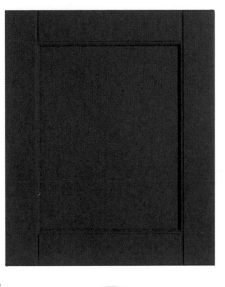

2

3

4   5

6

Practice restraint. If you're going to paint swathes of a blue as strong as the one McCarthy chose, try restricting your overall color palette to just blue and white to avoid busyness.

Let nature do the accessorizing. (1) A bouquet of sunflowers, a row of tomatoes on the sill, a tray of ripening peaches—they're all natural shades that will complement your blue.

Who said blue was only for cabinet contents? (2) Blue Oltremare cabinets from Arclinea will envelop you in blue.

Don't spare the nickel. (3) Hardware with a satin nickel finish jibes nicely with the gray veining in Carrara marble counters.

Go Carrara for your counters. (4) The marble's gray veining will enliven a broad expanse of island.

Show proper reverence to your ancestral Chinese porcelain. (5) Use the Temple Jar from Bungalow 5—a large Chinese blue-and-white jar hand-painted with blue and white jars—as your centerpiece.

Set a blue table. (6) Stemware from Treillage lends the perfect dash of blue to a place setting.

AGUA FRESCA

DIANNE BERNHARD,
designer, and homeowner

Can an outdoor kitchen ever
be as beautiful (and fully-
functioning) as one indoors?
Apparently the answer is yes.
Bernhard created an elegant
al fresco kitchen where
she can watch sailboats float
by while cooking and her
guests can tuck in beneath
twinkling chandeliers.

TOP: There are high-**BTU** burners on both sides of the 54 built-in grill, for lobster boils. Professional grill, burner units, and hood by Lynx—and, underneath, a Lynx warming drawer, a Viking Professional outdoor oven, and Lynx utility drawers—make it possible to cook a three-course meal out here.
"The grill is the main event. It's like having a fireplace in the room, and I wanted the hood to be massive and important. We ended up buying three hoods and putting them together so they would stretch over the burners on both sides of the grill. And then we had a custom panel made to go above it and disguise the vents."

BOTTOM: The Franke sink is paired with an industrial-style Sherisah Spring Spout Faucet by Westbrass that makes cleanup a cinch.
"I just loved that tall curve on the restaurant-style spray faucet. I bought it more for aesthetics than utility but there's nothing wrong with that! I've got two of those faucets, one on each sink. I wanted two sinks so I could have one for pots and the other for china—with a dishwasher at each of them. If you have the right equipment in the right place, it's amazing how easy it is to prepare a meal."

In this outdoor kitchen in Westport, Connecticut, Plain & Fancy cabinets with Nantucket-style doors and blue-toned CaesarStone countertops pick up the colors of the Long Island Sound just beyond the deck. Sub-Zero refrigerator drawers in the island allow easy access to beverages. Chandeliers from Kichler were antiqued with a metallic bronze finish to give them some age. Double rows of pendant lights are all from Sea Gull Lighting. Bernhard turns off the lights over the grill after cooking and dims the lights over the bar during dinner. Paint on floor and ceiling is Benjamin Moore Blue Springs to reflect the water view.

"I went with Caesar-Stone for counters. It's more consistent than natural stone and it's easy to clean and keeps a shine. And the color is so beautiful. As soon as I saw that deep blue I went straight to it."

"Cabinets are a smoky gray blue. To me, it was the only color that would fit with the water and the sky, which is not always bright blue."

"I handpicked each one of those stones on the walls. We made templates and laid all the stones on the deck so I could work out the patterning. It actually takes a lot of planning for something to look random."

"It's glass tile, in periwinkle verging on cobalt. It's the one big, bold stroke of color, but boy, is it big."

WALL ART

MARSHALL WATSON,
designer

You crave simplicity but still want pizzazz? A colorful kitchen but not colorful cabinets? Marshall Watson has a brilliantly simple solution to your conundrum. Make one wall—just one—an out-and-out scene-stealer and in that single bold stroke all your wishes will be granted.

THE BACKSTORY | "This is on Fire Island—no cars allowed. Once the kids get out here, they're stuck. It's all part of the summer camp atmosphere. People get to know each other. It's a Victorian cottage built in the late 1800s. The clients wanted a sense of tradition but didn't want it to look dowdy."

Veneto Glass Tiles from Stone Source cover an entire wall—all the way to the ceiling. Heavy-duty marine lights from Architrove above the island, and Deschutes sconces from Rejuvenation on the walls over the counters provide task lighting. The Pere Tranquille bistro stools from Annick de Lorme are made in France and can be customized in various colors and patterns; here they pick up on the blue-and-white theme.

"The blue-and-white palette feels beachy, summery, and clean clean clean."

That tile wall is very graphic. Almost like a piece of modern art.
That's good. Can I quote you? It's a small kitchen and it wasn't that expensive to bring it all the way up to the ceiling. And it's practical, because you can get grease splatters as high as three feet up.

So refreshing—a small kitchen.
You get a wonderful intimacy in a small space. I've seen 20 kids crowded around that table.

It feels shipshape, like a boat.
That's the concept. We're five miles out in the ocean. You've got to be very careful about what you build here. Look at the walls. They're all wood, which breathes and bends in a storm. No Sheetrock, because it will rot. These houses aren't insulated, because the whole community shuts down for the winter. Fabrics mildew. Metals rust. You've got to use durable materials, otherwise they'll be eaten up and spit out for dinner by the salt air.

So what works?
We used nautical lights with heavy plating. A porcelain sink, because stainless steel will pit, although we had to have a stainless-steel stove. The porcelain ones just aren't developed enough. Nothing fancy like a pot filler—you can't put water in the walls because it will freeze. And workhorse faucets from Dornbracht that don't break. You don't want anything that's too complicated for the local repairman.

CHOP CHOP
Prep work here is as easy as making a clean sweep from cutting board to undermounted farmhouse sink. White Manhattan Calacatta marble on the countertops blends in with the white-painted cabinetry. Window shades, made of indoor-outdoor fabric from Sonia's Place, bring the checkered feel of the tile over to the windows.

What's on the countertops? White Manhattan Calacatta marble. I put eleven coats of sealer on it. I always do. I've found that eleven coats works best. Granite would have been too hard-edged for this house.

The cabinetry is simple, which really makes the latches and pulls stand out. Are they old or new? New, from Restoration Hardware. They've created a lot of good hardware, and it's one of their greatest strengths. The bin pulls are long and easy to grasp. Your fingers move comfortably in them. Good hardware is like a great handshake. It just feels right. It's very important to touch and test hardware before you install it.

"My client said no transparent glass, because in two days it will be coated with salt. She taught me a lot, and so did the contractor, Ed Horton. This house is not air-conditioned and the doors are constantly open. Sometimes you see this mist moving through the rooms. It looks so romantic but it's filled with salt. So we did ribbed glass. Nothing shows on it and it does this wonderful distortion of what's behind it. This woman does not want to spend her time arranging cabinets. She told me, 'I want to be able to be messy.'"

COLOR FORMS
ALL PAINT IN THE KITCHEN IS RALPH LAUREN POCKET WATCH WHITE, A PERFECT SOFT COUNTERPOINT TO BRIGHT BLUE.

"This high gloss on the cabinets is like going up to the top of a mountain and breathing in that first view and the unbelievable fresh air. It's wipeable, and it lasts longer. This is all new cabinetry, and we didn't try to pretend that it was old. It will look old soon enough."

STALKING THE LOOK

1

2

3

4

5 | 6

Sit and be blue. (1) You could find your perfect blue fabric and customize the Kinsey stool from Rowe furniture.

Use a butcher block for a small kitchen multitasker. Is it a table or is it an island? Does it really matter?

Choose a faucet that overreaches. (2) The Gooseneck Faucet by Dornbracht is handy for filling a lobster pot.

Go all-out blue—from exhaust hood to cooktop. (3) The professional-style stainless-steel Garland range and Rangemaster hood look handsome against a blue background.

Let pattern peek in at the window. (4) A blue and white graphic pattern at the window like Tillett Textiles & T4 Fabrics' Argyle Crossing enlivens a strict blue-and-white palette.

Erect the Great Wall of blue glass tile— then use bright white grout to frame and emphasize every single glossy glistening rectangle! (5) The 2" x 6" glass tiles from Stone Source, laid in a traditional running bond, remind Watson of sea glass.

Ban recessed lights from your pretty beadboard ceiling. (6) Watson strategically placed Deschutes sconces from Rejuvenation on upper walls over the counters for task light with old-fashioned charm.

SPLASH

Backsplashes can be life changing. Install some stainless steel above the counter in your too-traditional kitchen and it's good-bye blasé, hello Bauhaus. You can choose a backsplash that melts into your counters like butter on an English muffin or one that just craves attention. Remember though, it's not only about looks—a backsplash also has to live up to its name. It's the last line of defense between your immaculate walls and the daily onslaught of percolating sauces, spattering oils, and unruly stews. Here is a raft of suggestions on how to make a splash.

MATERIAL MATTERS

Where should you begin when trying to pick backsplash material?
"It's very important to make sure the countertop material and the backsplash talk to each other so that color and pattern are balanced. For example, if you choose a busy granite for your counters you don't want to have too much texture in your backsplash. The last thing you want to do is to add to that busyness. But if you choose simple monolithic counters you could jazz it up with something like waterjet-cut mosaics or colorful glass tile. The simpler your countertops the more pattern you can use on your backsplash."

—**BARBARA SALLICK**, COFOUNDER AND SENIOR VICE PRESIDENT OF DESIGN, WATERWORKS

What is it about this subway-tile backsplash that feels so modern?
"I insisted that the tiles be installed in columns. Tile installers want to install randomly— it's easier. But we went to the Ann Sacks showroom and saw these tiles with the grout lines all lined up and loved the look immediately."
—**ANN WOLF**, DESIGNER

A SLAB OF MARBLE MAKES A TOTALLY BESPOKE BACKSPLASH. It's a custom look with a clean grout-free surface that's easy to clean. Slabs can go modern or traditional depending on the kind of marble you choose and the amount of veining. In this kitchen, the Carrara marble backsplash conveys an Italian country feel.

"The architect, Bob White, did a wonderful job of creating this Italianate character. His design has the simplicity and solidity of an old agrarian building. I wanted to keep that simplicity."

—MICHAEL SMITH, DESIGNER

DOES GROUT COLOR REALLY MATTER?

"Your choice of grout will greatly influence the outcome of your backsplash no matter what material you choose. If you choose a dark grout with a light tile, you will introduce a graphic element into your kitchen: the grid will be completely pronounced. On the other side of the coin, if your grout closely matches the tile color you won't notice the grid so much and you'll have a quieter background. You have to decide how much pattern you want to see. It's all about personal preference."

—BARBARA SALLICK, COFOUNDER AND SENIOR VICE PRESIDENT OF DESIGN, WATERWORKS

WHITE SUBWAY TILE IN A COTTAGE-STYLE KITCHEN IS A NO-BRAINER. But what if you ran those 3" x 6" beauties all the way up to the ceiling and around your contemporary cabinets? In this kitchen, the backsplashes' raised texture has extra impact alongside sleek metal, glass, and stainless steel.

"We wanted to cover the walls with inexpensive white subway tile, and we chose one that was handmade. Because it's made on a terra-cotta base, it has a little more irregularity than machine-made tile."

—DAVID MITCHELL, DESIGNER

An elaborately veined soapstone backsplash is the star attraction in this kitchen, where it sets off Lacanche's black Cluny stove.

"We used the same soapstone for counters and sinks, for seamlessness. And when I found that heavily veined slab, which most people don't want, I knew it would be the focal point of the room."
—MELANIE POUNDS, DESIGNER

BACKDROP DRAMA

Pick a Hue That's "You."
Create a one-of-a-kind backsplash! You can customize these handmade cement tiles, Quatro Foil from Original Mission Tile, by choosing your own color combinations.

Pick Smalls.
Mini subway tiles make a big statement. Savoy tiles by Ann Sacks (shown in Mint) come in 11 colors. They're only $1^{7}/_{8}''$ x $^{7}/_{8}''$, but they come on netted sheets to make installation easy.

Triangulate your Backsplash.
Invisible grout lines help the pattern of these cement tiles, Triangle Madness CW-2 from Laura Gottwald, to literally flow over your walls.

Go Old School or Better Yet, Ancient School.
Just look at the exquisite detail in the Damascus Tile from Lascaux Tile Company—ceramic tiles based on an ancient Syrian design.

Add a Touch of Marrakech.
Fretwork in Coral, Khaki, and Milk from Popham Design is a Moroccan cement tile with a modern look; handmade in Marrakech.

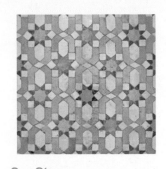

See Stars.
Handmade using a 1000-year-old technique, the Moroccan mosaic from Mosaic House has a stunning starry pattern.

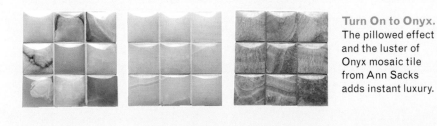

Turn On to Onyx.
The pillowed effect and the luster of Onyx mosaic tile from Ann Sacks adds instant luxury.

Earn your Stripes.
Gorgeous hand-cut striped tiles made from thin strips of colored glass, Phuze Tiles from Waterworks, provide a jazzy accent against a solid color. Or splurge and do the entire backsplash!

Remember Crackle Always Pops.
Classic brick tile from Urban Archeology has depth and character thanks to its hand-applied crackle glaze. Available in 65 colors, including Caribbean Crackle, shown.

MOSAIC TILES ADD BEAUTIFUL MOVEMENT TO A WALL WHILE ALSO MAKING IT IMPERVIOUS TO MOISTURE.
This mosaic tile wall, in **AKDO**'s **Mini Brick**, has an intriguing vintage restaurant appeal.

"Everything in the kitchen is clean-lined. We liked the mosaic tile backsplash so much we extended it all around the room. It's this expanse of tiny gray-and-white Carrara marble tile, and it makes it feel like some café in Paris."

—PAIGE SCHNELL, DESIGNER

What did you use for your own kitchen's backsplash?
I have 1" x 6" handmade tile from our Vintage line on my backsplash. It's creamy white with a slight crackle and it lends the space a slight reflective quality, a bit of life. My counters are cream-colored Danby Marble, honed. Those two materials complement each other because they're both really warm whites. I like turning on my under-counter lights and seeing just a little bit of backsplash shine. It feels so clean."

—BARBARA SALLICK, COFOUNDER AND SENIOR VICE PRESIDENT OF DESIGN, WATERWORKS

WALLS IN THIS KITCHEN ARE COVERED IN HAND-MADE STAR AND CROSS TILE THAT THE DESIGNER CREATED WITH THE LASCAUX TILE COMPANY.
The tile is a perfect counterpoint to the smoky color on the ceiling and cabinets, painted **Pratt & Lambert Glacier Sand**.

"I needed something strong to give this tiny kitchen character."
—CHAD EISNER, DESIGNER

GLASS TILE IS ALL ABOUT HIGH SHINE WITH A WIPE-DOWN FACTOR THAT'S UNMATCHED. The star of this kitchen is its backsplash of handmade glass tiles reminiscent of the nearby ocean, by Erin Adams through Ann Sacks.

....

"I used a bright turquoise blue and then put a lot of neutral color in the room so it doesn't end up looking like crazyland—there's a fine line, you know. I like to see color done in blocks."

—**FRANK ROOP**, DESIGNER

A SPLASH OF COLOR

How would you arrange a multicolor tile backsplash? "You might choose one main color, like green. Then run just green tile throughout the kitchen except under the range hood—the stove is generally where your tallest expanse of tile will be. Under the hood you could do a rectangular panel where you might mix colors—green tile with, maybe, blue and white tile, to create a color mélange. That way the colored tile will be a beautiful focal point because you've kept the rest of the kitchen quiet."

—**BARBARA SALLICK**, COFOUNDER AND SENIOR VICE PRESIDENT OF DESIGN, WATERWORKS.

Hand-shaped and hand-painted **Delft** tiles, from the **Royal Makkum** line at **Country Floors**, introduce a blue note to an elaborately carved range nook in a kitchen by designer **Beverly Ellsley**.

shop-keeper

OPEN SHELVES STYLED RIGHT DOWN TO THE GRAVY BOAT. A PLACE FOR EVERYTHING AND EVERYTHING IN ITS PLACE.

SHELF LIFE

JONATHAN KING and **JAMES STOTT**, *designers and homeowners*

Who knew tall stacks of plates and bowls and a shelf chockablock with pitchers could look as pretty as a Tiffany's display? And who'd have predicted a row of pans hanging in a window would glimmer so beautifully? This pair of chefs knows that keeping things handy can be gloriously handsome.

THE BACKSTORY | "The house had a small kitchen with heavy wooden cabinets. Last summer, we were building our very first cooking school and every day I'd walk through it with Bart Forbes, the architect, and come home and say, 'Oh my God, that cooking school looks so great! I'm going to move to the cooking school.' Finally, we asked Bart what it would take to do the same design in our own kitchen. It's new construction, although most people would think it was old because of the posts and beams." —JK

Hand-poured subway tile from Old Port Specialty Tiles feels antique. Paired with polished nickel hardware by Shaub & Company, this kitchen conveys the straightforward utility of an old general store.

Cabinets below hold linens, silverware, candles, and platters for one-stop table setting.

Imagine all the delicious meals served in this Cape Neddick, Maine, kitchen. It was built by the founders of Stonewall Kitchens—a company that makes jams, mustards, and other specialty foods. The everyday dishes all that great food gets served on are stored on simple open shelves, just to the left of the dish sink and two steps away from the dishwasher.

How did Stonewall Kitchen begin?

JK: It combined two passions—horticulture and cooking. We started making things out of our garden— herbal vinegars, jams, flavored mustards—and then a friend said, "You should sell these." And a business was born . . .

Is this the kitchen where it all began?

No, we bought this much later.

So this is new construction? It feels so authentic.

It's classic New England: shiplap, beadboard, clean white hand-poured tiles. I couldn't stop myself—they had to be hand-poured to get all those nice wavy imperfections. It's a modern farmhouse kitchen, and it has some of that early mercantile look you see in our stores.

You have two sinks. What happens at this one?

This is where the dirty dishes come to get rinsed and put into their own dishwasher. Then you empty it right onto those open shelves.

HERE'S HOW KING AND STOTT created open shelves both sculptural and intriguing: they kept it simple. Everything—tile, Carrara marble counters, floating shelves, and even the toaster—are in shades of bright white to keep the peace. Then they grouped "like" things together (proceeding as if their kitchen was an exceptionally cool housewares store). Plates are all stacked together on two bottom shelves on the left. Cups and bowls on the right. Large service-ware is restricted to the top shelf, and cutting boards are all grouped together, leaning against a wall atop the counter.

WHAT THE PROS KNOW. This design comes from years of professional cooking experience. First up, a clean-up sink for dishes set under the square window. Then, moving clockwise, there's a baking area; a bar area with ice maker, wine cooler, and stemware in the glass-fronted cabinet; another clean-up sink for pots; and a pantry cupboard. Countertops are solid Carrara marble, a hefty 2¾" thick to suit the large space. All the appliances, by Viking, are clad in stainless steel, and diner stools from Williams-Sonoma echo that workhorse material. A group of five industrial pendants by Urban Archaeology provide lots of task lighting and make up for the lack of recessed lights in the ceiling.

How big is this kitchen? It looks huge.

It's 47' long. We gutted three rooms and opened it up to the foyer so it feels like one big open space. The main island is 18' and the butcher-block island is 6'. It's a chef's dream, and it was a long time coming.

Why two islands?

Jim and I both cook, but like many people, we don't cook well together. We're both complete control freaks.

We've got duplicate knives, measuring cups, everything you need, on each island. The pots and pans are by the stove, and you can just turn around when you're done and there's the pot sink, with a big industrial spray. When we planned the kitchen we drew bubbles: cooking area, baking area, clean-up area. We put two refrigerator drawers in the butcher-block island, thinking we'd use them for produce, but they've ended up as our beverage station.

Where'd you get those great retro stools?

At Williams-Sonoma, years ago, but they still have them. They're real diner stools, and our nieces and nephews drive us crazy spinning around on them. They're very comfortable. I sit at the end of the counter every day when I come home and relax while looking at my mail.

WHAT IF...
YOUR POTS ALL HUNG
IN A ROW LIKE A PRETTY
WINDOW VALANCE?

Copper pots, which
the owners don't bother
to polish, hang over a
large stainless-steel sink,
31½" x 19½", equipped
with a restaurant-style
faucet; both by Franke.
No more digging around
in a drawer for the right
pot. And after wash
up? Just reach for an
available hook.

CRAVING...
TWO ISLANDS—FOR WHEN
YOU'VE GOT TOO MANY COOKS
IN THE KITCHEN

"This way I can be making a chicken
dish on the stove and Jim can be
making a salad on the butcher
block. We don't get in each other's
way, but we can still talk."

Dinner parties tend to happen in the kitchen where a curved wall of shelves shows off collections of ironstone pottery and American yellowware bowls. It's an intriguing backdrop for this old Danish table and chairs. The antique pine console is perfect for a buffet.

It's a white kitchen. Why does it feel so warm? The woodwork. It's local hemlock, just treated with a light oil to bring out the grain. The floor is reclaimed pumpkin pine, big boards 8" wide. What's great about it is it's very soft. You drop a can and it makes a dent. The dogs run in and their paws scratch it. Those marks tell a story. **Sounds like this is the true heart of your home.** This is where we hang out. I love to cook. On Sundays, you'll find me in my sweats, with the music on, making something I know is going to take a long time, like brisket. I'm never in a rush when I'm cooking. **I can just see you two, with a glass of wine, sitting at that round white table.** That's where we entertain. Our favorite thing is having two people over to eat in the kitchen. Even if there are six of us, we just squish in around that table. Everyone always wants to be in the kitchen. In my next house, I'm just going to have a kitchen, a bath, and a bedroom. That's all you need.

COLOR FORMS
THE GLUE THAT JOINS TWO CHEFS' SEPARATE STYLES IS
BENJAMIN MOORE ATRIUM WHITE

Beadboard ceilings, walls, and custom cabinets are sheathed in this modern white with pink undertones. It contrasts beautifully with the natural hemlock moldings and blends with the mottled white tile. It always feels crisp and lively, never gray, so it's perfect for an active kitchen.

STALKING THE LOOK

1

2

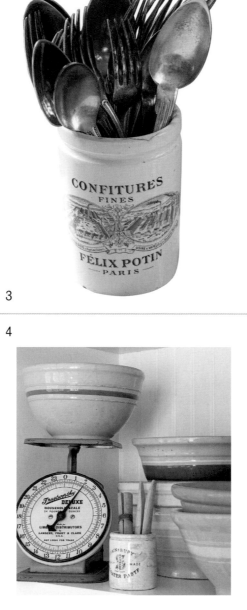

3

4

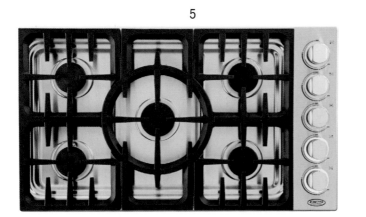

5

Be mercantile. Convey the straightforward simplicity of a country general store.

Group (1) olive oils, vinegars, and salts on an ironstone platter, with onions and garlic in a bowl nearby. And fill a big white pitcher with spatulas. It's convenient and charming, too.

Remember you can never have too much (2) antique English ironstone or old Burleigh ware.

Collect antique jam jars (3) to keep forks and spoons within reach on the counter.

Outline your kitchen in unembellished natural wood. Continue the trim around your windows and down through the corners to mimic the look of rural New England buildings of another age.

Pull in color with accessories (4) that jibe with your "general store" ambience like American yellowware bowls and a funky old scale.

Make two zones: a marble topped area for rolling out dough, and a butcher block counter for chopping.

Site your cooktop in the island to create copious space around the stove for utensils and ingredients you want within easy reach. (5) The Drop-In Gas Cooktop by Fischer & Paykel is pro-style all the way, with five dual-flow burners that deliver 11,00 to 17,00 BTUs yet can also simmer down to a mere 140 degrees.

A pewter platter on the top shelf sets off ironstone pitchers.

PARLOR GAME

JOAN SCHINDLER,
designer

What evokes fonder memories than an old-fashioned ice cream parlor? That was the inspiration behind this ravishing kitchen. Schindler found a vintage marble ice-cream counter, installed it as her muse, then gave herself permission to use elements found in commercial kitchens, like steel shelving and faucets piped directly out of the walls, for a deliciously cool result.

Antique French market baskets on the counter are a clever way to add texture to smooth marble and tile while keeping linens close at hand.

THE BACKSTORY | This Palm Beach, Florida, house is owned by a couple with many grandchildren. Its Mediterranean-style exterior offers no hint of the lively kitchen with a repurposed candy counter sitting at its center. The bluish cast of the counter hints at the water outside this oceanfront home.

A solid marble former ice-cream counter makes an incredible backdrop for a 17th-century French farmhouse table surrounded by 1920s French metal chairs. Steel shelves mounted on brackets and hung over white subway tile from Urban Archeology have "candy shop" appeal. Cream colored walls, in Benjamin Moore Cloud White, set off the bright white tile, and accentuate the arched ceiling.

"There's an old-fashioned thread running through here, but then I added more contemporary elements like open shelves made out of stainless steel. I think the mix of old and new is what makes it so interesting."

Chair cushions are in Cowtan & Tout's Iota Original, a lavender check that brings out the underlying French Country influence here.

What's the story behind that amazing cabinet?
It's actually an ice-cream counter. For years it sat in Urban Archeology, a store in Manhattan that specializes in architectural salvage, and I thought, someday this is going to make a terrific kitchen.

How did subway tile find its way here?
I just liked the look of it. It was clean, uncomplicated. It looked good with the counter, which feels very "American candy store" or "Ye Olde Ice Cream Shoppe."

The subway tile does have the feel of an old soda fountain but then there's this elegant arched ceiling. Did you create that?
Oh, yes. We created it. This was a gut remodel. We created everything.

Why the arched ceiling?
I'm always influenced by Europe. That feels very European to me.

Why go with open shelves?
I think they're very inviting. The client loves her grandchildren, and she wanted them to be able to come down to breakfast anytime and have everything all laid out—orange juice, croissants, fresh fruit. They don't have to go into the cupboards. The plates and cups are right there.

HANG TIME

A polished nickel rail from **Ann Morris Antiques** holds ladles and other utensils. Another rail under the cabinets holds tea towels. Vintage faucets function as pot fillers above a small sink that's great for washing vegetables before throwing them into the pot. For slicing, a long knife slot is built into the counter and there are two pull-out cutting boards on either side of the **Thermador Professional Series** range.

WHAT IF...
YOU KEPT YOUR RICE AND RIGATONI INSIDE A BLOCK OF OLD MARBLE THAT USED TO STORE ICE CREAM?

"Those are the original steel doors to the icebox. The whole thing is a solid block of marble, so heavy it's unbelievable. Anyway, we retrofitted the interior with shelves and kept the exterior exactly as it was with that band of black-and-gold marble all the way around."

CRAVING...
A PITCHER COLLECTION LINED UP LIKE A ROW OF DUCKLINGS

White ironstone pitchers from **Sentimento Antiques** look like an art installation lined up tall to small on an open shelf above the former candy counter. A large pewter tray propped behind the pitchers varies the scale for interest and adds another material so the shelves don't look like run-on white.

STALKING THE LOOK

1

2

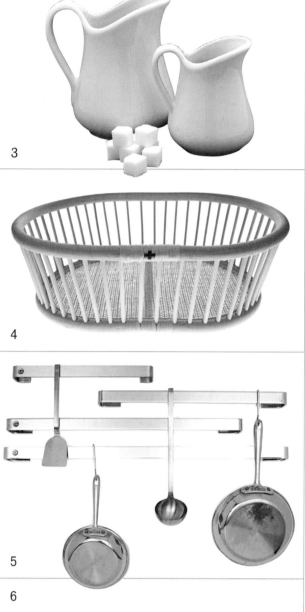

3

4

5

6

Search for one singular salvaged cabinet from an old store or restaurant and make it your focal point. Keep everything else in shades of white with hints of "old mercantile"—like hanging cheese graters, and faucets embedded directly in tile walls.

Use commercial-style pendant lights like the ones Schindler found salvaged from an old perfume factory.

Pick countertop material that helps the whole room to gel. (1) Schindler chose stone with a look to match the marble band in the candy counter. Black Portoro marble veined with gold.

Use oversized napkins with a splash of blue—all you need to set a beautiful table. (2) Paper guest towels with the look and feel of linen, Blue Linen Airlaid Guest Towels from Caspari, make terrific napkins.

Collect unmatched (only white) pitchers and arrange them like art on your steel shelves. (3) Start with Pillivuyt's Mehun Jugs that come in nine sizes.

Use open shelves made of steel with visible brackets—somehow 21st century and vintage at the same time.

Display your linens in baskets like you're a Parisian shopkeeper. (4) The Japanese Oval Basket from Tortoise Life will keep napkins prettily contained.

Get those ladles out of a crowded drawer and up on the wall. (5) Utensil Bars from Enclume, in stainless steel, brass, copper, or chrome will do the trick.

Find furniture that keeps quiet. Schindler used a very plain French antique table and chairs so nothing grabs attention away from the dominant element—the candy counter. (6) Jayson Home & Garden's Chelsea Dining Table with its reclaimed wood top and steel base is simply intriguing.

NORTHERN LIGHT

KATRIN CARGILL
and **CAROL GLASSER**, *designers*

Designers Cargill and
Glasser wrote a love letter
to Swedish style with this
Houston kitchen—clean,
pared down, and romantic.
Classic plate racks, butcher-
block counters, pale yellow
walls, and a pendant lamp
in a new wave Gustavian
shade of blue all capture that
covetable quintessentially
Scandinavian look.

TOP: An antique **Scandinavian** chest holds simple bone china made special with just the barest bit of gold embellishment—a capital "**T**" for the first letter of the owner's surname.

BOTTOM: The modern **Viking** range hints at "old **Scandinavia**" with its matte graphite finish and a hood detailed like an old dome-top chest. Utensils grouped in a basket partner with the plate racks on the opposite side of the room to further the notion that some utilitarian objects are just too pretty to hide away in a drawer.
"We gave in to the owner's wishes and designed an **American** chef's kitchen—the **Viking** range even has restaurant-style warming shelves. But the simplicity of the custom cabinetry and snowy marble countertops are 100 percent **Swedish**." —**CG**

The white linen roller shade is a traditional Swedish design.

Lefroy Brooks Kitchen Bridge Faucets have old-fashioned rural appeal.

"The work island has so much storage, we were largely able to do without wall cabinets, which I think weigh a kitchen down." —CG

The butcher block island goes well with a pale palette, and with no counter stools to get in the way, it provides all-around access for everyday food prep.

SCANDINAVIAN FANTASY

Milky yellow walls and gray-white cabinets convey the utmost softness. Even opaque glass-fronted cabinets have a misty muted feel. Rather than hang heavy cabinets on the kitchen's window wall, Cargill and Glasser designed plate racks to display a collection of French faience. The Charles Edwards toile pendant light is painted a gray-blue that's a modern twist on "Gustavian blue" and its nickel lining amplifies the island's task lighting.

To keep the space ultra-functional Garten likes to see her things out on the counter or displayed on open shelves. She even put a stainless steel shelf over the Viking Professional Custom Series Dual-Fuel range for the spatulas, kosher salt, and kitchen timers she uses all the time. Storage is doubled with cabinets on the stool side of the island for special-occasion items like Thanksgiving platters. And Garten chose long handles from KraftMaid because they're easier to grab than small knobs.

THE CHEF RECOMMENDS

ROBERT STILIN, *interior designer,* and **INA GARTEN,** *designer and cookbook author*

Judging by the kitchen they created, you don't want to trust Food Network star Ina Garten and her interior designer Robert Stilin with a secret. They obviously believe in getting everything out in the open— especially kitchen equipment in all its utilitarian glory. Of course, in the hands of this stylish pair even a potato masher looks chic.

THE BACKSTORY | Do you dream of stepping inside Ina Garten's celebrated East Hampton barn and getting some kitchen ideas from the Barefoot Contessa herself? The editors at *House Beautiful* certainly did. So for one exciting week *House Beautiful* recreated Garten's kitchen right smack in the middle of New York's Rockefeller Center. Here it is idea by idea (without the crowds) . . .

"I like really good equipment that you buy once, for a lifetime. All-Clad pots. A Viking range. Good-quality hotel silver. These are all things I've used for decades." —IG

Flour and sugar are always within reach in Crate and Barrel's two-gallon glass jars, next to the Cuisinart.

Garten likes to chop vegetables on an extra-large and thick Maple R-Board by John Boos.

You've got kitchen design down to a science. What's your secret?

IG: I think of design the way I think of my recipes: the simpler, the better. I start with the three major elements—stove, sink, refrigerator—and put them in close proximity to each other, with enough work space in between, and out of the flow of traffic, so if the kids and the dogs and the husbands are running around, they're not in my way.

How much counter space do you really need?

IG: As much as possible. And the bigger the island the better, because you can use it as a buffet. I love when people help themselves. They can choose what they want, and it makes them feel like family. It's also simpler for me. It can be stressful to entertain, so I do everything I can to make it easy and familiar. I never do a recipe for guests that I haven't done before. If you open my drawers, you won't see a thousand different pots and pans. I have a set of All-Clad and Le Creuset, and I'm really comfortable with them. I know how they work, so I know that what I'm cooking is going to come out well.

Garten likes gutsy countertops, super-thick and dark, so she chose ultra-durable **CaesarStone** in Raven. Light can be controlled with dimmers and directed wherever Garten decrees with **Thomas P. Richmond**'s flexible lighting system. Large-scale hurricane lamps from **Bloom** provide more visual interest than a collection of smaller accessories.

This is so much more than a kitchen. You've got a dining area and a desk area and big, comfortable chairs. Exactly. It's everything you need for living. Robert Stilin worked with me on the design, and when we built this out in my barn in East Hampton, we built it as a living room with a kitchen in it.

RS: It's that whole kitchen-dining-living thing. That's what people want these days. The kitchen has opened up into this big, multifunctional space. The husband can be cooking while the wife is reading. And guests want to be part of the action and see what's coming out of the oven, so I try to build comfort into a kitchen. To me, stools are not enough. Club chairs put people at ease. If you've got a small space, big furniture will make it feel bigger.

EASY DOES IT
The highly functional workspace is bookended by a **Viking Quiet Cool** refrigerator on one side and a freezer on the other. Custom wood panels on both appliances add warmth. **Visual Comfort**'s Column Lamp, in Sheffield silver, casts a pretty glow over a buffet.

WHAT IF...

EVERYTHING, YES *EVERYTHING*,
ON YOUR KITCHEN SHELVES
WAS EITHER SNOWY WHITE
OR SPARKLING SILVER?

"Everything I use all the time is
out on the counter, but it has to
be white or stainless steel. If it
were red and green and orange,
this place would look like a
bowl of M&M's." —IG

TAKE NOTE.
A desk area for planning
menus or just soaking in
the sunshine is sited by the
windows. Random laid wood
planks of solid hand-scraped
maple, in Pacific by Shaw,
convey a feeling of age. A
club chair from Lucca & Co.
pulls up to an antique Belgian
worktable to bring a little
history into the space. Slipcovered furniture has a casual
look. One of Ina's favorite
fabrics is Rogers & Goffigon's
Shaker Linen, and they made
this lavender color just for
her, named it Ina, and put it
in their line.

CRAVING...
A HIDDEN NOOK FOR
WET SPONGES

Garten prefers a wide
deep sink with no partitions,
like Kohler's 8 Degree Sink,
and clever use of space so
sponges dry out of sight.
Sink inserts like Kohler's
drying rack and cutting board
allow a sink to multitask.

How do you set the table?

IG: The first thing I'll do is go to the store, sometimes just the grocery store, and look at the flowers they have. I buy the best available— this time it was orange tulips. Not just one, because one just gets lost. The fundamental principle is to buy one thing, and buy a lot of it. Then I'll go to the fruit department and see what goes with the flowers that I could serve with dessert. Clementines! And again, *a lot* of clementines. They're gorgeous to look at and great with coffee. I have one set of dishes: white, from Crate and Barrel. Simple glasses, also from Crate. And I'll often use white Italian linen napkins from Bloom that you don't have to iron. They're already crumpled, and they look better that way. It's not your mother's linen. Even your mother doesn't want your mother's linen anymore.

What's the one piece of advice you'd give to a renovator?

RS: Don't do all new stuff. New cabinets, new countertops, but then bring in some antique pieces. It's nice to mix elements. Old furniture has a sense of warmth and realness. It takes off that hard edge. This kitchen feels fresh and modern, but it doesn't feel hard. And at the end of the day, it's fairly traditional. Ina and I decided that we were really not into the latest gadgetry. We wanted function, not fancy-schmancy.

Forget fancy centerpieces, Garten keeps it simple and monochromatic—the drama is in the abundance of clementines and tulips. **No** need for a formal tablecloth: take a piece of fabric, cut and fold it to fit, and use iron-on tape to make the hem! Garten doesn't go in for precious finishes. Trestle table from Restoration Hardware is made from old wood, which gets better the more it's used. **No** worries about spills when dining chairs are slipcovered in washable **V**intage **S**ugar Linen from Lee Industries.

COLOR FORMS

GARTEN AND STILIN ADDED WARMTH AND DEPTH WITH WOOD SMOKE ON WALLS AND WHITE ON WHITE FOR TRIM, BOTH FROM GLIDDEN

With so many windows, so much natural light, and a ceiling that arches high overhead, a dark color like this smoky gray works well on the walls. It not only grounds the room, it holds you safely inside so the space doesn't feel like it's seeping out the doors.

STALKING THE LOOK

1 2

3 4

5

Don't be shy. Get it all out on the table. (1) Organize wood and stainless-steel utensils in separate containers.

Make your island extra large so it can double as a buffet. Garten added table lamps to her island to make it feel even more like a sideboard.

Use a big basket (2) at the end of the island for large items that don't easily fit into cabinets—like stove racks and cutting boards.

Remember you don't need a garden (3) to have fresh herbs like rosemary.

Don't store anything way up high—on top of the cabinets—even when you have the space. Garten keeps everything within reach.

Keep serving spoons on the counter (4) so if something needs a stir you don't have to open a drawer.

Really serious about cooking? Consider following Garten's lead with a gas range against the wall and an induction cooktop in the island.

Fill a big bowl (5) with ice and champagne and it will immediately feel like a party.

SMALL MIRACLE

ELLEN O'NEILL,
designer and homeowner

Talk about living large in a small space. Design consultant Ellen O'Neill's tiny kitchen (the entire studio is only 450 square feet!) is hardworking and simultaneously gorgeous. Her carefully styled kitchen shelves look so beautiful it's a wonder she ever bothers to conceal them behind her lovely toile-covered screen.

TOP: O'Neill filled a snow globe with white ceramic napkin rings; just one of the many tools turned art objects on her floating white kitchen shelves. Wall, cabinets, and shelves are painted **Benjamin Moore Linen White.**

BOTTOM: A miniature stainless-steel sink set into a gray-and-white marble countertop keeps with the color palette. Because the sink is undermounted the lines of the countertop stay compatible with the horizontal lines of the two white shelves.

"The toile you see here on the screen is a toile with a capital T—really large scale."

"I've always had painted floors; I use automotive paint. Brown floors depress me to death and I knew from the start that I wanted a black-and-white palette. But just black and white can be too hard and cold, too optical. You need some creams and grays and sepias to ease you into a softer, gentler world and add a little romance."

MINI ME

There was no kitchen in this **New York City** studio apartment—it had originally been a servant's quarters—so **O'Neill** carved a petite but efficient one inside a skylit niche. A fabric screen, covered in **Cowtan & Tout's Siam**, can be pulled across to hide the kitchen, but when it's left open, the screen's sepia tone lends softness to the kitchen's black, white, and silver palette. The desk chair is one of **O'Neill's** "eclectic assortment" of vintage chairs and stools. Layering is one of the keys to this kind of intrigue—even the farmhouse faucet is set off by an elongated white ceramic tray. And multiples always make a statement—three large glass apothecary jars from **Crate and Barrel** are many times better than one.

TAKING STOCK

BERKLEY VALLONE
and **CAROLINE DECESARE,** *designers*

Everyone knows that some
pretty plates peeking out
from glass-fronted cabinets
look great, but have you ever
considered your canned
goods as art? And not just that
celebrated tomato soup either.
Vallone and DeCesare designed
a Las Vegas kitchen where
seltzer bottles and stacks of
canned yams provide as much
interest as a Warhol.

THE BACKSTORY | "My clients are a young couple with four children—
they have a 4-year-old, 3-year-old twins, and a baby who's just a year and
a half. It's insanity! A lot of this storage is for sippy cups and bibs! The
husband likes things to look very Old World but the wife likes things clean,
uncluttered, unfussy. This kitchen marries their two separate styles." —CD

" I divided this upper shelf into three horizontal sections because of my 'rule of odds'—odd numbers always look better. Three looks better than two or four to me." —CD

"Subway tile is timeless, classic. I think crazy backs-plashes can look dated after a while but subway tile never dates itself." —CD

White shelves with white beadboard backs, along with a honed Indian Premium black granite countertop—with no veining—are the perfect backdrops for color and pattern. Subway tiles in semi-gloss from Daltile add shine.

"We love the feel of these Rocky Mountain Hardware bronze pulls, they're sand cast to be more tactile; they feel so good to the touch." —CD

Apparently canned goods can be beautiful!

CD: I do this a lot. I like to make decorative accessories out of humble things, like cans, that are fun and colorful. It does take a certain amount of styling but these are honestly things these two cooks use all the time. I don't think everything has to be tucked away in a pantry. I mean, Andy Warhol made Campbell's Tomato Soup cans into icons. Why not do a shelf of them?

This is a big bright space in a new house, yet the details suggest an old-fashioned kitchen. What look were you going for?

CD: You know that Diane Keaton, Jack Nicholson movie, *Something's Gotta Give*? The kitchen in that movie was our starting point—a clean white traditional kitchen with subway tiles and glass-fronted cabinets, updated with stainless-steel appliances. We even did the same kind of brackets under the upper cabinets.

BV: The client wanted big, clean work surfaces. Originally, we did soapstone countertops like they had in the movie, but we replaced them with honed black granite after a year because of the maintenance. Soapstone has to be oiled, and when you oil it some areas absorb more and get darker while others stay lighter. It's very inconsistent, and that bothers some people. Indian Premium black granite gives a similar look, with less maintenance. We sealed it with a color-enhancing sealer.

Why did you decide on two separate islands?

BV: Originally there was only one; that's what the wife wanted. But it was so big you couldn't even reach the center. **CD:** You could have parked a car on it. So we redid it. Now husband and wife each have their own sink and their own workspace. Both sinks are big, with their own garbage disposals, trash on one side, and a dishwasher on the other. The days of those little round bar sinks on an island are over—they're too dysfunctional. **BV:** We did two dishwashers and two refrigerators, side by side, each with the refrigerator on top and freezer drawers below. There's also a beverage refrigerator under the counter where the glasses are kept.

How come you didn't match the sinks and faucets on the islands?

CD: The husband is Italian and he wanted a stainless-steel single-compartment sink that could handle big pasta pots. We all wanted the farmhouse look. He went online and found Franke's stainless-steel farmhouse sink. He's very particular about his space, which is why they have separate sinks, because she might leave a stray sippy cup around. **BV:** The double islands work really well when you're having a party. The inner one becomes the prep area and the outer one becomes a buffet. People can circulate all around the food.

TIMES TWO
With two cooks in the family, one island was split in half to give both husband and wife a workspace. Supremely comfortable Akira barstools from Royal Custom Designs are covered in indestructible Rustico leather from Cortina. On the front island, the Fairfax faucet and Undertone sink, both from Kohler, serve as a vegetable and salad prep area. The Single Prismatic Standard pendant lights from Urban Archeology hanging from the 12' high coffered ceiling make the space feel very loftlike. Grohe's 31-041 pot filler will extend to reach the farthest burner on the 48" Wolf range. The range hood, with its handy accessory rails, is from Viking. Roman shades in Jutis by Malabar "block the sun but don't take up as much space as curtains," says DeCesare.

WHAT IF . . .

EVERY BOTTLE AND CAN WERE AS EASY TO SPOT IN YOUR KITCHEN AS THEY WERE IN THE MARKET?

....

" You'll get the best effect if you pick your accent colors and stick with them—here we used mostly yellow and red cans. This kind of display doesn't really work if you've got a whole rainbow of different colored labels." —CD

NICE LEGS

A TURNED LEG ON EACH CORNER OF THE ISLANDS MAKES THEM LOOK MORE LIKE FURNITURE.

....

" Two large boxy cabinets would have looked too severe. Although the turned legs take up some cabinet space, it's worth it because they give the islands a softer, more custom look." —CD

CRAVING . . .

A FARMHOUSE SINK THAT PUTS A CITY-CAT SPIN ON THE COUNTRY-MOUSE LOOK

....

" This is a working kitchen with owners who love to cook, and this stainless sink is my nod to a professional restaurant kitchen, it takes this kitchen out of the realm of merely traditional." —CD

Is that the dining room, through the archway?

BV: It's the breakfast room actually, and it gets used all the time. It has killer light, with French doors on either side and then that big window behind the table. The table is new but made to look old. Super-casual black wicker chairs, with an indoor/outdoor fabric on the seats, and they can take the covers off and wash them. Important, with four young children. And then a banquette in back, with a leather seat they can wipe down.

CD: With a banquette, it's essential to be able to slide in and out, and that's easier if it's covered in leather instead of fabric. The kids love the sliding, and you can fit a bunch of little bums back there.

BV: With the two French doors to the barbecue and the pool, there's a lot of traffic here, and we wanted the table to be out of the way. With a banquette, you can push the table closer to the wall.

What's on the floor?

BV: They're 7' wide walnut planks. A wider plank feels older, more casual. It's a little country, just like the coffered ceiling, which we made with drywall, stock moldings, and beadboard. Then the industrial light fixtures and the stainless-steel appliances add a modern edge.

The archway bridging the kitchen and breakfast area echoes the Palladian-style window beyond. The chandelier from Allan Knight and Associates, hanging from the 12' ceiling, has the look of candles resting on an iron tray. A 9' long breakfast table by Bausman & Company accommodates a crowd and the Parlor Square chairs from **PALECEK** lend an indoor/outdoor feel.

COLOR FORMS

DECESARE USED SHERWIN-WILLIAMS PURE WHITE FOR HARMONY

"We used this same white on the cabinets and walls because it's pure white, not at all creamy. So it goes well with bright white subway tile as well as the KitchenAid mixer. I don't like seeing creamy white in a room where there's also lots of bright white." —CD

STALKING THE LOOK

1

4

2

5

3

6

Canned goods as accessories? Give it a try. Colorful labels feel graphic and modern when you group "like" cans together on one shelf. Bring in tall bottles on other shelves to vary the scale.

Find dark brown woven chairs that convey a casual indoor/outdoor feel. (1) The durable Butterfly Loom chair from Bluefish Home picks up the color of the dark grain in a wood plank floor.

Sprinkle strategic pops of lipstick red. (2,3) A red scale, a red colander, bright red tomatoes and Dransfield & Ross Linen Wave napkins enliven a strict black-and-white palette.

Choose a chandelier that's one part post-modern and one part pre-Edison. (4) The designers chose an electrified wax candle chandelier to look relaxed by day and romantic at night.

Use modern black and white roman shades for surprise. (5) Missoni's Leipzig in black/cream at the windows will keep even the most traditional kitchen from looking like granny's place.

Put a knife block right next to the range, (6) so veggies go right from cutting board to pot. Customize your knife block with Insieme kitchen knives by Berti. Choose from 23 handmade ox-horn-handle knives, each with its own magnetized wood block.

Clad tall ceilings in coffers and beadboard for an airy SoHo loft feel.

Hang your television high enough to be viewable from both the work area and the kitchen table.

STONE COLD GORGEOUS

HARRY SLATKIN,
designer

Think stone is just for backsplashes and counters? Slatkin will make you think again. His kitchen stars white marble, mosaics, and dark Pietra del Cardoso stone in roles you might never have cast them in. The wall that features Slatkin's pasta pots looks as exquisite as a snow sculpture.

The shelves on either side of the stove extend out farther than the ones in the middle making them wide enough to store large stockpots and serving bowls.

THE BACKSTORY | The Slatkins live in this New York City townhouse with their two children. They've got a big family kitchen on the first floor and this small kitchen on the second floor because, as Slatkin explains—"the dining room is on the second floor and food would be cold by the time it was carried up from the downstairs kitchen. So we created this caterer's kitchen right next to the dining room. When we entertain—anything from a seated dinner for ten to a buffet for eighty—this little kitchen facilitates that."

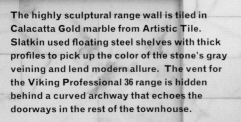

The highly sculptural range wall is tiled in Calacatta Gold marble from Artistic Tile. Slatkin used floating steel shelves with thick profiles to pick up the color of the stone's gray veining and lend modern allure. The vent for the Viking Professional 36 range is hidden behind a curved archway that echoes the doorways in the rest of the townhouse.

The microwave is in a marble niche.

The butcher-block island, at left, is sited against a wall because of space constraints. Steel base cabinets by St. Charles of New York have drawers for utensils and open shelves (instead of a towel rack) for baskets where tea towels and pot holders are stored within easy reach.

Tell me how all this lays out.
The idea is that you can stand at the island and turn in any direction to grab what you need. You can open the oven or reach for the salt or get the cream out of the refrigerator. There's so much work that goes into thinking out that process. My brother, Howard Slatkin, is an interior designer and he helped. My wife and I don't always listen because we have our own opinions, but he does this for a living so he's usually correct. He'll suggest where outlets should go, for instance, and then we'll argue about it and put them elsewhere and the next thing you know, we're redoing the outlets.

Very smart, the way those outlets are done in black and hidden in the dark stone backsplash. Also, you didn't let the small space stop you from having an island. You just cut it in half, and put one end against the wall.
You need a central work table. It's where everything happens.

I like how you take traditional elements and use them in a more modern way. The marble, for example, is not old-fashioned slabs, but tiles.
We wanted a modern kitchen with an old-fashioned look that would feel like it belonged in this beautiful Beaux Arts–style town house. Think of those wonderful old working kitchens in Palm Beach or Newport. This is our version, without the huge staff.

It's so unusual to see backless cabinets attached directly to marble. They almost seem to float.

I like seeing straight through the glass to the marble. It doesn't break the line.

Even a farmhouse sink looks more contemporary when it's black. What is it made out of?

Pietra del Cardoso stone, which is similar to soapstone but harder. It doesn't show stains. It doesn't show dirt. It's really easy to take care of, and the black adds a nice weight to the kitchen.

Why did you make the lower cabinets out of stainless steel?

I think there's a warmth to stainless steel, and again, like the appliances, it gives me that professional look. Any color would have been wrong, and white would have made it look ordinary. The stainless steel ties the whole kitchen together.

Do you worry about scratches?

At first I did, but you know what? We have to live in the house. If anything, I think the scratches give it more charm.

Does that mean you actually chop on the butcher block island?

Absolutely. If it's perfect, it doesn't look like a working kitchen. It's kind of like people. As you get older, you show your marks. We should be proud of them. They add character. There's no Botox in this kitchen.

FINELY CARVED
The curve over the range wall is repeated again in the backsplash above the sink, both custom-made by **St. Charles of New York** in honed **Pietra del Cardoso** stone. The custom cabinets' handles seem to have sprung naturally from their smooth steel fronts. It's a contemporary look that meshes delightfully with the **Old World** treatments like marble walls and mosaic tile floors in **Giallo Svevo** mixed with **Calacatta Gold** marble tiles. The refrigerator is to the right of the dishwasher.

WHAT IF . . .

YOUR KITCHEN FEATURED MOSAICS RIGHT OUT OF AN ANCIENT ROMAN BATH?

Delineations like *modern* and *old-fashioned* start to blur when stainless-steel open shelves adjoin antiquity-inspired mosaics on the walls and floor. "I like mosaic. It's a nice accent on the wall and it makes such a pretty floor. And it feels great on your feet. Very comfortable," says Slatkin.

ENTERTAINMENT TONIGHT

Slatkin switched to white cabinets for the glass-fronted bar cabinet, conveniently located in the same corner as the refrigerator, because a floor-to-ceiling stainless steel cabinet would have felt too laboratory-like. It contains antique glassware that still sees duty at dinner parties. The door handles match the ones on the steel cabinets for consistency.

CRAVING . . .
A CEILING AS LIGHT AND MOUTHWATERING AS A MERINGUE

Old-fashioned tin ceiling tiles in a fleur-de-lis pattern from AA-Abbingdon Affiliates were installed, and then painted on site. It's a little finishing touch that's a joy to discover. The pendant light fixture in nickel and crystal, another gracious note, is based on a 1920s design by Hector Guimard and is available at Lampworks.

STORE YOUR STUFF

Choosing your kitchen cabinets is your defining moment. Think Caesar crossing the Rubicon or Washington crossing the Delaware. It's your chance for glory but also your point of no return. Whatever else goes into your kitchen—islands, appliances, furniture—it will have to respond stylistically to the look of your cabinets. So choose carefully, second guess yourself a couple of times, and then strike boldly and don't look back. The possibilities are beautiful—you're sure to be victorious.

THE DOWN LOW

If you could give only one piece of advice about kitchen cabinets, what would that be? "Maximize the use of lower storage space. The higher a space is, the harder it is to work with. The exception to that is slotted storage. I have a cabinet above my wall ovens with ten structured slots for cutting boards and sheet pans, but everything else is down low—mostly in huge drawers. We have a large island as well and had cabinets built along one side that holds all our glasses and plates so that my 5' 2" wife and 4' daughter can reach anything anytime."

—ALTON BROWN, COOKBOOK AUTHOR AND FOOD NETWORK STAR

This kitchen is all about the cabinets. Where's all the stainless steel? "I like to build everything in and panel it. If I could panel the oven, I would. There's no reason to leave your dishwasher or refrigerator exposed. That's like showing off your appliances, and what's the point in that? Paneling makes a kitchen feel more like a real room than strictly a work space." **—JAY JEFFERS,** DESIGNER

Yes, the traditional white cabinet can be reinvented! This Manhattan kitchen is "a contemporary interpretation of a classic prewar space," says designer Garrow Kedigian. "It's pure, simple, and white." The cabinetry has a gridded detail that borrows its lines from the windows.

When the kitchen is open to the family room, open shelves can help the two spaces hold together. "Open kitchens seem to call for open shelves. Still, soup cans and cereal boxes have to hide somewhere, so plan for closed storage under counters or in a nearby pantry and keep those shelves simple and organized."

—**BARBARA WESTBROOK,** DESIGNER

One sure route to choosing the right style for your cabinets is to do something in sync with your home's architecture.

"I like kitchens to feel like they've always been there, to match a style appropriate to the age of the house—this is a Tudor, built in the early 1900s. I hate to see a super-modern kitchen in an old house. This kitchen is part of the dining room, and I felt it needed to maintain some formality. White would have looked way too kitcheny. The dark gray looks like furniture at night. It's so sexy when the light hits it and flickers off the Calacatta marble."

—BENJAMIN DHONG, DESIGNER

What's the most common mistake people make when choosing cabinets?

"Too much uniformity. Cabinets that look like an assembly of mass-produced boxes, all the same height and depth. That has more to do with the standards of the industry than the comfort of the person working in the kitchen. You don't have to follow the masses."

—FU-TUNG CHENG, DESIGNER

CABINETS HAVE THE POWER TO MAKE A TRADITIONAL KITCHEN FEEL MODERN AND VICE VERSA.

In this kitchen, contemporary cabinets and hardware mix with reclaimed distressed wood on the island. The bright colors of the island and the stove read "country kitchen" but the cabinets' ebony stain keeps the mood citified.

"It is a very modern kitchen. The cabinets are from Boffi and the counters and backsplash are stainless steel, but I had the island made from old wood. That and the vintage lights are just enough to keep the cabinets from looking sleek."

—HEATHER SMITH MACISAAC, DESIGNER

Even the refrigerators have a furniture-like enclosure. "I wanted an Early American language, a traditional American kitchen. It is an assemblage of furniture—the antithesis of the contemporary kitchen in which everything is standardized and integrated. New, handcrafted storage looks like real furniture with cornices and random raised panel fronts."

—KEN PURSLEY, DESIGNER

WOOD CABINETS, WOOD FLOOR, AND A WOOD CEILING! THEY CAN WORK BEAUTIFULLY TOGETHER. If the cabinets are light, a dark floor will ground pale wood above. In this kitchen, alder wood cabinets are completely compatible with merabu wood floors and a cedar ceiling.

....

"Building most cabinetry below eye level keeps this kitchen more roomlike, and diminishes the utilitarian feel. There is plenty of drawer and under-island storage, and a pair of tall cabinets with sliding steel garage-style doors, on the far left, conceals the inevitable jumble of small appliances."

—ANN WOLF, DESIGNER

OPEN SHELVES CREATE A SENSE OF LIGHTNESS IN A SMALL KITCHEN. Upper cabinetry was removed in this kitchen and it was replaced with open shelves painted Farrow & Ball's Teresa's Green. Cabinets have dark bronze bin pulls and knobs by Rejuvenation.

....

"You can get too airy. You need something dark like this hardware to keep a room grounded."

—ALEXANDRA ANGLE, DESIGNER

Antique mirrored glass on the cabinet doors enlarges the feeling of space and pulls light into this small city kitchen by Jonathan Berger. And mirroring is a completely unexpected way to jazz up plain white recessed panels.

FITTING IN

Crouch no more. It's easy to see what's in lower cupboards when you have pull-out drawers.

Save your aching back. A undercounter pop-up shelf means never having to hoist your KitchenAid mixer again.

Shout "presto" and pull out a pantry. Bulthaup's pullout pantries are accessible from both sides.

Cook up a couple of tempting sliders. Typically only the bottom 2″ are used in a cutlery drawer, but this sliding drawer by Christopher Peacock takes advantage of the extra space for more storage.

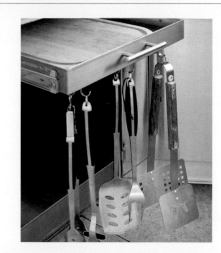

Hang in. In an outdoor kitchen cabinet by Kalamazoo Outdoor Gourmet, utensils hang inside the cabinet, out of the way until needed.

Tear open your shutters. A shutter rolls up to reveal a microwave and other appliances in this Bulthaup kitchen.

Revere thy daily bread. Buy good bread, and keep it fresh and crusty with KraftMaid's bread bin.

revival

Rooted in history, these kitchens hearken back to our culinary past while leaving room for innovations to come.

CHAPTER 7

belle de campagne

**PRIED FROM THE LUXURY OF THE LOIRE?
SHIPPED FROM A CRUMBLING COTTAGE
IN CALAIS? LOOK CLOSER.**

C'EST CHIC

MICHELE ALLMAN,
designer

Do your domestic fantasies
extend to French chateaux with
massive limestone fireplaces?
Are your dreamscapes papered
head-to-toe in toile? If so,
this is your kind of kitchen.
Here Allman shows how she
imagined *une très belle cuisine*
so perfectly detailed you'd
expect to see fields of lavender
through these toile-framed
windows rather than the oak-
lined streets of Houston.

THE BACKSTORY | "This is an all male household except the mom. It's
new construction and although it's very feminine we made sure that it's also
comfortable for the boys. The whole house is French provincial inspired.
She's a big collector. She's collected porcelain and linens from France for
years and years and this new house is her joy!"

The blue-green walls and cabinets that envelope the room were glazed
and antiqued to look like a centuries old chateau. Vaughan's Pagoda
red tole lantern picks up the colors in the portières (interior curtains)
made with Bailey & Griffin's Canton Toile in Cherry Vanilla, backed
with Brunschwig & Fils' Paola taffeta check in Pepper Red.

The French antique inspired Minton-Spidell stools are covered
in Brunschwig & Fils' La Mer in Pompeian Red complementing
the curtains' toile. Pavia Antico walnut travertine tile on floor
from Walker Zanger is a classic European touch.

"My client is so creative and well traveled. She studied the details of old French chateaux and that's how we came up with the cabinets and the moldings."

Toile fabric always takes me straight to France. And there's something so luxurious about all this fabric.

It really softens a large room. We even made portières for the doorways. My client knew she wanted a red toile, but this is no fire-engine red. It's a pinkish cranberry. And the ground is not white, but cream, so the effect is more subtle. We looked at many different toiles because we wanted not only the right color, but an appropriate subject too. This one happens to be a country scene, which is perfect for a kitchen. Still, it's amazing how many people don't even notice what's actually portrayed on the fabric.

The cabinetry is beautiful, with its French country curves. And you've camouflaged everything but the stove.

The kitchen functions like a family room, so we didn't want people to feel like they were sitting next to an appliance. And we built the cabinets high to lift your eye. We don't want you to miss the 12' ceiling with the beautiful reclaimed wood beams.

That's a very long island. How did you keep it from looking like a boat?

I broke it up with wrap-around bookcases at each end, and made space for four stools in the middle. You've got to create some interest and variety in the base, or it will be way too boring at 12'. We also cut the granite countertop into a curve at both ends to soften the edges and echo the arches in the room.

A wall behind a stove always cries out for something and this mural is fantastic!

Those are hand-painted tiles. You pick your images and your colors and they make them for you. It almost looks like a painting. We picked images of chinoiserie and pagodas—we thought the typical painted tiles with chickens or little children would have looked a lot less sophisticated. Tile works well behind a stove because it's easy to wipe down.

Is this wall the focal point for the whole space?

Oh, yes. As you walk into the room, you focus on the stove and the windows. So that's where we put the cabinets, with glass doors to show off her collections of china and stemware. Even the sides of those cabinets are made of glass. She really enjoys looking at her things, and the glass makes that area feel even more open. The whole kitchen is very light and airy.

Why granite and not marble?

Because it's sturdy and holds up well and my client fell in love with this rich color. Also because its speckled pattern is tighter than the veining in something like Calacatta Gold marble would have been. Veins in this island would have been too distracting with all the other pattern in the room.

OLD SOUL
A hand-painted tile mural from the Chinoiserie series by Tempest, available at Architectural Design Resource, accents the 60" dual-fuel range by Wolf. Harrington Brass Works pot filler in satin nickel feels antique. Cabinets for stemware on either side of the stove are open—Allman designed them with see-through glass sides—so they don't close off the space. Bianco Tuscano granite counters have lots of green speckles, which pick up the color of the cabinets.

WHAT IF...
YOUR STOVE SURROUND LOOKED LIKE A HEARTH OUT OF *THE THREE MUSKETEERS*?

....

"It's not an old mantel, it's new, carved out of limestone. This area is meant to look like a big old cooking fireplace you might see in a chateau in the Loire Valley. We stuccoed the top of the hood to look like a chimneypiece—it would have looked too large if we'd brought the limestone all the way up to the ceiling. And we put a carved plaster artifact found in France on the mantel to dress it up a bit."

CRAVING...
THE *PLUS PARFAIT* PAPER TOWEL HOLDER.

....

A niche in the island to the left of the sink keeps the paper towels accessible, yet out of sight.

"No one sees it, it's like the cook's little secret back there."

A CUT ABOVE
A pull-out cutting board in the island to the right of the sink has a hole to make it easy to brush the scraps straight into the trash bin.

"We thought it would be so clever to have this cutting board over the trash bin! And it turned out great."

Did you agonize over the color of those chairs around the kitchen table?

My client already had those chairs and we talked about redoing the finish, since it's a very strong green. But then I went through her stacks of dishes and pulled out those majolica plates in the same deep green. When I put them on the wall it pulled the whole room together. After so many white, utilitarian kitchens this is a surprise, as if you've left Texas and been transported to a whole new place. I feel very French in this room.

Why did you switch from limestone to wood floors here?

For a warmer look. We went to great lengths to make sure they looked old with premium walnut scraped by hand to give it an antique look. And the table is an old rustic French farm piece that the owner used as a garden table in her previous house. We think it looks wonderful here in the kitchen on this wood floor.

What's in those two huge cabinets?

That's where she keeps her enormous collection of linens and porcelain. She's been collecting them all her life; she can set a beautiful table at a moment's notice.

GALLIC WONDER
The working kitchen is to the right of this breakfast area, where reproduction chairs surround an old zinc-topped table. An antique French starburst clock is the focal point of the display on the breakfast room wall. The portieres to the left frame doorways leading to the house's central hallway. The sofa, upholstered in Brunschwig & Fils' Chancellor Strié in Pompeian Red, faces a fireplace.

COLOR FORMS
ALLMAN CONJURED A FRENCH SPIRIT WITH BENJAMIN MOORE NOVEMBER RAIN.

"We started with Benjamin Moore November Rain and then added layer upon layer of pigment and glaze to build up this crusty finish. My client loves color and was very involved in mixing this. Some days it looks a little more gray. On others it's more greenish. The granite we chose had a greenish hue and this blue-green color seemed to make sense with it. We wanted the cabinets to look like old worn pieces of furniture, the sort of thing you'd find in France."

Keep your balance. Allman calmed the swoops and curlicues of the architecture by keeping her layout symmetrical—two identical tall cabinets flank the centrally located range niche.

Stay in denial. Pretend you're cooking in pre-Bastille France and put a panel over anything that smacks of 21st century—especially the refrigerator.

Find a place for a lantern. Nothing says "French chateau" like a candle flickering inside a lantern. (1) Fourteenth Colony Lighting's Galvanized Interior Lantern will add a Gallic glow to your kitchen.

Plop down on cushions fit for royalty. (2) Allman upholstered the kitchen chairs' cushions in a French inspired print, Brunschwig & Fil's Durbar Strié in Pompeian Red.

Choose counter stools with a French accent. (3) Whitewashed and antiqued Minton-Spidell stools are reproductions that lend a Gallic touch.

Be brave with color. Paint cabinets a bright hue and then use an antique finish to soften it.

Remember it's all in *les détails*. (4) Breakfast room seat cushions with silk tassels like Les Tuileries in green from Scalamandré put a luxurious spin on everyday life.

Finish with metal. Allman chose an antique zinc-topped table. (5) The unexpected combination of a limed-oak ball-and-claw base with a metal top lends this table from Design Workshop an antique European feel.

VIVE LA FRANCE

DANA LYON,
designer

You're wandering the
cobbled streets of a small
French village when a
dimpled matron invites you
into her charming kitchen for
a cup of tea. No, wait. This
is Phoenix. Here's how Lyon
used authentic accessories,
red tile, and a curtain that
looks like a vintage tea towel
to create a dream of the
French countryside.

TOP: The beautifully carved island is topped with galvanized metal to be
both authentic and practical. A cake stand from **Williams-Sonoma** and a
white earthenware fruit basket from **Tiffany & Co.** are just a few of the
accessories that lend this kitchen its French spirit. The antique bench is
covered in indestructible **Relieve Faux Leather** by **Brunschwig & Fils.**

BOTTOM: The outdoor dining area off the kitchen, under a wisteria arbor,
exudes provincial charm. The **Essex** dining table by **Kingsley-Bate** is
beautifully weathered and **Patio Terrace** chairs by **Palecek** have the classic
look of French wicker chairs—but they're made from rattan and wicker-like
(natural colored) plastic with high **UV** resistance. Square concrete pavers
from **Ancient Stone** are laid in a grid with the same **Chicago** bricks that
cover the kitchen floor.

Cheery red-and-white tiles from Craftsman Court Ceramics are set off by dark soapstone counters. Curtains in Ralph Lauren's Brass Lantern Ticking in Red (turned sideways to make the border) and brick flooring from Chicago Brick are shorthand for French country style.

"The kitchen has a French country feeling with the open shelving for pots and pans and the island with the French panel detailing."

"It's definitely a color blast. But it's a nice deep red, which gives you a little richness. Adding the warm golds toned down the starkness of the red and black, too. You have to limit your palette severely—two colors, maybe three, never more."

"The builder gave the island and door that weathered look. He used layers of stain, and sometimes wirebrushing, so the wood picks up the color not so evenly."

"You have to have the absolute right accessories to pull off a kitchen like this, like the baguette and grape baskets, and the vinegar bottle, all antiques, that you see here. Everything has the look of age."

FRENCH CONFECTION

LISA COHEN,
homeowner

Talk about going all out. Cohen didn't just give a little nod to European flair when she designed her kitchen, she shot for the moon. Her New Jersey kitchen rolls up all the romance of an old French patisserie with details like leaded glass, hammered copper, turned posts, scenic tiles . . . the list goes on. And yes, you can try this at home.

THE BACKSTORY | "We have five kids in here every day. Big house, big family, and we really use this kitchen. The kids come in and sit after school. And everything has held up so far! I'm like a frustrated decorator. I studied art history in college and fell in love with all those Flemish tapestries and old master paintings. The romance and drama of that old-world look is very special to me and I think it comes out in this kitchen."

The 12' high ceiling is sheathed in pressed tin tiles between the coffers.

Custom cabinets by White Eagle, applied moldings by Enkeboll, leaded glass—not to mention blue-and-white scenic tile—firmly establish the fanciful French theme. The dark wood island provides added drama when contrasted against Calacatta Gold marble counters. A butcherblock insert in the island is a built-in chopping block.

The massive iron chandelier, made friendlier with blue fabric-covered shades, was originally in an Addison Mizner house in Palm Beach.

The level of detail is astounding. Is that leaded glass on the cabinets?
Yes. And it's real leaded glass, done the old-fashioned way, with each pane individually cut. The house, which we built from the ground up, is English Tudor, and I wanted leaded-glass windows. But it's a lost art, and it was like pulling teeth to get someone to do it. I don't have a problem with it on the cabinets but we had to redo certain windows. When you have rain hitting it . . .
Well, it may not be practical, but it sure looks romantic.
And it's great here. Everyone says this is their favorite room in the house. I worked with Alexa Hampton on the whole project, but I took over the kitchen because I knew exactly what I wanted—the tile, the tin ceiling.
Why did you do the pressed tin between the coffers, to make these tall ceilings feel more intimate?
Actually, the pressed tin is all part of going for a French patisserie feeling. It's silvery and unexpected, and it works with the nickel sink. It all blends.
All the cabinetry is painted white, except the island. How come?
I like the way the dark wood looks with the white marble on top. And it blends in with the old Russian oak floor and contrasts nicely with the white cabinets.

Where do you find people to carve turned posts these days?

Those are applied moldings. Molding companies and lumberyards have these books, and you look through and pick out what you want and then you integrate them into the cabinetry. My builder, James Nigro, put it all together for me. He's great with woodwork.

Why did you choose marble countertops?

I wanted that black-and-white marble like you see in a French patisserie. You know the kind—as it ages, it gets even better. Then my builder showed me this Calacatta Gold, with brown and gold veins that make it feel a little warmer. And it picks up the color of the wood on the island.

This extra deep sink is opposite the chopping block that's set into the wood island, making it convenient for washing vegetables before chopping. The sink area has a toe-kick space instead of a baseboard between the floor and base of the cabinet so it's easier to stand close. Calacatta Gold marble counters are finished with a double ogee edge—which means the countertop's edge has two cascading carved ridges for extra allure. And the finishing touch on the doors and drawers are classic French spiraling handles from LB Brass.

DÉJÀ VU
Details like curlicue posts on either side of the main sink and between windows conjure up another time and place. A hammered-copper sink by **Native Trails** paired with **Perrin & Rowe**'s satin-nickel faucet furthers the mood. Two dishwashers on either side of the sink are hidden behind wood panels that match the cabinet fronts.

WHAT IF . . .

YOU SHEATHED YOUR REFRIGERATORS (BOTH OF THEM!) IN FANCIFUL HAND-PAINTED TILE?

. . . .

Two Sub-Zero refrigerators are totally transformed with hand-painted French faience tiles—portraying a fishmonger and a bread baker—from Country Floors, and carved panels over the bottom freezer drawers from Enkeboll Designs. A pull-out pantry between the refrigerators holds a selection of teas.

"You know what? We don't ever use those cabinets above the refrigerator. I don't even know if they open. You have to understand, the ceiling in here is so high—it's like 12 feet."

CRAVING . . .

BASKETS FOR POTATOES, ONIONS, AND GARLIC DIRECTLY UNDER YOUR CHOPPING STATION.

. . . .

The thick chopping block that's incorporated into the island has baskets— with elaborate carved handles—underneath.

What was your inspiration here?

Blue and white. I love that feeling you get when you look at blue-and-white porcelain. It's so fresh. And I've always loved blue-and-white tile. You see it all over Europe, and it was in my mind.

Did you choose the range for its blue knobs?

No, because it had everything I wanted—it's the 60" Blue Star range—two full ovens, six burners, plus a grill on top.

Those scenic tiles have an old-world look and add a sense of age. Where did you find them?

At Country Floors. The circular scenes on the backsplash are four different landscapes, with great details like a man with a net leaning over the water to catch a fish. Then there's a big fruit bowl on the tile behind the range.

The ornately carved corbels affixed to the backsplash only appear to be holding up the cabinets. They gracefully divide the blue-and-white patterned tile from the circular scenes. For balance, Cohen sited two same-size hand-painted scenes on either side of the range and placed a painted basket of fruit—of the same scale—under the pot filler. The painted tile border on the range hood echoes the feel of the swirling carved columns dividing the base cabinets from the stove.

PLAYING THE BLUES
Blue-and-white tile from **Country Floors** wraps around the entire room. Even the stove hood has a hand-painted tile border with a ribbon detail.

COLOR FORMS

COHEN'S USE OF BEIGE AND BLUE RECALLS SAND AND SEA IN CAP D'ANTIBES.

"Cabinets were painted in a beige bone and then antiqued. The finish is very forgiving, which is good because we have lots of children in here every day. And then we mixed up our own shade of French blue for the walls. Very fresh and yet it has a certain depth because of that bit of gray in it. It makes me feel as if I'm back in France."

STALKING THE LOOK

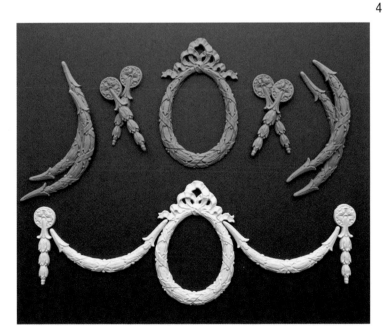

1   2   3   4   5

Paradoxically, sometimes the best way to create harmony when working with ornate detail is to make things even more ornate. (1) Repeat big dramatic gestures many times all around the room. Six leaded glass cabinets work better than one. Five painted tile scenes are less distracting than just a few and so on . . .

White it out. This level of confident detail begs for a bashful background. An antiqued white finish on cabinets and pale Calacatta Gold marble countertops keep the strong details in this kitchen from overwhelming.

Look up. Extra tall ceilings are perfect for a cozy material like pressed tin tiles—they bring the feeling of space down to human scale.

Make a scene. (2) Vinyl-protected and prepasted, this Dutch Faux-Tile Wallpaper from Warner looks charmingly antique and hand-painted. Plus it's washable!

Turn into a basket case. (3) Store things that need a dry environment, like garlic, close at hand in strategically placed baskets.

Embellish the story. (4) The Composition Ornament (1116F) from Decorators Supply Corporation comes in a natural wood finish that looks great when painted white and applied to a cabinet. (5) Wood trim rope molding from Architectural Depot looks *très chic* flanking a range.

Swing wide. Wide plank floors with a dark finish ground the room without creating yet another busy pattern.

The Busby Gilbert Arabesque tiles on the backsplash and the Antique Terra Cotta Dark tiles on the floor, both from Ann Sacks, have a chic French Riviera feel. Rugs from Dash & Albert enliven the floor while a window shade in Chelsea Editions' Acorn and Leaves on Gold Linen blocks the hot sun. Weston barstools from Janus et Cie add texture to the limestone counter. White ceramic hardware is nice and cool to the touch.

Danby, a marble from Vermont, is on the countertops and French limestone is on the island.

MADE IN THE SHADE

CATHY KINCAID,
designer

To counter the harsh Arizona sun, Kincaid cultivated a kitchen full of soft shadows. She used dark moody hues and a surprising brick-covered vaulted ceiling to keep things cool and peaceful. Old-world materials like a zinc range hood and terra-cotta floors convey the feeling of a castle somewhere in Joan-of-Arc's France.

THE BACKSTORY | "My client likes dark rooms. Have you ever been to Scottsdale in August? The heat is unrelenting. Your skin prickles. But the minute you walk into this kitchen it's cool and dark. There aren't any bright overhead lights. And my client likes these muted muddy colors."

"Every house needs at least one antique light fixture. These are from Ann-Morris Antiques."

"Wallpaper like this, Persian Miniature from Brunschwig & Fils, gives a room a past."

OBJECTS OF DESIRE

HILARY MUSSER,
designer

This kitchen is the ultimate collector's fantasy with blue cabinets showing off collection after collection of antiques and—in the center of it all—an island that was carved by hand in France. Musser took her love of Quimper faience pottery and old milk pails, and built a whole kitchen around it. It's a delicious taste of France, although there may not be much room for the food.

THE BACKSTORY | "I designed the kitchen around the collections. This is not an old Nantucket house. I designed it. I built it. I picked every piece of hardware. The idea was to make it look like an old house—but with all the modern conveniences."

Subway tile runs all the way up to the ceiling in keeping with the theme.

Vintage light fixtures, the pot rack, and many of the old English milk pails hanging from it are from Ann-Morris Antiques (the small pails on the windowsill held cream).

In this new water-view Nantucket kitchen, Musser channeled the look of an old French butcher shop. She commissioned French craftsmen to make an industrial size butcher-block island—she even embellished it with a black iron bull's-head medallion and her initial "M" on the front—and had it shipped stateside.

The German silver sink, found at Joanne Hudson Associates, is fitted with a brass farmhouse faucet. Who says silver and brass don't belong together?

You've chosen traditional materials—beadboard, subway tile, white marble, honey-colored wood— that help convey a sense of age.

I gravitate to those type of things. All the wood floors are old. I considered using old wood for the cabinets, but I didn't want drawers that stick. I ended up going with new but making it look old. I had those barley-twist details hand-carved and then sent to the factory in Canada to be colored to match.

I recognize the spongeware pitchers next to the sink and the yellow Quimper faience pottery on the blue shelves, but what are those objects hanging from the pot rack?

They're old milk pails that were used by dairies in England in the 19th century. The milkman would bring fresh milk in a pail to your door.

Did you smuggle that huge island out of some French butcher shop?

A friend had something similar and I copied the idea, with her permission, and had mine made by the same people in France. They shipped it in three pieces. I put in the marble and the cooktop myself. There's a downdraft right behind the cooktop, which rises up at the push of a button. I didn't want a big hood over the island—it would ruin the view.

I notice you don't have much art on the walls. All the artwork you need is in your collections.

The great feature of the house is my pottery, and I want to show it off. People have said, "Hey Hil, we're trying to serve dinner. Get all this stuff off the counter." But I like having it around. I couldn't live in one of those dull, ordinary kitchens with everything out of sight— that's no fun.

Tell me about your tricks for achieving artful display.

Quantity is quality. Almost anything can be interesting if you have enough of them. Group objects rather than scattering them around. You want to get a snapshot of the whole collection with one glance. And you don't want your display to look too planned. I like the casualness of open shelves.

Musser's motto: every single space must feature something intriguing to contemplate. To that end, her cabinets are as intricately carved as antique furniture. There's an array of old English tea cozies tucked on top of the cabinets and antique Italian apothecary jars line up on the marble countertop. Surprisingly, this mash-up of objects, pattern, and texture holds together because everything is essentially blue, yellow, and white.

COLLECTING BEAUTY

Musser's charming collection of contemporary yellow Quimper dinnerware is displayed very casually—stacks of plates are easy to transfer directly to the table. The cabinets, which were custom-designed by Joanne Hudson and built by Downsview, have ornate carved moldings that contrast beautifully against their humble beadboard interiors and the beadboard ceiling. The antique French blue color was chosen specifically so the pottery's bright colors would pop.

WHAT IF...

THE COFFEE POTS ON YOUR
SHELVES HAD NO USE BUT
TO NOURISH YOUR SOUL.

In another part of the kitchen,
Musser has assembled an army
of vintage French enamelware
coffee pots which were called
biggins. The biggin, originat-
ing in France around 1800, was a
two-level pot that held coffee in
its upper compartment; hot water would be poured in to drain
through the coffee and into the
coffee pot below.

GOOD SEATS

Seats at the bar face the island
and have views across the
main sink and out the window.
A wine cellar is on the other
side of the bar in the bottom
cabinet. Stemware and more
French china is safe and dust-
free behind tall glass-paned
double doors.

CRAVING...

AN ISLAND OUT OF A
PROVINCIAL *BOUCHERIE.*

The Viking range-top with
its white marble surround
was retrofitted into the island
because Musser wanted
to face into the room while
cooking. The marble insert
that surrounds the cooktop is
a place to rest a hot pot or a
warm serving dish. Pressing
a button to the right of the
cooktop raises the exhaust
hood. Small brass rings
embedded in the side of the
island are handy for hanging
potholders and tea towels.
Two wall ovens by Therma-
dor fit snugly into the wall
beyond with a cabinet above
for storing baking dishes. Old
ceramic milk pails displayed
atop the cabinets further the
old-world feel.

Where did you get that creamy white marble on the countertops?

I searched the country and found it at a place called Vermont Quarries. It's almost pure white, like Italian Carrara. Then I had it specially cut in 2" thick slabs with a honed edge. They had never cut a piece that thick before. I like it that way—more dramatic.

What is the farmhouse sink in this pantry made of? Great patina!

It's all handmade of nickel silver, which is also known as German silver. As soon as water stays on it for a few minutes, it starts to turn color. Same with the one in the kitchen. You have to polish them if you want to keep them shiny.

So do you polish them?

No, not really. The patina is part of the charm. I don't worry about scratching the silver, staining the marble, or cutting the butcher block. I want everything to look used. I like antiques.

"**Pottery like my blue-and-white Cornishware is an easy way to introduce color and warmth into a room.**"

PANTRY EXTRAORDINAIRE

The adjacent pantry, with reclaimed terra-cotta floors from **Country Floors**, is where the microwave, espresso machine, and toaster live. The room also doubles as a mudroom. An extendable **KWC** faucet paired with Linkasink's nickel silver farmhouse sink is a delightful throwback to another time and another place. The bull's-head theme continues with busts on the wall to the left of the sink and on an antique butcher block from **Howard Kaplan**. Musser eschews window treatments so her collection of antique Cornishware, displayed on white tile shelves between the windows, and her collection of vintage kitchen storage tins, on shelves to the left, can be bathed in sunlight.

COLOR FORMS

FRENCH GRAY BLUE ON CABINETS IS A STRONG NEUTRAL THAT HOLDS ITS OWN AGAINST MUSSER'S COLORFUL COLLECTIONS.

"**I was looking through samples at Joanne Hudson Kitchens in Philadelphia—she custom designed the cabinets—and saw this blue and liked it. I thought it was warm and different and would go well with my collections.**"

1

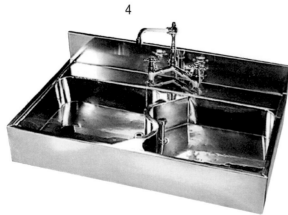

2   3

4

Quick, start collecting. (1) Accumulating the kind of sizeable collections that add so much personality to Musser's kitchen could take years. Get started! (LEFT) Begin with Cornishware from T.G. Green pottery in England—they've been making ceramics the same way since 1920. (RIGHT) Fill some shelves with Soleil Yellow Quimper, hand-painted in Brittany, from Faienceries de Quimper HB-Henroit Quimper.

Design a real working island (put your barstools elsewhere)—maybe one that looks like an enormous antique French butcher-block.

Take subway tile all the way up to the ceiling to add shimmer and shine behind antiqued cabinets with a more muted matte finish.

Scatter a few cow heads around. (2) The Abattoire Cow Bust from Pennoyer Newman looks just like the ones outside European butcher shops, but it's of lightweight, weather-resistant resin stone.

Find cabinets with all the charm of antique French furniture. (3) The Pilaster Kitchen Dresser, like every component in a Smallbone kitchen, is custom-made which means you can have the moldings you dream of—and custom-colored, so you can have your favorite blue, too.

Follow Musser's lead and make the mudroom double as your pantry.

Search for sinks with big personalities. (4) Similar to Musser's kitchen sink, this German Silver Sink from the German Silver Sink Company has a ton of charisma.

HUE LA LA

SUZANNE TUCKER,
designer

Colors taken right from the bucolic Provençal landscape put a gloriously Gallic spin on this new California kitchen. Tucker used sage green, mustard yellow, porridge beige, and rustic terra-cotta to create a kitchen with a distinctly French farmhouse feel.

TOP: Just beyond this kitchen's island is a cozy dining area. Green painted lower cabinets (in the background) on either side of the kitchen are 42" high and provide more storage while also functioning as a room divider.

BOTTOM: Two separate stainless-steel sinks by Franke allow this homeowner to pile dirty dishes in one while washing vegetables in the other. The Domo faucet by **KWC** swivels for use at either sink. The dishwasher by Bosch is hidden behind a green wood panel. "I'm partial to Bosch," says Tucker. "Their dishwashers use a minimal amount of water and they're very quiet." The classic French spiraled iron knobs are from **Golden Lion**.

Tucker found a pair of rusty antique rooster lanterns and then designed a crosspiece to connect them.

"We basically gutted the building and brought in everything you see, including the reclaimed old beams, to give it a farmhouse feel."

"This is an old stone house that was built 100 years ago as a winery. It felt very much like the South of France so I pulled in all those Provençal colors."

"The kitchen cabinets are new but made to look old with seeded glass in the doors and about six layers of paint, all worn back, to give it that nice aged quality."

Integrally colored plaster walls and a distressed finish on the tongue-and-groove cabinetry add the patina of age to this new kitchen. Beauharnais limestone was used for the countertop, backsplash, and floor as a quiet background for color. The island has a butcher block top in keeping with the farmhouse theme. Richard Mulligan's Mama Bear chairs—with cushions in Pineapple Plaid in Olive from Marvic Textiles—"look so battered it feels like you've had them for 50 years," says Tucker.

KITCHEN ISLANDS

....

BUSTLING OR SPARE, ISLANDS ARE ALWAYS OPERATION CENTRAL.

"Before islands, what were kitchens all about? Remember those old TV shows where the wife in the apron would have to squeeze by the kitchen table in the middle of the room, crowded with relatives waiting to be fed, just to get an egg? Islands serve so many purposes. People can sit there out of the traffic pattern; they provide work space for a variety of activities—not just for cooking; and they can provide a place for an ice-maker, microwave, or wine cooler."
—T. Keller Donovan, designer

A Provençal craftsman built home-owner Marie Nygren's kitchen's handsome anchor: a weathered French oak island with open storage below.

A chandelier from BoBo Intriguing Objects provides a romantic glow when Nygren serves a buffet dinner from her island.

The cabinets, by designer Smith Hanes, are also in French oak to keep the mood calm.

The bottom shelves are perfect for storing oversize serving dishes and wide drawers are a great place to store place mats, napkins, and other table linens.

HOW MANY CONVENIENCES CAN YOU FIT INTO ONE ISLAND?

- **Butcher block**—chop without fear, right on your island top.

- **Cookbook shelves.**

- **Cooktop**—stir and stir the risotto, and still be a part of the conversation.

- **Dishwasher drawers**—take two: dirty dishes in one, glasses the other.

- **Filtered faucet**—find one that dispenses hot, cold, and filtered water all from the same faucet.

- **Ice maker**—parties, 'nuff said.

- **Knife drawer**—a slot for every knife and every knife in its slot.

- **Linen drawers**—wide enough to store your place mats without folding.

- **Marble slab**—ideal for rolling out cookie dough.

- **Microwave drawer**—hide it away and pull it out when you need it.

- **Prep sink**—with a mandatory garbage disposal, scrape scraps in and be done.

- **Pull-out pot drawers**—tall enough to store your stock pot, lid on.

- **Pull-out trash and recycling bins**—in the middle of the action, what could be more convenient?

- **Refrigerator drawer**—create a soda and juice station.

- **Silver-cloth-lined drawer**—don't let granny's ice tongs tarnish.

- **Tray storage**—stack them sideways in narrow open cubbies.

- **Warming oven drawer**—so what if soccer practice ran late, dinner's still toasty.

- **Wine chiller**—the perfect temperature with every pour.

ISLAND ALTITUDE

"A kitchen island should be about 38" high—a little taller than the countertops—to be comfortable for prep."

—THOMAS O'BRIEN, DESIGNER

HAVING TWINS

These large twin islands, each with its own Kohler sink, drawers, cabinets, copious counter space, and even a Bosch dishwasher, don't overwhelm the room because they're painted a soft color, Benjamin Moore Danville Tan, to blend with the pebbly beige color of the limestone stove surround. And the Gerber hardware has an antiqued brass patina that's harmonious with the cabinet color. Painted white? An entirely different room.

"I think it's very important to limit color, to be restrained. I introduced green and gray into the stain on the floor, and that gave it a cooler tone. And that's Costa Esmeralda granite on the counters. It was very difficult to find a granite that lends itself to a cool palette."

—SUSAN FERRIER, DESIGNER

1. TURN THE TABLE.
Make one end of your island a great big lazy Susan. "If I've got a square, I'll usually throw a round shape against it," says designer Barry Dixon. "I did that in this kitchen, where that circular lazy Susan table is cantilevered over the adjacent rectangular island." In the evening, an Asian fish-trap lantern from Gore Dean casts beautiful patterns over the lazy Susan's eminently durable hammered-metal top.

2. CULTIVATE SWEETNESS.
"I used to bake a lot when I was a party stylist. So this huge 6' x 6' island is covered with white baker's marble, which stays cool, and a marble sink in the middle of the island," says Jamie Gottschall, designer. "I have very weird luck with things. After the kitchen was done I had nothing to put in the shelves under the island. I walked into Marshalls and there were these pink-and-white striped tins and I just about fell over. They say laundry on one side, so Joyce Danko, a muralist, labeled the other side with the names of French pastries and delicacies."

3. AGE GRACEFULLY.
"We wanted an aged, casual feeling, with distressed finishes," says designer Ray Booth. "This center island is oak, treated with ammonia and wire-brushed to pull out the grain." The kitchen island by St. Charles, with its "X" detail and no prep sink, looks like an elegant European antique. It's comfortable for a casual dinner, provides enough counter space to spread out food prep, and maintains a certain elegance when the kitchen is viewed from afar.

COOK UP AN ISLAND THAT MELTS INTO THE LIVING ROOM.

"I designed the island to look like a table, with turned wooden legs and open shelving that faces the living room. The wooden top has butterfly joints that look like little bow ties. It has gateleg ends reminiscent of early American tables. You swing them away from the island and pull up the rounded leaves to make it bigger. If you swing the gates toward the island, the drop leaf falls and the island gets smaller."

—STANLEY DIXON, ARCHITECT

TAKE YOUR COLOR CUE FROM YOUR COUNTERTOP.

This island is painted Farrow & Ball Lamp Room Gray to complement the veining on the Carrara marble counter-top. An antique pot rack and the turned leg details at its corners add old-world soul to the island. "This is where my two kids do their homework while I cook, and everyone talks about their day," says designer Dana Abbott.

1. MASTER ZEN.
"We built the cabinet and the island out of mahogany. What makes them truly elegant is their finish. I had these Dale Chihuly glass bowls in this dark black squid-ink purple, showed them to Tony Giacalone, a master refinisher and asked, 'Can you get this color?' He said, 'Of course.' The steel countertop reflects light, but we scarred it up real fast to knock it back a bit. The more distressed it gets, the better. And I collected these egg-shaped rocks from an island in Penobscot Bay."
—MALLORY MARSHALL, DESIGNER

2. SHINE BRIGHTLY.
"The kitchen is designed to be an extension of the living and dining areas," says designer David Mann. To give it a pristine, dressed-up look he designed the island of gleaming crystallized glass and chose Philippe Starck's sparkly Hudson aluminum counter stools.

3. TAKE TWO.
"We built two islands, which makes a lot more sense than one giant island. So many islands these days are like aircraft carriers. You could land a jet on one! I find them so obtrusive. You end up having to do laps around the room just to get to the fridge. With two, there's a better flow."
—MADELINE STUART, DESIGNER

JUST ROLL WITH IT.

This island is made of cold-rolled steel, covered with reclaimed oak matched to the floor for a continuous flow. "Someone suggested we put a concrete top on the island, like the counters," says designer Erin Martin, "And I just felt . . . the answer was **NO**! It needed to morph up, roll up from the floor, and then roll back down. This is not about being furniture in the room—it's an organic part of the space, so it's not overwhelming. I think this is a very successful kitchen. It has clean, modern elements, but the island, the dark, walnut-stained cabinets, the old wood planks on the floor give it the softness of history."

—ERIN MARTIN, DESIGNER

BE SWELL ON WHEELS.

"Originally our architect designed the island as a peninsula, but that seemed to cut off the room, so I pulled off the connecting piece and created this floating island. You can roll it over to the stationary island if you need more work space, or push it up to the French doors and use it as a bar or service cart to the outside."

—PETER FISHEL, DESIGNER

CHOP & ROLL

People get emotional about their countertops. Some love the "character" added by stains and water rings, while others go all Lady Macbeth if a lemon drop lands on their limestone (*Out, damned spot!*). Some worship the way granite's shine resists anything short of a jackhammer, but others are staunch advocates of the matte look of classic honed marble. And *do not* get kitchen professionals started on countertop edges, unless you're prepared to listen to a long soliloquy on "ogee or not ogee."

GETTING EDGY

What is an ogee edge? What are some other types of countertop edges?

- **AN OGEE EDGE** is an ornate profile that typically mimics an inverted crown molding. Used in traditional style kitchens, it echoes details found on the cabinet doors and moldings. While pretty to look at, this edge is difficult to keep clean, so it is often saved for just one working zone—such as the island—with a square edge used everywhere else.

- **A DOUBLE OGEE EDGE** is just what the name implies—twice the profile of the single ogee profile. Different materials, finishes, and shapes create layered interest in a kitchen—so an edge like this is a nice detail in just one zone. It takes a skilled eye to place a double ogee edge so it doesn't look overwrought and forced. And of course it's doubly hard to keep clean.

- **A ROUNDED (OR BULL-NOSE) EDGE** is a profile that was typically used in the 1980s, but I still see it from time to time. This type of edge has taken a back seat for the last couple decades along with shoulder pads and big hair, but things do recycle so you never know . . .

- **SQUARE EDGE** profiles are classic and, in my opinion, the best. Whether used in traditional or contemporary designs this edge rules! When edges are square the eye isn't distracted and the counter material can be admired. The edges aren't saying, "look at me." This is also the easiest to keep clean!

—**BILL PROCTOR**, SHOWROOM MANAGER, PARIS CERAMICS USA

BUTCHER-BLOCK COUNTERS ARE ALL ABOUT THE EASE OF ONE-STOP CHOPPING. "The maple butcher-block island and countertop add a softening element into this kitchen, an old-fashioned settled look. They're porous, so time and wear will inevitably confer imperfections—your family's history in stains and rings. Treasure them!" —**ROBIN BELL**, DESIGNER

Which kinds of stone are easiest to keep clean?
Granite is good and strong. Marble is more porous than granite, but it's tougher than you'd think. I've had honed, sealed white Carrara marble counters for ten years. I really abuse them and they're just now beginning to develop a patina, with slight weathering and chips that I love. I suggest French limestone for kitchens, too. It's more durable than the lighter limestones from Greece or the Baltic regions. Slate and soapstone are beautiful too, but require maintenance and constant mineral oil treatments and soapstone has the added problem that it's soft and easily chipped. I only recommend them if it's a no-cook situation.
—**FLORENCE PERCHUK**, KITCHEN DESIGNER

"I like beautiful old-fashioned kitchens, so I made this one kind of traditional. I used soapstone on the island because I love the light charcoal gray and the fact that you can get grease out of it. Soapstone is very old-fashioned and American."
—**WALDO FERNANDEZ**, DESIGNER

Granite is dense, hard, and very tough, making it one of the most durable materials for counters. In this kitchen, honed Galaxy granite countertops provide powerful dramatic contrast against creamy white cabinets.

"I wanted contrast in my kitchen but I didn't want to use a solid black granite like Absolute Black. This Galaxy granite has speckles that give it a lot of life and depth. And it's incredibly strong. We've had big buffets, hot plates, spilled red wine—it's even tolerated the acid of lemon juice really well. It's a granite that hides all sins."
—**ATHALIE DERSE**, DESIGNER

Travertine is a porous stone; its pitted surface is most often filled and sealed to make for a better work surface. When paired with light wood cabinets in this small kitchen, the pale stone helps to expand the feeling of space.

"Travertine is rustic. I love the texture and color. It's a little darker than the wood, which adds just the right amount of contrast. And the edge is rounded, so it's not sharp. I guess travertine is more porous than some other stone but it doesn't bother me. People are so paranoid about stains, and I know everyone always says, well, that's the patina, but I really do believe that! It is sealed, but that doesn't mean it's going to stay spotless."
—**PATRICK WADE**, DESIGNER

What's easier to maintain, honed surfaces or polished?
It doesn't matter, really. But we recommend honed—it looks more interesting, and is more user-friendly for fingerprints than polished, which can be too sleek and off-putting. —**FLORENCE PERCHUK**, KITCHEN DESIGNER

"Onyx really is beautiful. The light goes through it and it just glows. I'm a limestone-concrete gal, and I was nervous about this stone, but we fell in love with it. People will tell you it's not for kitchens because it's soft, but look, you go to Europe and everything's beat to pieces and they don't care. We're not trying to make it look like a showroom. Let it have a life of its own. These counters will look even better in ten years when the edges are chipped. Chips and scratches give it character. The island countertop is twice as thick as the other counters because I hate it when everything matches." —ERIN MARTIN, DESIGNER

How do you deal with fingerprints on stainless-steel counters?
We recommend a wax-based aerosol spray for that. It's called Stainless Steel Cleaner/Polish, from a company called Ball (drillspot.com). Once or twice a week you spray on a light mist. Don't put on too much—you don't want to soak the surface and make it greasy. Wipe the mist with a clean, lint-free cloth. Just make sure you wipe in the direction of the grain lines in the steel. The spray will bring back the original luster and leave a thin layer of wax. It's not hard or sticky, but it resists fingerprints. And if fingerprints do show up, they can be easily wiped away.

—ADAM KAMENS,
CEO, AMUNEAL
MANUFACTURING CORP

A glass countertop is a low-maintenance and surprisingly durable finishing touch for a modern kitchen. In this kitchen a pair of architect's old drafting tables, found at a thrift store were modified with a glass top to serve as an island.

"I took off the tilting wooden tops of the old drafting tables and wondered what should replace them. Then it dawned on me, why not glass? It's frosted on the underside, which makes it look like ice. Now the tables kind of float. It's hard to scratch it, but if you do manage to destroy it, it can always be replaced. And nothing stains glass, not even red wine. Friends can sit down with a drink and I can put them to work, chopping and nibbling. After they're gone, I just wipe it down with Windex."

—ELDON WONG, DESIGNER AND HOMEOWNER

Why do you like Corian?
I think I've become allergic to granite. You see it in every remodeling show, every real-estate ad. Corian is a very sensuous material—cool to the touch. And practical—if some catastrophic stain occurs, you can just sand it down. I specified an eased edge on my counters, which just takes the sharpness off the 90° angle."

—T. KELLER DONOVAN, DESIGNER

Why do you love stainless steel?
There's something about stainless-steel counters that I find very warm. I mean, it's crisp and clean and slightly reflective, but there's also a softness to it. The more you use it, the more surface-scratched it gets. Once it develops that patina, it's really welcoming.

—MADELINE STUART, DESIGNER

"The advantage of concrete is that you're not limited to a slab size. It's cast in place and there are no seams. Plus, we carved out a drain board. You can work like that with concrete. It's user-friendly, warm to the touch, and easy to clean. It doesn't chip easily or react negatively to citrus or wine the way stone can. We made the counters thick because thick countertops immediately say, 'This is special.' Countertops are usually about an inch thick. These are two inches, and the island is three inches. It feels substantial and serious, almost monolithic." —ANIK PEARSON, DESIGNER

Countertops made from recycled materials are an eco-friendly alternative to quarried stone. In this kitchen, Squak Mountain Stone on the island top is made from recycled paper, recycled glass, and low-carbon cement.

"Squak Mountain Stone, which looks like slate, is on the island, and then the other counters are edge-grain black walnut to add more texture. Again, the walnut is a natural, earthy look. Our choice was limited because many green products are contemporary-looking, and we wanted a traditional look. Nothing here is shiny or glitzy. Everything feels organic. I like the kind of things that get better over time."

—MICHAEL DEL PIERO, DESIGNER

How do you remove stains from marble?

There are a host of tips listed on the Marble Institute of America's Web site (marble-institute.com). You can poultice away rust. You can remove soap scum or mildew with a solution of a half cup of ammonia in a gallon of water. And you can remove most coffee or juice stains with a little hydrogen peroxide in water, plus a few drops of ammonia. For everyday wear-and-tear, buff away small scratches with superfine dry steel wool called "grade 0000." But if you're really worried about your counters, put in those new engineered quartzes, like Zodiaq or Silestone. They're almost impervious and indestructible. Or be extra careful to cover the counters completely with cutting boards whenever you work in the kitchen.

—FLORENCE PERCHUK, KITCHEN DESIGNER

Lava stone countertops are made from volcanic lava glazed with enamel. Its lustrous crackled finish is highly resistant to stains and scratching and it can be custom colored to match your palette. Here turquoise lava stone countertops pair beautifully with a colorful harlequin pattern tile backsplash.

"Lava stone delivers a clear, clean, shiny color that you can't get with any other countertop material. It's impervious to hot and cold and doesn't develop a patina."

—WILLIAM DIAMOND, DESIGNER

"I'm fascinated with the look of European butcher shops—the shine of white marble—it's all about a pared-down aesthetic, not much color but a lot of texture. That's what I wanted my kitchen to look like. This Martha Stewart table in the kitchen had a tile top, but plates wobbled. So I put this honed piece of marble on it."

—JILL SHARP BRINSON, DESIGNER

new victorian

OLD-FASHIONED AND UNABASHEDLY ROMANTIC, KITCHENS THAT RECALL THE REGAL SENSIBILITY OF ELEGANCE GONE BY.

BRIDGING THE CENTURIES

CRAIG KETTLES,
kitchen designer and homeowner

In his Georgia kitchen, Kettles channeled his childhood affection for the 19th-century stylings of his grandmother's home. The timeworn, burnished pieces he's spent years collecting are scattered throughout the space: so charming and intriguing you hardly notice all the modern kitchen bells and whistles.

THE BACKSTORY | "We moved from Atlanta to this property, eleven acres on a lake, because we wanted a more relaxed country life. And I wanted our new kitchen to have the feel of a 19th-century farmhouse that's been renovated over the years. If I'd given this kitchen a more current look I'd already be planning the renovation; this is a style we can live with for the rest of our lives."

The pantry is hidden behind the stove, through the door on the left, and the island, in the foreground, is stepped up to hide any mess in the kitchen. The flicker of candles in an iron rack with 12 votives by Jan Barboglio lends pre-electric charm. Rhone pendant lights and Pacific City sconces above the range—all from Rejuvenation—add to the *fin de siècle* mood.

"We put the antique china cabinet on a riser so we don't have to bend down too much to reach the lower levels."

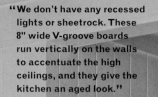

"We don't have any recessed lights or sheetrock. These 8" wide V-groove boards run vertically on the walls to accentuate the high ceilings, and they give the kitchen an aged look."

"I think the biggest mistake people make in doing a kitchen is going to someone who sells cabinets, because you wind up with every square inch covered in cabinets, and of course you fill them. I'd do the reverse. First figure out how much stuff you really need, and then design cabinets to fit it."

"The trash is in this old tin from Belgium that was once used to sell coffee beans."

I'm surprised this kitchen is new! It feels so nice and old-fashioned, as if it were cobbled together from found parts.

That's exactly what my partner Michael and I did. We collected pieces like the china cabinet and the marble-topped table and the butcher block, and designed the kitchen around them.

Why two islands?

We have a division of labor— he cooks and I bake—and that's supported by a division of space. The middle area, between the two islands, is my domain. I roll out pastry dough on that table and the marble keeps it cool. I've got my cookie sheets and measuring things nearby, my own sink, and my own oven, a Fisher & Paykel, which I like because it bakes extremely evenly. It's a high-tech oven with a simple interface—just two knobs to turn. I can't stand that digital stuff—too many buttons to push.

It does look like someone actually cooks here. Those copper pots on the pot rack look like they get a pretty good workout.

Michael loves old copper pots, which are very good at conducting heat quickly and evenly. He's got the area by the range, and I never get into his space when he's cooking and he doesn't get into mine. It works really well for cleanup, too. He has a regular dishwasher in his island for pots and pans, and I've got dishwasher drawers in mine for plates and stemware. We can knock it out pretty fast after a party.

The stone fireplace is so dramatic, and it's raised. Why?

That's so you can see it from the dining table. It's nice having it up higher. People can walk over and warm their hands. The fireplace is the centerpiece of this big, theatrical space, and it's open on both sides, so you can also see it from the keeping room. That's an old-fashioned name for this neat little room, paneled in old barn wood, where we have a sofa and a desk. We spend a lot of time there in winter, reading by the window overlooking the lake.

What's on the island countertops?

Soapstone. Soapstone has that timeless look, and it's fairly easy to maintain. You just oil it once in a while. By now it's got a few chips along the edges, but I don't mind. I've got some clients who like perfection, but I don't.

The stone in the fireplace really draws your eye.

It's Tennessee Fieldstone. It feels rustic and it's readily available here in Northern Georgia.

Why an antique marble topped table and not a marble insert in the island?

It's an old French table with a lot of character and so we put a marble top on it. Sometimes we use the table as a bar or a coffee station and sometimes I clear everything off and roll out pastry dough. I'm not very tall so the counter is still comfortable even though it's a little lower.

HOT HOUSE
The fireplace is centrally located perpendicular to the islands. Old Belgian beer bottles are arrayed on the dry-stacked stone fireplace for added interest. The island is equipped with a KitchenAid Architect Series ice maker, perfect for parties.

WHAT IF . . .
YOUR KITCHEN LOOKED JUST LIKE YOUR GRANNY'S?

"My grandmother's kitchen was all fantasy. It's still a sacred place for me. She was Julia Child before Julia Child. Her kitchen was all open which is the reason our kitchen is so exposed. We used lots of antique furniture because my grandmother had furniture—like a cabinet for dishes and one for storing silver, that sort of thing. We hope to create the kind of family memories here that my grandmother created in her kitchen."

TRICKS AND TREATS

"We really like to cook, and a good stove was important to us. We fleetingly considered a restored gas range, but Michael finally went for the reliability of a Wolf. And with a Sub-Zero glass-door refrigerator, you can see what you have at a glance. But I do find myself styling the shelves. The red box is an old bread box."

CRAVING . . .
A PLACE WHERE THE CANNED PEACHES HAVE NOWHERE TO HIDE.

In the pantry—which is in a separate room behind the stove—one set of shelves is about 4" deep, just the size of a typical jar, so things don't get hidden behind each other. The library ladder is an antique from Belgium.

> " If the table had been round I would have done a round fixture. This old billiards fixture has the right amount of age and it's linear which looks good over a rectangular table."

That window seat looks so inviting, what can you see?
It has a view of Lake Rabun, a very special lake in North Georgia with an Adirondacks feel. Our property is all terraced down to the lake. I stretch out on that window bench with a cup of coffee in the morning and a glass of wine at night and just stare at the water. Outside the French doors there's an herb and vegetable garden.

How did you create floors with such beautiful aged patina?
They're antique heart pine taken out of a 19th century house.

The whole space, even the pantry behind the stove, feels very open.
There's a logical progression— you move from the pantry to the islands, where the food is prepped, to the table. What makes it work so well is that everything is exposed. Food is life, and the process of preparing it is beautiful, so I have no problem seeing the spices and the pots and the plates. It makes for a warm, soulful kitchen, and it's great for guests; they don't need to open a lot of doors to find things.

HISTORY LESSON
Open shelves in the island hold dishes and glassware, and silverware is kept in a drawer in the old French farm table, which makes it very easy to set for a meal. The billiard light is antique, and so are the heart pine floors.

COLOR FORMS

BAYBERRY GREEN FROM THE OLD FASHIONED MILK PAINT COMPANY ON THE ISLANDS PULLS THE OUTSIDE IN.

" This green just appealed to me and my partner, Michael McGaughey. The house is on a lake, surrounded by trees, and it was a way of connecting the kitchen to the outdoors. It's milk paint, which I like because it's got a lot of texture and variation. It adds character to a new house."

STALKING THE LOOK

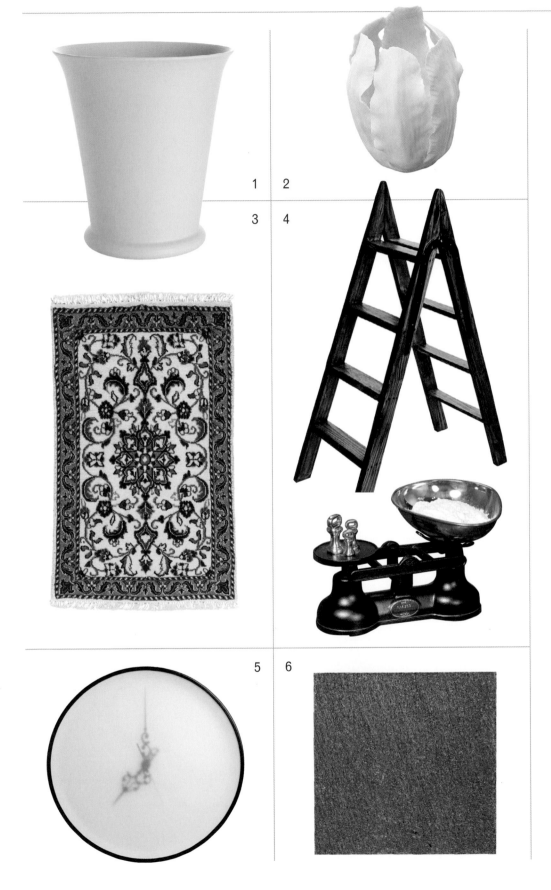

1 2

3 4

5 6

Keep cabinets to a minimum. Find antique furniture that fits your notion of a romantic old kitchen and build around it.

Collect antique copper pots. A few burnished copper beauties hanging from your pot rack lend a big shot of charm.

Bring in shots of crisp green to freshen old-fashioned elements. (1) The small Porcelain Garden Pot from Cultivated Gardens is glazed in a perfect springlike shade of green.

Light candles. What better way to get a pre-Edison mood? (2) Porcelain petals protect the flame in Ted Muehling's sculptural Tulip Votive for Nymphenburg through Kneen & Co.

Warm your reclaimed heart pine floors with small rugs that show a little age. (3) The Persisk rug from Ikea, shown in Pattern 2, may be new but its inspiration is an antique passed down through generations.

Layer on the atmosphere with bygone-era staples like a wooden ladder and an antique kitchen scale. (4) (TOP) Global Views ladder through High Fashion Home is perfect for the pantry (BOTTOM). The Balance Beam Scale through Lehman's looks antique because it's handmade in England of brass and cast metal.

Place a large clock on a wall—a classic Victorian-era touch. (5) The Mystic Wall Clock from Umbra is a majestic 2' in diameter. Frosted glass fogs the Victorian-style hands, evoking the mists of time.

Choose countertop stone with vintage cred. (6) Kettles chose all-American soapstone, from Vermont Soapstone, for counters and sinks. "Even honed granite would have looked too new for this kitchen."

SOUTHERN HOSPITALITY

TY LARKINS,
designer

Who doesn't love the
Old South? Larkins pays
proper obeisance to Dixie's
traditions while turning the
oh-so-formal style on its
head. Same heavy moldings,
same ornate flourishes, but
somehow all made fresh
and new. It's the traditional
Southern vernacular, but
looking as relaxed as a belle
waking from a nap.

TOP: A white pottery collection silhouettes beautifully against this kitchen's brown painted cabinets. "It's the **David Hicks** philosophy," Larkins says. "When you take things with common traits and put them together, they take on more importance."

BOTTOM: A kitchen chalkboard by **Ballard Designs** caters to Larkin's seven-year-old twin daughters. **Rhone Pendants** from **Rejuvenation** and a large wall clock from **Target** lend the space schoolhouse appeal.

This Baton Rouge, Louisiana kitchen has the soul of an old Southern mansion but it reads more modern. Walls and woodwork are painted the same color, **Classic Gray** by **Benjamin Moore**, which calms decorative flourishes like **Palladian** windows and deep crown moldings. Tall backsplashes in creamy subway tile and countertops in honed **Carrara** marble are old-fashioned touches while **Indecasa** stools from **Design Within Reach** add modern vitality to the traditional setting.

"The kitchen gets the most traffic. It's family central, where everything happens. The marble island's got pen marks, but it's nothing that a little stone cleaner can't handle."

"This house is completely new construction. I grew up in New Orleans, and being around all that history really influenced me. I wanted to capture some of the magical quality of the fine old houses there, but decorate in a modern way."

ENGRAINED BEAUTY

MCKEE PATTERSON,
architect

This is the kind of elegance that only seems to exist in PBS branded mini-series. And like any good Masterpiece Theatre its inspiration came from England. The kitchen features carved pilasters and an island with as many nooks for books and newspapers as for pots, a welcoming spot for his lordship to relax with his pipe and the *Times*.

THE BACKSTORY | "This is a working couple with teenage children. Their kitchen is a very important pass-through because it runs the length of the house. The formal foyer looks directly into the breakfast room so they wanted it to look nice, kind of library-ish, and we carried that idea into the kitchen. We wanted a wood that isn't dark in tone but still has a beautiful richness to it."

All the cabinetry, paneling, and beams in this Connecticut kitchen—designed by Austin, Patterson, Disston Architects—are made of butternut wood; its pale color keeps the mood light. The island has open shelves on one side and deep storage drawers on the other. Barstools from Wood & Hogan look antique. The white-painted butler's pantry is visible through the door on the far left.

"The main thing is that the butternut wood warms up the room, but there's also a practical side. When you ding butternut, it doesn't show. If you hit a painted surface with a pot or a chair you see the ding. And butternut also resists cracking and warping."

This kitchen is a cocoon of honeyed wood. What was the inspiration?
We refurbished the whole house, which was built almost a century ago. It was a mishmash of styles that we pared down, but the architectural detail, the long columns with the ribs and broad shoulders, was derived from the original 1860s or 1870s door trim. I was the architect and Rosemary Browne was the decorator. The owner, Liz Lynch, says what she loves most is that there's no division between cabinets and walls. It's seamless, all of a piece. And there are wood beams. I always think that when you're doing wood spaces, the ceilings should have at least a gesture of wood.

Even the stove hood is wood.
It's such a big feature, and we didn't want to distract. A company called Best makes innards for any hood you want. Stainless steel lines the underside.

What kind of wood is this kitchen made of?
Butternut, which is a favorite of woodworkers. It's soft and relatively light in weight.

What did you choose for counters?
Green granite. The butternut wood has a beautiful reddish tone and so this green seemed a good choice for counters. Red and green complement each other. And we did the backsplashes in the same material. I like tall backsplashes like this because they're such a clean look.

Why did you use open shelves on one side of the island and drawers on the other?

The Lynches like to cook; it's part of the joy of the house for them, and with only one child at home now, they often eat at the island. There's a counter at one end for stools—the other end has a Bosch dishwasher—and the whole thing has a neat, tidy look. Liz said, "I like the convenience of open shelves, but I'm messy, and I don't want my friends having to look at the mess while they're at the table."

At the table?

The table in the breakfast room. Liz and Dan usually entertain small groups, and they use the breakfast room rather than the dining room. So the open shelves are on the side of the island you can't see from in there.

And the French doors actually got paint!

The idea is not to get slavish about the use of wood— even if it's as beautiful as butternut.

No recessed lights and the pendants don't hang directly over the island. Does the work space get enough light?

Oh yes. I'm not a big fan of recessed lights. When you're working on one side of the island the lights on the opposite side provide ample task light. I really like the way these brass pendants play off the wood, stainless would have been too silvery and bright.

SUNNY PERSONALITY
Three sets of French doors with gleaming Federal-style brass cremone bolts are painted Benjamin Moore Ancient Ivory—they open onto a terrace and a leafy yard. Even the 36" Viking stove sits inside a butternut wood niche. White oak floors are "easy on the feet," says Patterson.

WHAT IF...
THE ONLY ART ON YOUR WALLS WAS NATURE'S BEAUTIFUL BUTTERNUT GRAIN.

When you look from this house's formal front entry hall through the breakfast room and into the kitchen, the mood reads more *library* than *kitchen*—and that was the whole point. Keeping walls art-free enhances the experience of the elegant moldings and dignified ceiling coffers, which adds up to a gracious vista.

CRAVING...
A ROMANTIC BUTLER'S PANTRY TO SHOW OFF YOUR WEDDING CHINA.

The butler's pantry is "all about the china, the good stuff," says **Patterson**. A weathered copper sink and fittings by **Herbeau** along with ash countertops convey the look of a traditional butler's pantry. **Cabinets are painted Benjamin Moore Cayman Islands**, a creamy color that mixes well with brass and wood.

Most cooks would kill for all this storage space—there are cabinets all the way to the ceiling!

So many people don't want overhead cabinets, but if you eliminate them, you have a storage problem. If you have lower cupboards and want a rollout shelf—so you can reach things easily without hitting your head—you lose lots of space, including three inches in width for the door. I said, "Let's just make drawers and not lose that space." It's so much easier to get plates, and even pots and pans, from a deep drawer than from a cabinet.

What about those long horizontal cabinets above the doorways? What are those for?

Big platters, lobster pots—things that aren't used very often. The doors have special hinges. You only have to pull one of the knobs and the door lifts itself. That's necessary when you're on a footstool holding a pot—you can't be using both hands to open the cupboard.

Why did you choose this dark hardware?

It's a wonderful deep chocolate-brown finish, a very good neutral. More like a piece of ebony than a shiny metal. It really keeps things calm by not making a big deal out of the knobs.

All this wood but then you chose not to cover the refrigerator?

We wanted a little looseness. We didn't want the kitchen to look too compulsive.

SOFT FOCUS

Stainless-steel appliances—Sub-Zero refrigerator, General Electric microwave and wall-mounted oven with Trivection technology—gleam against the burnished wood. Cabinet hardware by Ball & Ball has an aged feel. The tall cabinet to the right of the ovens holds large platters and canned goods.

COLOR FORMS

PATTERSON ENVELOPED THE ROOM IN A GOLDEN GLOW WITH CABINETS IN BUTTERNUT WOOD.

" Butternut has a wonderful grain and a rich, lustrous, satiny patina when it's oiled. We didn't want mahogany or anything dark—wood can swallow up light. "

STALKING THE LOOK

1

2

3

4

5

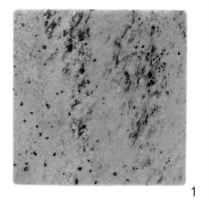

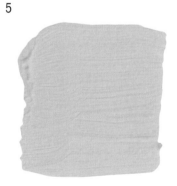

Keep it flush. When cabinets are flush with moldings it quiets the architectural detail and lends elegance.

Use restraint with paint. Because the only painted surfaces in the kitchen are the French doors, your eye is drawn to them, and the view.

Don't let your countertops shout. (1) Patterson used mottled Typhoon Green granite countertops with thin profiles that stand back and let the butternut woodwork shine.

Install the 19th century's version of can lighting. (2) In this kitchen Circa Lighting's Sloane Street Shop Lights provide period appropriate task lighting while still staying tight to the ceiling.

Choose a woodsy color for your table linens. (3) Homeowner Liz Lynch uses Deborah Rhodes napkins from Lynnens to pull out one of the livelier hues in the wood grain.

Match your breakfast room chairs to your kitchen counter stools. (4) Ladderback breakfast room chairs by Guy Chaddock echo the look of the kitchen barstools.

Don't let your range hood spoil the atmosphere. Patterson designed a wood casing around the range hood with a flat front that looks like an upper cabinet.

Invert your palette in the butler's pantry. (5) Ash countertops and cabinets painted Benjamin Moore Cayman Islands 952 in the butler's pantry are a surprise.

OLD SCHOOL

CHRISTOPHER PEACOCK,
kitchen designer

No English boarding-school dining hall could possibly be as beautiful as this elegantly restrained space, but that schoolboy memory is what Peacock claims inspired his design for this *House Beautiful* model kitchen—built not in the Shropshire countryside, but right in the middle of Rockefeller Center as part of a special event.

THE BACKSTORY | If you build it—especially smack in the middle of Rockefeller Center—they will come! New York City crowds loved this model kitchen by wizardly kitchen designer, Christopher Peacock. It's old-world gorgeous, and it puts the cook at center stage.

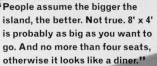

"People assume the bigger the island, the better. Not true. 8' x 4' is probably as big as you want to go. And no more than four seats, otherwise it looks like a diner."

Walnut refectory cabinets by Christopher Peacock, centered around a pair of Euro-Style French-Door Refrigerators by Jenn-Air, honor the straightforward practicality of an age gone by. CaesarStone countertops in Misty Carrara have the look of white marble. Counter stools by Little Bird Furniture Studio feel like English refectory stools while hanging lights by Urban Archaeology have a turn-of-the-last-century industrial appeal.

What a kitchen! These wood cabinets look like old-fashioned iceboxes.
Actually, I was thinking of the large paneled cabinets in my old school dining hall back in England. That was the inspiration for our Refectory Collection, and the hardware is a big part of the look. When I couldn't find the right kind of antique hardware, I designed it myself. They're overscaled and made of polished nickel. I've worked with chrome, copper, brass, and bronze but I keep coming back to polished nickel. I just love that soft sheen.

Are you moving away from white kitchens?
I still love and champion white kitchens, but it doesn't have to be all white. I think a room needs a balance of elements. I love the contrast between dark and light cabinetry. The wood accentuates the white and the white accentuates the wood. It's walnut, left natural. The beauty is in the wood itself, which we handpicked. There's no stain on it, just a very low-sheen lacquer so you can wipe it down. If you put a high-gloss finish on it, you just see the reflection of the light bouncing off and you don't see the grain.

Why not panel the refrigerators?
I like stainless steel. It looks professional, and I needed it to break up the cabinets. There are two refrigerators because in this huge room just one would not have been enough visually.

Do you always recommend two sinks?

Not always. If the main sink is close enough to the island, there's really no need for another, although it's nice. I love these big Kohler stainless-steel sinks, wider at the bottom so you can scrub a roasting pan. I usually start the layout with the sink. Put it under a window where you can look out and watch the kids play. And make it large. I think one big sink is invaluable. The countertops are made of CaesarStone, a quartz composite that looks like marble. But it's not going to stain. You can set down a hot pot.

What else do you recommend?

Trash storage in different areas can be useful. You don't want to walk across the room once you've unwrapped the chicken.

Do you believe in lots and lots of counter space too?

Having miles and miles of countertop is a complete waste of time. It's a lot to wipe down, and it just becomes an area to dump stuff. All you really need to prepare a meal is four feet of counterspace.

Any surprises inside these cabinets?

I'm crazy. I pay more attention to the inside of the cabinets than the outside. But I'm not big on gadgets, so any kind of special interior has to be useful and simple.

HANDLES WITH FLAIR
Polished nickel hardware from **Christopher Peacock** feels substantial to the touch and gleams against the white cabinets. Glass-fronted cabinets, open on two sides are convenient to the table on one side and the sink on the other. They hold crystal and china from **Wedgewood** so setting the table is a cinch. Pullout willow baskets for onions, potatoes, and garlic are handwoven in England.

CRAVING...
A HANDS-FREE FAUCET!

"This is the first time I've used these Pilar Faucets from Delta that go on and off at a touch. Say you've been battering up the chicken and your hands are covered in muck. Just nudge it with your wrist and it turns on. Very practical."

WHAT IF...
YOU KEPT YOUR FOOD IN DRAWERS WITH EMBOSSED LABELS AND STITCHED LEATHER PULLS?

"The bins in our pantry cupboard have leather handles, which is a nice surprise, lovely to the touch. I'm very much about trying to tap into people's senses. If you think about what gives you pleasure, it's the little things. There's no reason why we can't have luxury in what we use every day."

It's so great that the cooktop is in the island!
This is a wonderful kitchen for someone who loves to cook and socialize at the same time, because you stand and prepare the food facing out into the room. You're interacting with family and friends. And as large as the kitchen is, you're not running up and down to prepare a meal because everything you need is close by. You've got the cooktop and a sink on the island in front of you, with plenty of counter space. You turn around and there's the refrigeration. It's as efficient as a galley kitchen.

Speaking of efficiency, if you're going to invest in two of something, what should it be?
Dishwashers, definitely. Not necessarily placed together. Think about the process of cleaning up: You need counter space nearby for the dirty dishes, as well as a trash can and a sink so you can scrape and rinse the plates. Then you don't want to walk way across the room to put them away.

Any more expert advice?
If you're going to put a sink on an island, make it a good size. The little ones are hopeless. And the first rule of lighting is to have plenty of it. Put it on dimmers so you can control the quality and create mood. I like halogen lights because they give a very bright, natural light. Stay away from old-fashioned fluorescents, which can be cold and flat.

DOMESTIC BLISS
The Modular Electric Downdraft Cooktop from Jenn-Air's Expression Collection eliminates the need for an overhead vent so it could be installed right in the island. Jenn-Air's Pro-Style SteamClean Dishwasher, which offers a flexible racking system, is sited conveniently near the sink and stove. The Epic Legends hardwood floor in Gold Rush Walnut by Shaw Floors is partially composed of recycled wood fibers. Each plank is hand-scraped, so no two are the same, lending a soft aged quality.

COLOR FORMS
SCULLERY WHITE BY CHRISTOPHER PEACOCK PAINT ON CABINETS IS ULTRA-DRAMATIC AGAINST LONG SWATHES OF DARK WOOD.

Even though there are dark moments in this kitchen the striking white color on cabinets makes it feel always awash in light.

STALKING THE LOOK

1   2

3   4

5

Create a fantasy English boarding-school dining hall, then mix in sleek white cabinetry to lighten the look.

Go big or go home with old-fashioned oversized nickel hardware. (1) This kitchen's polished nickel roller latches from Christopher Peacock are modeled on antique originals.

Keep root vegetables (2) dry, dark and impossibly charming in pullout wicker baskets.

Stay true to your old school theme with rich, dark wood stools and padded leather seats. Peacock used counter stools by Little Bird Furniture.

Bring your back-up refrigerator in from the garage. Twin fridges, like Peacock used here, can hold enough cold beverages to hydrate a rugby team.

Set a formal table in a flash with your good silver tucked right beneath your fanciest china. (3) The sterling silver drawer in this kitchen is fitted with a felt cover and its accompanying Oberon Fine Bone China by Wedgwood is stored directly in the cupboard above.

Un-jumble your junk drawer. (4) Christopher Peacock's Anything Drawer has adjustable inserts to organize all your junk.

Find towel racks (5) that appear when needed and disappear when not.

NEWFOUND GLORY

THOMAS JAYNE, *designer,*
and **PETER PENNOYER**, *architect*

Tradition is taken seriously
in the Old Dominion state.
So refitting a gracious Virginia
home meant honoring its
historic walls. Jayne and
Pennoyer created a kitchen
that looks like it was gently
shoehorned into this 18th-century
beauty during the mid-1930s—
and they did it without spilling
a drop of Southern charm.

The furniture-like feet on
base cabinets and brack-
ets underneath upper
cabinets are details that
were fashionable in 1930s
American kitchens.

The refrigerator is
behind a painted wood
panel; it just looks like
another cabinet.

THE BACKSTORY | "It's a four-over-four room Georgian house, circa 1750.
Two wings were added in the early 20th century, and the current owner had
them taken down and rebuilt in the Federal style." —TJ

The appliances may be new, but the cabinetry details and the curtain panels in the glass-front cabinets have a vintage look. The Miele gas cooktop is inside the island's countertop so chefs can enjoy the leafy Virginia landscape while manning the stove. Window valances and the flowery fabric they're made of, Cowtan & Tout's Coniston linen, have a nostalgic feel. Getting back to pre-war basics (World War II that is), Franke undermounted sinks are paired with single lever Victorian Faucets from Harrington Brass Works.

This kitchen is a perfect fit for an historic Virginia house. How did you do it?

TJ: The idea was to make it look as if the kitchen had been retrofitted into one wing back in the 1930s

PP: We didn't want anything slick. In fact we wanted it to look like it had been a challenge fitting it all in.

The cabinets have lovely brackets and little legs—to look more like furniture?

TJ: We didn't want them to feel like brand new built-ins. Which is why they stop and start, instead of going all around the room.

PP: And the cabinets have no pretensions. My pet peeve is islands so dressed up with pilasters that they become these little architectural follies. This cabinetry is intentionally humdrum.

The contrast of light cabinets and dark counters is gorgeous and so is the way they blur into the backsplash. What is that material?

TJ: Old-fashioned soapstone, like they used in Colonial times. It has a warm, soft touch and it's amazingly durable. Doesn't burn or stain. Nothing can penetrate it, which is why you see it so often in science classrooms.

PP: New materials would not have felt comfortable with all the texture and patina of the old house. This place has the kind of soul you get only in the South.

What's the story behind this peekaboo window?

PP: In that corner, you can see back through a window that's original to the 18th-century house. We just built the cabinetry around it because we didn't want to spoil the symmetry of the paneling in that room by bricking it over.

How did you get new cabinets to look original to the house, like they'd been painted over and over again across the years?

PP: The finish is very soft. Also, all the millwork—every corner, every edge—has been sanded down a little bit, so nothing looks too sharp and new.

Why, if you're constructing cabinets with glass doors, would you put curtains behind them?

TJ: You see it a lot in 18th-century England and France. It contributes to the overall discretion, making the kitchen look more like a room. Putting the refrigerator behind paneled doors is another camouflage technique. We chose a cooktop instead of a range because it basically disappears. The island is part of the same impulse—besides offering a lot of storage, it also hides the ovens so when you're seated at the table you don't see any appliances.

VIEW INTO THE SOUL
The line of upper cabinets breaks to accommodate one of the original 18th-century windows, offering a glimpse back into the interior of the old house. There are two built-in Miele ovens on the opposite side of the island. The floors are 126-year-old reclaimed Southern pine.

COLOR FORMS
JAYNE PICKED BENJAMIN MOORE SCARECROW FOR CABINETS FOR ITS COMFY RETRO FEEL.

" The paint color Thomas came up with for cabinets is something I can't even begin to describe—he'll study how a color looks in every kind of light and even in the corners, where it intensifies. He calls it the reverberating effect." —PP

" That stone color is easy on the eyes and authentic to the period. I wanted something neutral, so you would look beyond the cabinets to the views." —TJ

WHAT IF...
YOU TOOK PAINS TO BE SURE EVEN YOUR NEW CEILING READ "1930S RENOVATION"?

······································

" The wires for the lamps on the ceiling are run through old pipe, as if it was rigged up in the 1930s. I like the informality of exposing the old timber framing." —PP

The new wing was built with old beams—salvaged from a munitions factory constructed in 1872—and painted Benjamin Moore Dove White. The Willis light fixtures, with white glass shades hanging from old-fashioned cloth cords, are modeled on classic pendant lights that were popular in the 1930s; from Rejuvenation.

1930s REDUX
······································

The working area in the kitchen is relatively compact, to allow room for a big tavern table with blue painted Sheraton legs and a plank top. The table and the red Windsor chairs are by Barton Sharpe. The windows and door leading out to the porch are curtained in Cowtan & Tout's Coniston linen, the same fabric that is used for the kitchen valances.

CRAVING...
THE OLD-FASHIONED CHARM OF GLASS-FRONT CABINETS WITHOUT THE PAIN OF KEEPING PLATES PERFECTLY STACKED.

······································

Inside the cabinets, shirred curtains run on two simple rods.

GLOW

You'll never get a perfect sear if you can't see the salmon. It takes all five senses to create great food, so don't let form trump function when choosing your kitchen lighting. That pretty Venetian glass chandelier you're desperate to hang is not going to make you the next top chef. If you don't know a Kelvin from a Kenmore, read on. This lesson should be illuminating.

AT FIRST SIGHT

What's the most important piece of advice about planning kitchen lighting?
Avoid the standard grid—contractors often recommend a square grid of recessed lights that don't do much more than provide a wash of light. You need layers. First, you need the right kind of designated task lights in places where you're prepping or cooking a meal or where your kids do their homework. But don't forget to provide for ambient lighting as well! Kitchens aren't always about preparing a meal. Sometimes you're in your kitchen for a glass of juice before the sun comes up, and you certainly don't want a big bang of light, right? It's nice to be able to flip a switch and have your pathway softly lit by sconces or in-wall LED lights.

—CASEY PENRY, OWNER, GLOW CONTRACT LIGHTING.

Dessin Fournir lanterns with burnished iron shades contrast beautifully against an island topped with smooth Imperial White marble.
"I like to mix corroded surfaces with technological ones." **—JOHN SALADINO,** DESIGNER

THERE'S NO RULE THAT SAYS ALL THE PENDANT LIGHTS OVER YOUR ISLAND HAVE TO MATCH. Designer **Thomas Hamel** hung three different styles of **Tom Dixon Beat** lights over this large island for maximum task lighting and to avoid punching recessed lights into the limed wood ceiling. Style-wise, everything is pared down and low-key except the pendants—proving light fixtures don't always have to play supporting roles.

THE PENDANTS ARE ONLY PART OF THE STORY. There are two islands and two sets of cheerful ruffled pendant lights from **Vaughan** with **Chelsea Plaid** silk inserts. They are supported by light from recessed ceiling lights, under-counter lights, and halogen lights that illuminate the long cabinet at the back.

"The built-in breakfront was designed to look like a piece of furniture, with glass fronts and mirror-backed cabinets to reflect the glassware. The lights in the cabinets are halogen lights on rheostats. Actually the under-counter lighting and the hanging lampshade lamps are all on dimmers so we can set the mood when we entertain."

—ANNE MILLER, DESIGNER AND HOMEOWNER

PLANTING BULBS

Can the lightbulb you select really make a difference?
Very much so. Lightbulbs with the right CRI and Kelvin number are very important in recessed cans and on tracks. I like a bright, crisp white light in a kitchen. I recommend a low-wattage halogen with a high CRI (*an index measuring the way a light source renders color*) like 80–86 or above, and a nice crisp white Kelvin (*a scale reflecting whether a bulb's light is warm or cool*). The perfect Kelvin number for a kitchen is 3000K. Those numbers ensure the colors in the room will read true—in other words, your granite, your wood, your fabrics will read close to the color they would read if they were out in the daylight. You don't want things to look muddy or dingy. And think of all the colors in foods, like meats and vegetables, that you need to see clearly to get a good result. For example, what if you're cooking chicken and it looks done on the stovetop, but when you get it to the table you can see very plainly that it's not? Not good.

—CASEY PENRY, OWNER GLOW CONTRACT LIGHTING

Large pendant lamps from **Visual Comfort** provide focused task lighting for the island in this kitchen by designer **Ken Fulk**. Stylistically, their gleaming metal unifies all the silver finishes in the kitchen—from the chicken wire in the upper cabinets to stainless-steel appliances to the nickel hardware and stainless stools.

GUIDING LIGHTS

Bring Darkness into Light.
Create drama over your cooktop with Kichler Lighting's Ripley sconce.

Downsize.
The George pendant, from Rejuvenation, with its ruffled opal-glass shade, is a pretty option for a petite kitchen.

Prepare a Moveable Feast.
Adjust the Maxine Side-to-Side Articulating Lamp from The Urban Electric Company to focus light where you need it most.

Add a Touch of Chic.
The Mode Pendant, from Pagani for Baker Furniture, has style to spare.

Chalk it Up.
A stylish pendant to light your island with a chalkboard shade to scribble your shopping lists. Chalkboard Peter pendant from John Beck Paper & Steel.

Color Your World.
Add a pop of red to your white kitchen with this glazed parchment pendant, Fashionista from Motif Designs.

Speak Softly.
Soften your kitchen with a graceful silk-pleated pendant from designer Thomas O'Brien, The D'Arcy Hanging Light through Visual Comfort.

Mix Your Metals.
Hang this reproduction pendant, Model 7721-1 in Antique Brass/Copper from Fourteenth Colony Lighting, over your island for vintage style.

Look Industrious.
The Garey Medium Industrial Light by Thomas O'Brien for Visual Comfort has old warehouse appeal.

Sync your Fridge.
The polished stainless-steel Orson light from Remains partners beautifully with stainless-steel appliances.

SWITCHED ON DESIGN

Is under-counter lighting a must?
I do think it's necessary but this is an area of conflict between designers and lighting consultants like me. Designers sometimes confuse under-counter lights with task lights. They often think under-counter lights are all that's needed for food prep at the counter. Not true: under-counters are basically mood lighting. I always suggest cans or track lights to supplement in areas where there are a lot of kitchen tasks being performed

Do you love recessed lights?
I do like them because they can be completely customized. But people in high-rises with concrete ceilings don't have the option of recessed lights so I recommend a good track or monorail system, as opposed to a light fixture in the center of the room.

—CASEY PENRY, OWNER
GLOW CONTRACT LIGHTING

THIS BARN-LIKE KITCHEN POSED AN ESPECIALLY PERPLEXING LIGHTING PROBLEM:
How do you provide task lighting in a kitchen with triple-height ceilings. The answer was to use custom island-top table lamps rather than overhead pendants, supplemented by track lighting angled to direct light exactly where it's needed.

. . . .

"Lighting a barn is really hard, because the overhead tracks are so high up. Greg Yale, the lighting designer, said, 'You'll need much more light than you think,' and of course he was right. I prefer low dramatic light, so they're all on rheostats. The ceiling is up-lit so it sort of glows at night. There's directed light down the middle of the counter and we lit the cabinet."

—INA GARTEN, COOKBOOK AUTHOR AND HOMEOWNER

Architect **Ken Pursley** put a new spin on task lighting by installing two double candlestick sconces by **Dennis & Leen** directly onto the backsplash inside this kitchen's range niche. The sconces provide sufficient light for cooking while their dark patina, elongated silhouette, and silk shades bring newfound elegance to the simple task of stirring a stew.

Chandeliers in the kitchen?

In a farmhouse? Why not! In her own rural kitchen, Kelley McDowell used a pair of wood and iron chandeliers from Circa Home Living and supplemented them with lots of spots on the rafters to direct light onto countertops. And the chandeliers' curves play beautifully off the square windows.

OVERSIZED BLACK LANTERNS ARE NECESSARY TO BALANCE AN EXTRA-LONG ISLAND AND HIGH CEILINGS.

·····································

"We needed a huge gesture over that 12' island. So we had double-size lanterns made, then used a pair."

—T. KELLER DONOVAN, DESIGNER

How do you pick a pendant light to hang over an island?

You know, that's a question I've been answering for ten years. When I first started in this business I was recommending those low-voltage mini-pendants over islands, just to keep things low key. But now kitchens have completely changed, they've become much bigger and islands are enormous. So pendants have to be larger too. You can't have a 12' island with a few small pendants above it, they'll disappear! I think to pull together these big, open family-room kitchens you need the kind of large-scale fixtures all the big manufacturers are coming out with. Little tiny lights over a big island look messy, almost like tchotchkes.

—CASEY PENRY, OWNER, GLOW CONTRACT LIGHTING

scullery

FORM FOLLOWS FUNCTION WITH
ECHOES OF THE BACK-OF-THE-HOUSE
PRACTICALITY OF AN OLD-WORLD
SERVICE KITCHEN.

REPEAT PERFORMANCE

JOAN SCHINDLER,
designer

Every great old country house
once had a kitchen like this.
"Cook" was queen of all she
surveyed and when she was
serving up a white-tie dinner
for forty her kitchen had
better work! This beautifully
updated version of that no-
nonsense kitchen combines
modern utility with the
romance of an age gone by.

THE BACKSTORY | "This kitchen in Lakeville, Connecticut, came together
through a happy marriage. I wanted the kitchen to look beautiful, and the
client, who's a really good cook, wanted it to work very, very well."

The hexagonal floor tile is
from Urban Archeology, but
the custom flower-pattern
design is based on a floor
Schindler saw in England

The Traulson glass-front fridge on the right is a "pass-through" refrigerator that opens on two sides—it can be accessed from the prep kitchen too. Nero Marquina marble countertops and twin 18th century light fixtures are understatedly elegant. The massive custom-made center island, with a butcher-block top, is on casters, but just for visual effect—it's too heavy to really move.

Pans, trays, and mixing bowls are stacked on the island's bottom shelf for easy access.

The tile floor is certainly beautiful. What was the inspiration?

I got the idea for the geometric flower pattern from a floor I saw at Harrods in London. For the white field, I used sheets of 12' x 12' meshed hexagonal tiles from Urban Archeology and then I had each flower mounted individually on 6" x 6" sheets. The subway tile on the walls is also from Urban Archeology, and it has a crackle finish that suggests mellowed age.

What about the floor plan?

Well, that great pass-through refrigerator that opens on both sides—into the main kitchen and the prep kitchen—was the client's idea. That really affected how the space laid out.

That fridge is a showstopper. Where did you find it?

It's custom. We found out no one made one, so we went to Traulsen. They were reluctant because they don't really do custom work, but I convinced them! So now the client has a 48"-wide, double-front, eight-door refrigerator.

HOW DID SCHINDLER SPEC SO MANY CONVENIENCES WHILE KEEPING AN ENTIRE BANK OF WINDOWS CABINET-FREE?

Four freezer drawers and an icemaker, both from Sub-Zero, plus two Incognito dishwashers from Miele— all with stainless steel fronts—sit underneath the counters. And Thermador warming drawers are in a lower cabinet next to the range.

THROUGHWAY

The little prep kitchen offers a more intimate scale for whipping up a snack or a quick meal for two on the Italian bluestone counter. The two-sided Traulsen refrigerator is on the left. Note Schindler's detailed use of rounded subway tiles on all edges. "We like the idea of soft and continuous flow of the walls, no sharp corners," she says. The use of white bronze for the hardware, from Sun Valley Bronze, also lends the kitchen a visual richness. Cabinets are painted Benjamin Moore Decorators White and all panes in the cabinets are restoration glass, which is uneven—for an old-fashioned feel.

BACKWARD GLANCE

IN THIS BUTLER'S PANTRY, A CABINET-MAKER BUILT LOWER CABINETS TO LOOK LIKE DRAWERS—DOWN TO THE WHITE-BRONZE PULLS FROM SUN VALLEY BRONZE— BECAUSE SCHINDLER THOUGHT DRAWERS UNDER THE COUNTERS WOULD BE IN KEEPING WITH THE 19TH-CENTURY MOOD.

"In the pantry, which is a kind of hall leading into the breakfast room, I felt that a bank of drawers should go under the counters because the horizontal lines look so beautiful, but my client wanted cabinets. So we compromised. They're cabinets, but the cabinetmaker made the doors look like drawers, right down to the custom white-bronze drawer pulls—so we're both happy! "

WHAT IF...
YOUR REFRIGERATOR HAD TWO FACES?

The custom stainless-steel pass-through refrigerator by Traulsen opens into the main kitchen on one side and into a small prep kitchen on the other. It feels very modern and yet old-fashioned at the same time.

TRIPLE PLAY
The polished nickel Franke Triflow Corinthian faucet has three levers— the front handle dispenses filtered water.

CRAVING...
A TILE FLOOR WITH AN EDWARDIAN VIBE.

A black-and-white hexagonal tile floor runs throughout the space, including this butler's pantry that connects to the breakfast room—it makes the whole layout feel like a country house's servants' kitchen (albeit one with formal panache). A hefty bronze towel rack, an English cow painting, and an antique chair with a drawer all pick up the color of the dark tile in the floor. Tile is installed the way it would have been done in an old utilitarian space, with large square tiles serving as a kick plate below rectangular subway tiles that extend to the ceiling.

The breakfast room really feels like an extension of the kitchen. That's why we used the same floor tile in there. We wanted it to feel like a gracious room too, so we chose this Italian Renaissance–style oak refectory table and a set of 1940s Belgian chairs. My favorite touch is the built-in china hutch, made of reclaimed pine, with a warm French polish. It's both useful and elegant—a great home for the client's mismatched blue-and-white English china. This room can be informal, for just the family, or more formal, for guests. I hate it when dining rooms don't get used. What's the point of a dining room if you don't eat in it?

A wide pantry connects this room to the main kitchen. This is both breakfast room and dining room. A simple Louis XIV chandelier lends the space a low-wattage opulence, and the client's collection of English blue-and-white china (extravagantly mis-matched) displayed in the pine hutch gives the room a homey sense of elegance and fun. The dining chairs, upholstered in Hinson's Warren Windowpane linen and walls papered in Hinson's Cumberland Stripe take the chill off the tile floors.

STALKING THE LOOK

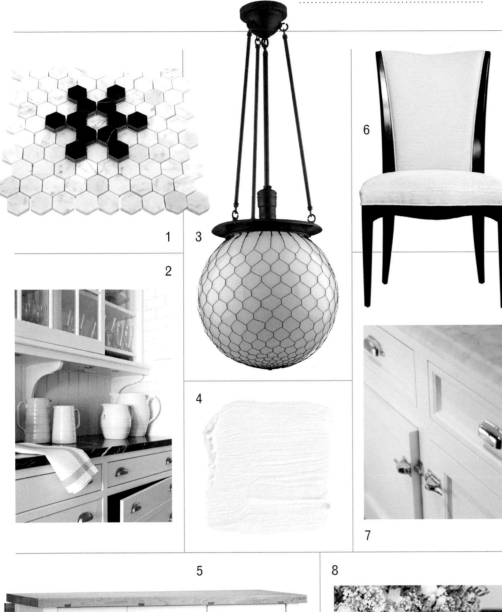

1

2

3

4

5

6

7

8

Start staring at your feet. Lower your gaze and be on the lookout for an old-style tile floor with a pattern you can copy and let loose underfoot in your kitchen. (And don't stop at the kitchen, run it under your dining table too!) Get creative with Walker Zanger's Tribeca Hexagon Field Tiles. (1)

Go to great lengths to maintain 19th century cred. (2) In the butler's pantry Shindler designed wavy window-paned upper cabinet doors that slide to open.

Find dramatic pendant lights that lend instant age. (3) This pendant's net design from 1908 was meant to catch glass if the globe broke. Rejuvenation's Hood with Wire Net comes in three globe sizes and thirteen finishes.

Don't get fancy. Drawers are flat fronted and cabinets have simple inverted panels and both are painted a very basic color, Benjamin Moore Decorators White, (4) in semi-gloss (for easy wipe-down).

Roll with it. (5) Get the look of this kitchen's industrial island-on-wheels with the Somerset Kitchen Island from Crate & Barrel.

Find chairs with crisp silhouettes to calm your patterned floor. (6) A Barbara Barry side chair feels elegant and comfy at the same time.

Remember you need closure. (7) Authentic details—that's what Christopher Peacock's Scullery Cabinetry is all about.

Convey a convivial French bistro. (8) Uncomplicated Gallic chic is born when an antique ironstone pitcher filled with garden flowers mixes with floral French dessert plates and white linens on the breakfast room table.

AMERICAN SPLENDOR

STEVEN GAMBREL,
designer

A genius blend of past and present, Gambrel's mission was to restore the Gibson Girl good looks of this 19th-century all-American beauty. He did such a masterful job concealing all the modern conveniences you half expect to see bell pulls and bustle-skirted maids.

TOP: It's hard to believe that the oak butler's pantry off the kitchen is brand new—it's such an authentic interpretation of a 19th-century pantry. Drawers for linens, windowed cabinets for glassware, and doors that slide aside to reveal stacked plates are tailored to fit the owners' needs. Brass hardware from **Nanz** was chosen for its period feel.

BOTTOM: Some shelves in the butler's pantry are backed in mercury glass which adds sparkle and shimmer to the rich dark wood. The door to the dining room is a copy of the kind of swinging door that would have been installed originally in a house of this era.

"These walls are brick with a crackled glaze. The grout is black. It was originally used for service kitchens. We referenced a kitchen in a 19th-century Vanderbilt mansion designed for a large staff. Of course, nobody has a staff wing anymore. The back of the house is the front of the house these days, right?"

"This is a large 19th-century Shingle style house in an old Connecticut port town, but it was in extremely bad shape. We redid it with authentic details but geared it toward a modern lifestyle."

"The client wanted her range in the island, facing out, so she could participate in the activity in the kitchen when she cooks."

AT YOUR SERVICE

This kitchen is modeled after the service kitchens found in grand old 19th-century American houses. Walls covered in Grove Brickworks from Waterworks and counters in Absolute Black granite have a utilitarian industrial look (once meant for hosing down). Gambrel designed the doors of the glass-front Klondike Case refrigerator to look like period cabinetry. The Lacanche range sits in the island beneath a hood designed by architect John Toates. Vintage stools further the strong masculine feel of the space.

ENGLISH COMPLEXION

DIONNE TRIFIRO,
designer

The duck-egg blue
cabinetry, the soft green
glass tiles—this kitchen looks
like you could fling open
its windows onto the lush
Devonshire countryside.
Trifiro mixed several different
Smallbone cabinet styles and
finishes to create the illusion
of a serviceable old farmhouse
kitchen that's evolved
over generations.

THE BACKSTORY | "This kitchen is an addition to an old house in Hewlett, New York, for a large family with young children. The house was built in 1913 and we wanted to keep that old-country-house feeling."

The mix of cabinetry by Smallbone of Devizes—two islands in the foreground from the Pilaster collection in oak, and an island/bench from the Original Hand Painted collection—contributes to this kitchen's easy nonchalance. A 48" Wolf range with two ovens, a Wolf Pro 48" refrigerator with glass door, and a 42" side-by-side Sub-Zero refrigerator convey the serious functionality here. A pot rack from Howard Kaplan with built-in lights and numbered hooks is based on an old French design.

"This is a brand new kitchen with all the latest appliances, but it doesn't have that hard edge. You walk into this lovely old house and it's just what you would expect to see—solid oak and hand-painted cabinets. You can feel the warmth."

Three islands! Why do you need three?
The first is kind of a mini-mudroom right by the back door. It has a bench where you can sit down and pull off your boots, a drawer for mail, and a counter for flower arranging just opposite one of the sinks. Then there's a prep island next to the Wolf range, the main refrigerator, and the main sink. The third island is more of a coffee bar, with stools facing the TV. The kids can do their homework or friends can sit there and have a glass of wine without getting in the cook's way. This is a large kitchen addition for a large family, and we broke it up into three areas to fit their day-to-day routine.

I notice you also broke up the cabinetry by doing several different finishes.
The oak was a logical choice for the two cooking islands, because it's hard-wearing and doesn't scuff as easily as paint. The cabinets against the wall were painted ivory to blend into the background. Then a decorative painter from Smallbone—this is all Smallbone cabinetry—came out on-site and custom-mixed that beautiful duck-egg-blue paint to highlight the beadboard around the bench and the old-fashioned china cabinet. That made them look more like separate pieces of furniture rather than built-ins.

"You know how you can never get a vase under the tap very easily? That's why you need a faucet with a tall spout, or better yet, an industrial-size pull-out sprayer. You can use it to fill a bucket or scour a roasting pan too."

Did you ever think about paneling the refrigerators? We had nothing to hide. After all, this is the 21st century and Sub-Zero has gone to a lot of effort to make them attractive. I did set the secondary refrigerator/freezer into the wall, and wrapped the main refrigerator with woodwork so the first thing you see as you come through the door is not the side of a refrigerator. But the front is quite appealing.

What are the counters made of? CaesarStone, in a color called Champagne Limestone. It's extremely hard-wearing. I much prefer it to granite, which is too speckly for me. You can't find a pure color in granite unless you're going for black. But if you want something light, it's CaesarStone or marble, and a lot of clients don't like marble because it can stain. I prefer to think of it as developing a patina, but some people don't see it that way.

TO BOOT
The bench seat, which is done in a natural finish, lifts up for more storage and cookbooks are stored in a shelf on one side. Pendant light from Ann-Morris Antiques stays true to the Old English mood. The industrial faucet at the sink that's used for flowers is the Dornbracht Meta.02 two-hole mixer with professional spray set. CaesarStone countertops in Champagne Limestone unifies and calms all the colors and finishes.

WHAT IF...
YOU "MIXED" AND DIDN'T WORRY ABOUT "MATCHED"?

White cabinets mix with a blue hutch, which mixes with oak islands. There's even an appliance garage with a stainless-steel door in the wall opposite the stools, which pulls down to hide the **TV** and coffee machine. Then to put a modern spin on country charm, **Case Study** stools from **Modernica** cozy up to the island and an under-counter **Sub-Zero UC-24R** holds beverages.

OUT OF THE COUNTRY
THE MHK110 FIRECLAY SINK BY FRANKE IS 28" LONG AND ALMOST 8" DEEP— AND SEEMS EVEN DEEPER SINCE IT HAS BEEN UNDER-MOUNTED. IT'S PAIRED WITH FRANKE'S MK28-36C STAINLESS-STEEL GRID, WHICH ALLOWS DISHES TO DRAIN. THE META.02 FAUCET AND RINSING SPRAY ARE BY DORNBRACHT. SMALLBONE ALSO MAKES THE PEWTER KNOBS THAT OPEN THE CABINETS.

"**N**othing says tradition quite like an old-fashioned farmhouse sink. I think the apron front is beautiful and you don't have to worry about scratching fireclay."

CRAVING...
A PLATE RACK THAT ISN'T JUST FOR SHOW; IT HOLDS *ALL* YOUR EVERYDAY DISHES.

"**T**he **P**ilaster plate rack in oak is one of **S**mallbone's signature pieces. **D**ishes and glassware used every day are within easy reach. "**M**ake sure your everyday dishes are stored near the dishwasher so you can unload straight onto the shelves."

"Hire a lighting designer—a very good investment. Contractors tend to put lights in willy-nilly but a lighting designer will know just what you need to achieve the right effect."

You've placed two thick slabs of marble on this cabinet just for rolling out dough?

Yes. I'll often tuck marble into a place where there's not so much traffic. That piece is called the pot board dresser, and it's been part of the Smallbone line from the beginning. The big square drawer has stainless-steel inserts for flour and sugar, and the lower level is just the right height for little helpers. **These special inserts are amazing . . .**

I think that's one of the real pleasures of Smallbone cabinetry. There are pull-outs and inserts for everything—cutlery, whisks, spice jars. They have a good-looking appliance garage with a tambour door that comes down and hides the coffee machine. I always put a stainless-steel liner in the cabinet under the sink to catch any drips. Pull-out stainless-steel bins in the pantry cupboard hold bread and pasta. Once you choose the pieces you want from the various collections, each item is individually made and custom-designed down to the square inch. I even did his-and-hers drawers, lined in gray felt, for sunglasses.

CAKEWALK
The pot board dresser in oak is the perfect baking stand and the freestanding dresser in duck-egg blue on the left keeps bowls and utensils nearby—both are from Smallbone's Pilaster collection but look as if they might have been found in an antiques shop. Glacier Bay glass tiles from Waterworks have a glossy finish and extend up to the ceiling, so any stray flour can be easily wiped down.

STALKING THE LOOK

Don't be afraid to divide your island acreage in half or even thirds. "When an island is too big it becomes dysfunctional. If you have to walk halfway around to get to the refrigerator or serve a bowl of cereal to your children it doesn't work," says Trifiro.

Turn a marble-topped cabinet into a baking station. (1) Thomas O'Brien's Lenox Kitchen Island through Hickory Chair is perfect for rolling out dough.

Hang a pendant with presence over your boot bench. (2) A replica of a vintage London streetlight, the Vintage Prism Pendant from Restoration Hardware, casts light up and down for even illumination.

Add a shot of modern. (3) Case Study Stools from Modernica are contemporary, fun, and easy to care for too.

Keep accessories within your color scheme. (4) Classic containers, contemporary colors—Martha Stewart Collection ceramic kitchen canisters at Macy's.

Be informal. (5) In a kitchen this easygoing any old pot on the shelf can turn into a vase.

Choose a floor that takes the pressure off your housekeeping. (6) This kitchen's floor is tiled with French flagstones, Bourgogne Claire limestone tiles from Paris Ceramics, distressed to look old then laid in a random pattern. The natural variation in color helps hide dirt and also breaks up the expanse of the room.

Pick blues and greens reminiscent of a misty morning in an English meadow like the (7) Glacier Bay glass tile in a glossy finish from Waterworks that Trifiro used in this kitchen.

Find a pot rack simultaneously beautiful and utilitarian. (8) Trifiro chose a pot rack from Howard Kaplan copied from a French antique with sliding hooks and built-in pendant lights.

HISTORY LESSON

JEFFREY BILHUBER
designer

Now here's an idea.
Do a retro-renovation and
return to a time when kitchens
were meant only for cooking.
Bilhuber created a single-
mindedly serious new kitchen
for his own 19th-century Locust
Valley home, then covered it
in a turquoise color so
lighthearted you can't help
but smile to see it.

TOP: Pots and pans hang casually floor-to-ceiling near the range. Bilhuber says parts of the house date back to 1668 and the scored-plaster walls and ceiling are meant to evoke the scratch coat found underneath the **D**elft tiles in **N**ew **Y**ork's early **D**utch settlers' kitchens.

BOTTOM: Set inside a sunny window, backless salvaged cupboards combine utilitarian glassware storage with decorative display.

Woodwork and open shelves in this new kitchen, painted Pratt & Lambert Pacific, both have a 19th-century aura. Floors painted Benjamin Moore Courtyard Green hide all manner of sins. Vintage lamps are mounted above salvaged sinks and black pendants from Ann-Morris Antiques hang from a scored-plaster ceiling. An enormous glass-paned refrigerator from True Manufacturing is the only visible nod to the 21st century.

"This is a working kitchen, not a place to congregate."

"A lot of household things are just the way they are. It's not just about being pretty. The details here are not invented flourishes. They have a reason for being, a function."

SMALL TALK

MICHAEL S. SMITH,
designer

It's as if Smith took an
enormous old service
kitchen and squeezed it into
a space the size of a butler's
pantry. With its Arthurian
looking range hood, hammered
from antiqued pewter, this
place looks like it might have
provided sustenance to
the Round Table. Or at
least their squires.

THE BACKSTORY | Smith transformed a 1950s ranch into a classic
English house for himself. "The kitchen is smaller than I would want—
I was restricted by the footprint of the old house—but it's really functional.
Everything is within reach."

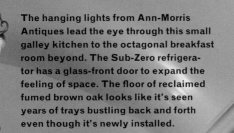

The hanging lights from Ann-Morris Antiques lead the eye through this small galley kitchen to the octagonal breakfast room beyond. The Sub-Zero refrigerator has a glass-front door to expand the feeling of space. The floor of reclaimed fumed brown oak looks like it's seen years of trays bustling back and forth even though it's newly installed.

How would you describe your kitchen?

It's not pretty English, it's more masculine English. My favorite rooms in English houses are entrance halls and kitchens because I like the severity of those spaces. Form follows function. In movies like Gosford Park, I'm always looking at all the back-of-the-house stuff. I wanted to play up the idea that this was a great old service kitchen.

It's a galley kitchen, but who even notices with that arched ceiling?

Edwin Lutyens, the great English architect, was all about shape, and this is my Lutyens barrel-vault ceiling. It gives a sense of ceremony to a narrow space.

Is the ceiling height what makes this kitchen feel so much bigger than it is?

That and the fact that the house is laid out as a sequence of rooms—laundry, pantry, kitchen—culminating in the breakfast room, like the light at the end of a tunnel.

So the enfilade of rooms lets you borrow space, in a way.

Exactly. The architecture sets up the vista, and the eye automatically goes to the farthest point. The glass-fronted refrigerator and cupboards also help by giving a sense that there's more depth, which makes the room feel less closed-in.

CREATIVE FLOW
On the backsplash, handmade Moroccan Bejmat tiles by Mosaic House have an opalescent quality. The grout is tinted taupe to suggest age and echo the Lagos Azul limestone counters from Walker Zanger. Both sink and faucet are from the Michael S. Smith Town Collection for Kallista. Architect Oscar Shamamian found room on the left for a shallow cupboard to hold a selection of teas.

It's both grand and modest—there's the vaulted ceiling, yet the cabinet hardware is straight out of the servant's quarters.

But every piece including the faucets and doorknobs is sterling-plated, which is softer and more beautiful than regular nickel. It's a finish that shifts with the light and changes, just like the limestone countertops. Citrus stains them, so every once in a while I'll have them cleaned, but I like the fact that they're not static.

People admire old stone but when it comes to their own house, they want something pristine. Not me. The floors are just waxed, no urethane. Everybody tried to talk me out of it, but putting anything else on them just doesn't give the same effect. I try to walk the walk. If I have counters that stain and floors that need to be waxed, then I can say with great confidence, "Hey, don't be afraid. It requires some maintenance, but it's worth it."

What prompted the octagonal breakfast room?
I just think it's pretty. It may be unfashionable these days to define rooms instead of leaving it all one giant unformed space, but I think humans like pleasing geometries and regular shapes. I leave the French doors open all the time. It's easy to go in and out—a standard part of the deal in California.

WHAT IF...
YOUR BREAKFAST ROOM LOOKED A LITTLE LIKE A GREEK TEMPLE?

The octagonal breakfast room gives Smith the pleasant sense of eating outside, while shielding him from the direct sunlight. Five pairs of French doors lead out to the terrace paved in Turkish travertine.

CRAVING...
AN EXHAUST HOOD THAT'S THE BIGGEST PERSONALITY IN THE ROOM.

"Oscar Shamamian, the architect who worked with me on the house, designed the hood—very Jules Verne meets the Industrial Revolution. The stove is a BlueStar, the best professional stove you can get for a house, according to my research."

TAKE A SEAT

You've got your whole kitchen pulled together—top to bottom, tile to flooring—everything is perfect! Time to pull up a stool at your fabulous new island and *relax*! You deserve it. What's that you say? Can't seem to find a barstool that fits? Here are some suggestions that'll knock you off your feet.

RESERVED SEATS

Why have counter and stool combinations become so popular?

"As dining rooms get squeezed out of existence, kitchen tables and islands now share all the family and entertaining seating. Parents have become short-order cooks with all their kids' activities. For empty nesters, counter stools are a place to sit and share in the meal prep with a spouse. And then for parties, counter stools invite guests into the cooking space with the host. They can sit with a glass of wine and chat with the cook. Stools fit all lifestyles."

—**KIMBALL DERRICK,** CKD AND PRESIDENT, BENTWOOD OF CHICAGO

" If we'd used regular backless stools, the kitchen might have looked like a luncheonette. The Windsor chair stools bring a furniture feel into the room."
—**T. KELLER DONOVAN,** DESIGNER

Sometimes the barstools are the coolest things in the room. Who knew truck springs could make such intriguing perches?
"These stools are giant springs, literally taken off a truck. I saw them at a salvage yard and thought they would look great by the island."
—**KEN FULK**, DESIGNER

ADVICE THAT HAS LEGS

What's the biggest mistake people make with counter seating?
"Too many stools. Each stool should have at least 24" of its own designated counter space. And watch out for the apron that runs beneath the counter. Aprons can be as much as 3"–6" deep. So if you've chosen a stool with a cushion and the counter itself is thick, you can end up with very little space between the top of your legs and the underside of the counter. Now you've got no crossing of legs, no moving of legs. It's a mistake a kitchen designer makes only once."
— **KIMBALL DERRICK,**
CKD AND PRESIDENT,
BENTWOOD OF CHICAGO

COUNTER STOOLS HAVE THE POWER TO MAKE A NEUTRAL KITCHEN SNAPPY.
Upholstered stools are a comfy way to infuse life, as long as the fabric is durable and sealed against stains. In designer Ruthie Sommers's own "California Beach-y" kitchen, vintage stools at the Calacatta marble island covered in laminated Pintura Studio linen, add a fresh dose of color to her all-white kitchen.

Stools can help the entire kitchen design hold together. Matching barstools to your breakfast area chairs is a great way to unify the space and keep the peace. In this kitchen by designer Markham Roberts, matching the Fouquet chairs to the Alma stools, both from **T&K French Antiques**, joins the separate zones and keeps all the pattern in this kitchen from overwhelming.

PRETTY PERCHES

Modernize.
Of powder-coated steel, Blu Dot's Real Good stool adds a lively jolt of contemporary style.

Add a Tropical Beat.
The Palm Garden from Baker Furniture is the perfect beach house perch.

Go for the Glam.
The Bel Aire stool from Currey & Company has a jazzy Hollywood Regency feel.

Hoof It.
The Bungalow Classic stool by BoBo Intriguing Objects has a whitewashed beech base with a contemporary take on hoof-foot legs.

Rock the Rococo.
The Lynx Armless stool by Drexel Heritage Furniture flaunts its curves!

Look Substantial.
The Marcello stool from Ballard Designs is as comfortably enveloping as a living room armchair.

Feel Closer.
The Slipcovered Counter Bench from Lee Industries is a homey departure from the two-stools formula for the kitchen island. It seats two comfortably (or romantically!)

Make it Go Away.
CB2's Vapor Stool is so streamlined, it's barely there.

Get the Laboratory Look.
With its aluminum frame and vinyl seat, the Nine-O from Emeco has chic industrial loft appeal.

Get Two Stools in One.
The seat on this Peddler's Home Design stool adjusts from 26" to 30" for either counter or bar height. And the backrest is removable for a more minimal look.

Get Naturally High.
The BassamFellows collection's Geometric stools from McGuire Furniture are crafted of natural materials—rattan and leather.

LEG ROOM

How much do you worry about knee space?

"Everyone is very careful to get the height of their stools right—usually 24" high for a counter stool and 30" for a bar. But that won't matter if you don't think about the space under your counter too. You don't want to be constantly banging your knees into the cabinetry. If your counter is bar height, 42" then you want at least 12" of knee-room for someone sitting there on a stool. As your counter heights go down you need more space, because the sitter's knees will protrude more. So if you have the standard 36" counter height, you need at least 15" of depth, and for something 30"tall (kitchen table height) you want to leave at least 18" for knees."

—KIMBALL DERRICK,
CKD AND PRESIDENT,
BENTWOOD OF CHICAGO

EVEN THE SIMPLEST BARSTOOLS CAN PACK DECORATIVE PUNCH. In this kitchen by designer **Tom Scheerer,** the pale wood legs and contrasting seats of **Thomas Moser's Coal Shovel** stools pick up the lively golden shades in the backsplash tiles.

Upholstered backless stools can blend into the background in a tight space.
Three Bongo Stools by Lee Industries are upholstered in fabric that echoes the color of the cabinets. "In a small space everything should blend, and using colors that blend is a way to unify furniture so it all becomes the same gesture, even though there are parts and pieces."

—SUSAN FERRIER, DESIGNER

A BIG MONOLITHIC ISLAND SEEMS SO MUCH LESS SERIOUS IF STOOLS HAVE A SENSE OF HUMOR. MYRA HOEFER'S A LA REINE STOOLS WITH GOAT'S FEET TUCK UNDER THIS OVERSIZED ISLAND.

"I'm in love with anything that has feet! You need a little eccentricity."

—MYRA HOEFER, DESIGNER

SIMPLE DARK BARSTOOLS BECOME DRAMATIC DIVAS IN AN ALL-WHITE KITCHEN. IN THIS KITCHEN, THE CURVES OF CHERNER STOOLS FROM ZINC DETAILS STAND OUT IN STRONG RELIEF.

"I like repeating geometric patterns. Look at the way the barstools line up in the kitchen, the organic rhythm of them—that feels right to me."

—JEAN LARETTE, DESIGNER

What goes through a kitchen pro's mind when choosing barstools?
"A stool with a high lacquer finish is going to pretty quickly show wear. Stained or naturally finished wood on the other hand can be touched up and it can take a lot of abuse without showing, and of course metal always wears well. You'll get the most comfort from a cushioned surface but the fabric needs to be laminated or treated to prevent stains. Leather is durable, but leather and vinyl can be a problem in summer because they stick to bare skin, making it difficult to get down from the stool."

What if I want a back on my stool?
"If your stool has a back it's going to protrude into the room more so you have to make sure you have enough space. Measure to be sure that there is approximately 60" of space from your overhanging countertop to the cabinetry in the wall behind. You need 24" for the stool to be pulled out from the counter and then at least another 36" so someone sitting on the stool doesn't block traffic. In a very confined space it's better to go with a backless stool that pushes all the way under the counter."

—KIMBALL DERRICK,
CKD AND PRESIDENT,
BENTWOOD OF CHICAGO

"This kitchen has a classic, timeless quality," says designer Mona Ross Berman, "with a few fun pops of color to keep it from being staid and predictable"—like the fanciful valance in Arcadia Sulphur by Raoul Textiles and the Modwalls glass tile backsplash.

PHOTOGRAPHY CREDITS

COVER
Photographed Francesco Lagnese/Studio D. Prop styling by Penelope Bouklas
6 Victoria Pearson

CHAPTER 1
8-9 Ngoc Minh Ngo
10-11 Reed Davis
12-13 Reed Davis (4)
14-15 Reed Davis (stove, 3, 6); David Turner/Studio D (4); Lara Robby/Studio D (5)
16-17 Thomas Loof
18-19 Thomas Loof (4)
20-21 Thomas Loof (dining room, 4); Lara Robby/Studio D (3)
22-23 Eric Piasecki (3)
24-25 Reed Davis
26-27 Reed Davis (4)
28-29 Reed Davis (patio, 1); Philip Friedman/Studio D (5, 6)
30-31 Luca Trovato
32-33 Luca Trovato (4)
34-35 Luca Trovato (dining room, kitchen, 4); Lara Robby/Studio D (2, 3)
36-37 Pieter Estersohn (4)
38-39 Clockwise from top middle left: Karyn Millet; Erik Kvalsvik (2); Nathan Schroder (2); Ngoc Minh Ngo; Jonny Valiant; James Carrière
40-41 Clockwise from left: Thomas Loof; Laura Moss; James Carrière

42-43 Clockwise from left: Karyn Millet; Victoria Pearson (2)
44 James Carrière
46-47 From top: José Picayo; Karyn Millet

CHAPTER 2
48-49 Ngoc Minh Ngo
50-51 Ngoc Minh Ngo (dining room); Lara Robby/Studio D (2, 4); Philip Friedman/Studio D (5)
52-53 Francesco Lagnese
54-55 Francesco Lagnese (4)
56-57 Francesco Lagnese (kitchen, 3, 4, 5); David Turner/Studio D (2); Lara Robby/Studio D (6)
58-59 Victoria Pearson
60-61 Eric Piasecki
62-63 Eric Piasecki (floor, 2, 5, 6)
64-65 Laura Moss
66-67 Laura Moss (4)
68-69 Laura Moss (kitchen); Lara Robby/Studio D (1); Philip Friedman/Studio D (6)
70-71 Thomas Loof
72-73 Thomas Loof (4)
74-75 Thomas Loof (kitchen, 1, 4); Jose Picayo (2)
76-77 Eric Piasecki
78-79 Mikkel Vang (3)
81 Nathan Schroder (2)
82-83 Clockwise from middle left: Durston Saylor; Eric Piasecki; Simon Upton; Ellen McDermott; Dominique Vorillon (2); Thomas Loof

84-85 Clockwise from left: Victoria Pearson; Karyn Millet; Ellen McDermott
86 From top: Victoria Pearson; James Carrière
88 John Kernick

CHAPTER 3
90-91 Eric Piasecki
92-93 Eric Piasecki (4)
95-96 Eric Piasecki (kitchen); Philip Friedman/Studio D (3); Lara Robby/Studio D (4)
97-98 William Abranowicz/Art + Commerce
99-100 William Abranowicz/Art + Commerce (3)
101-102 William Abranowicz/Art + Commerce (kitchen, 2); Ellen McDermott (4); David Turner/Studio D (6)
103-104 Don Freeman (3)
105-106 Ellen McDermott
107-108 Ellen McDermott (4)
108-109 Ellen McDermott (cabinets); Philip Friedman/Studio D (6)
110-111 Victoria Pearson (2)
112-113 Clockwise from left: Ellen McDermott; James Carrière; Michael Grimm
114-115 Thomas Loof (kitchen); Karyn Millet (pot); Julian Wass (sink)
116-117 Karyn Millet (left)
118-119 Victoria Pearson (top left); Miki Duisterhof (bottom left); Lisa Romerein (bottom right)

CHAPTER 4
120-121 Julian Wass
122-123 John M. Hall
124-125 John M. Hall (4)
126-127 John M. Hall (kitchen, 1); Philip Friedman/Studio D (5)
128-129 Amy Neunsinger
130-131 Amy Neunsinger (dining room, 1); Philip Friedman/Studio D (2); Lara Robby/Studio D (3)
132-133 Karyn Millet
134-135 Eric Roth
136-137 Eric Roth (4)
138-139 Eric Roth (kitchen, 3); Lara Robby/Studio D (2)
140-141 Jonny Valiant (2)
142-143 Julian Wass
144-145 Julian Wass (4)
146-147 Julian Wass (kitchen); Lara Robby/Studio D (3, 4); Philip Friedman/Studio D (5)
148-149 Francesco Lagnese (3)
150-151 Francesco Lagnese (8)
152-153 Laura Moss (kitchen); Gridley + Graves (1)
154-155 Clockwise from bottom right: Simon Upton; Eric Piasecki
156-157 Karyn Millet (kitchen); Philip Friedman/Studio D (rug)
158-159 Clockwise from top left: James Merrell; Jonny Valiant; Jonn Coolidge; Joshua Allen

CHAPTER 5

160-161 Gridley + Graves
162-163 Gridley + Graves (kitchen); Jose Picayo (3); Philip Friedman/Studio D (4, 5)
164-165 Eric Piasecki
166-167 Eric Piasecki (4)
168-169 Eric Piasecki (sink, 1, 3, 5)
170-171 Quentin Bacon
172-173 Clockwise from top right: Quentin Bacon (3); David Turner/Studio D
174-175 Quentin Bacon (kitchen); Lara Robby/ Studio D (5, 6)
176-177 Francesco Lagnese (3)
178-179 Julian Wass
180-181 Julian Wass (kitchen, cabinets, 2, 3); Philip Friedman/Studio D (1); Lara Robby/Studio D (4)
182-183 Clockwise from left: Ngoc Minh Ngo; Thomas Loof; Eric Piasecki
184-185 Thomas Loof (left)
186-187 Clockwise from top left: Jonny Valiant; Francesco Lagnese; Laura Moss; Dominique Vorillon

CHAPTER 6

188-189 Gridley + Graves
190-191 Gridley + Graves (3)
192-193 Gridley + Graves (5)
194-195 Frances Janisch
196-197 Frances Janisch (kitchens, pitchers, 1); Lara Robby/Studio D (2); David Turner/Studio D (3, 5); Jose Picayo (4);
198-199 Karyn Millet (3)
200-201 Julian Wass
202-203 Julian Wass (4)
204-205 Julian Wass (6)

206-207 Thomas Loof (3)
208-209 Joe Schmelzer
210-211 Joe Schmelzer (4)
212-213 Joe Schmelzer (kitchen); Philip Friedman/Studio D (1, 5); Lauren Burke/Getty Images (2); Lara Robby/ Studio D (3)
214-215 Annie Schlechter
216-217 Annie Schlechter (4)
218-219 Clockwise from left: James Carrière; Pieter Estersohn; Frances Janisch
220-221 Clockwise from top left: Jose Picayo; John Gould Bessler; Victoria Pearson; Ngoc Minh Ngo; Pieter Estersohn
222-223 Clockwise from left: Francesco Lagnese; Julian Wass; Nathan Schroder; Trevor Tondro; Julian Wass; Annie Schlechter (3)

CHAPTER 7

224-225 Simon Watson/ Trunkarchive.com
226-227 Nathan Schroder
228-229 Nathan Schroder (4)
230-231 Nathan Schroder (dining room, 3); Lara Robby/Studio D (4); Philip Friedman/ Studio D (5)
232-233 Reed Davis (3)
234-235 Julian Wass
236-237 Julian Wass (4)
238-239 Julian Wass (stove, 1); David Turner/ Studio D (2, 3, 4); Lara Robby/Studio D (5)
240-241 Reed Davis
242-243 Gridley + Graves
244-245 Gridley + Graves (4)
246-247 Gridley + Graves (kitchen)

248-249 Julian Wass (3)
250-251 From left: Amy Neunsinger; Don Freeman
252-253 Clockwise from top left: Tria Giovan; Francesco Lagnese; Amy Neunsinger; Eric Piasecki; Lizzie Himmel
254-255 Clockwise from top left: Laura Moss; Victoria Pearson; Karyn Millet; Victoria Pearson
256-257 Clockwise from left: Christopher Baker; Tria Giovan; Jose Picayo; Oberto Gili
258-259 Clockwise from left: Luca Trovato; Don Freeman; Victoria Pearson; Joshua McHugh
260-261 Clockwise from left: Eric Piasecki; John Kernick; Tria Giovan (2)

CHAPTER 8

262-263 Gridley + Graves
264-265 Gridley + Graves (4)
266-267 Gridley + Graves (kitchen); Lara Robby/ Studio D (1, 2); Philip Friedman/Studio D (4); David Turner/Studio D (5)
268-269 Thomas Loof (3)
270-271 Lucas Allen
272-273 Lucas Allen (3)
274-275 Lucas Allen (kitchen, 3, 4)
276-277 John Kernick
278-279 John Kernick (4)
280-281 John Kernick (6)
282-283 Ellen McDermott
284-285 Ellen McDermott (4)
286-287 Clockwise from bottom right: Eric Piasecki (2); William Abranowicz/Art + Commerce
288-289 Left: Francesco Lagnese

290-291 Clockwise from top left: Simon Upton; Victoria Pearson; Pieter Estersohn; John Gould Bessler

CHAPTER 9

292-293 Lucas Allen
294-295 Lucas Allen (5)
296-297 Lucas Allen (kitchen, 4, 8); Lara Robby/Studio D (3)
298-299 Simon Watson/ Trunkarchive.com (3)
300-301 Miki Duisterhof
302-303 Miki Duisterhof (4)
304-305 Miki Duisterhof (kitchen, 5); Studio D (4)
306-307 Thomas Loof (3)
308-309 Grey Crawford
310-311 Grey Crawford (3)
312-313 Clockwise from left: John Gould Bessler; Victoria Pearson (2)
314-315 Left: Thomas Loof
316-317 Clockwise from left: Matthew Hranek; Francesco Lagnese; Reed Davis; Thomas Loof

PHOTOGRAPHY CREDITS

318 Jonny Valiant
321 Victoria Pearson

GENERAL INDEX

322 Miki Duisterhof

In designer Summer Thornton's Chicago kitchen, high style means high contrast. Black cabinets by Custom Woodcraft are topped with white Carrara marble from the Countertop Factory. The Fairmount Art Deco pendant by Rejuvenation picks up the black-and-white theme. Bentwood barstools from Kurt Petersen.

GENERAL INDEX

A

Accent wall scene-stealer, 178–181

Accessories. *See also* Collections

authentic-item example, 232–233

backlighting, 53

canned goods as, 209, 213

color of, 193, 305

natural, 175

unusual, 15, 51

white, 51

"Addicted to Alabaster" kitchens

about: definition of, 122

Balancing Act (sleek modern), 140–141

Carte Blanche (white-on-white-on-white chic), 142–147

Set Piece (Hamptons movie set–inspired), 132–133

Simply Spotless (clean and pristine), 134–139

Tickling the Ivories (quintessential white kitchen), 122–127

White Noise (industrial elegance), 128–131

Antique collection on display, 242–247

Armoires, 39, 145, 146

B

Backsplashes, 182–187. *See also* Backsplashes (tile)

balancing counter pattern with, 182

bamboo, 37

bluestone, 38

boulder/stone, 13, 14, 15

concrete-look, 16–17, 18–19, 21

contrasting against cabinets, 283

Dutch "gable," 91, 95

glass, 99

granite, 67, 166, 271

lesson on, 182–187

marble, 72, 98–99, 138, 141, 183

material selection, 182

mirrored, 61

outlets hidden in, 215

Pietra del Cardoso dark stone, 215, 216

ranges with, 101

soapstone, 184

stainless-steel, 68, 182, 220

subway-tile, 182

tiles and flooring, 186, 187

Backsplashes (tile)

Arabesque/Moroccan/ Syrian, 185, 240–241, 310

crackle, 185

diamond-shaped/ hexagonal, 115

French-style, 81, 83, 238

gallery of, 185

glass, 187

handmade vintage-look, 186

harlequin pattern, 261

Kariota, 53

lively golden shades, 316

Mexican white, 162

mini subway-tile, 185

mosaics, 185, 186

multicolor, arranging tile, 187

one-of-a-kind, 185

onyx, 185

scenes in, 238

striped, 185

subway-tile, 123, 143, 149, 173, 185, 208–209, 269, 293

Baking

marble countertops and, 251, 252, 263, 304, 305

station, cabinet as, 304, 305

Bars

classic authentic-feel, 41

high buffet, 33

outfitting, 41

sinks, 66, 210

stainless wet bar, 41

stools and chairs, 22, 24–25, 41, 77, 210, 245, 271, 313, 314, 315–317

Basalt countertops, 25

Baskets, 75, 161, 163, 194, 197, 198, 205, 215, 233, 237, 239, 278, 279

Beige paint colors. *See* Paint and stain colors

"Belle de Campagne" kitchens

about: definition of, 226

C'est Chic (French-chateaux inspired), 226–231

French Confection (romantic patisserie feel), 234–239

Hue La La (colorful farmhouse look), 248–249

Made in the Shade (old-world castle feel), 240–241

Objects of Desire (antique collection on display), 242–247

Vive la France (charming French country feel), 232–233

Benjamin Moore paints

about: Aura low-VOC collection, 152

Ancient Ivory, 272

Atrium White, 20, 192

Aura in Hancock Green, 148

Blue Springs, 177

Cayman Islands, 273, 275

Champion Cobalt, 174

Classic Gray, 269

Cloud White, 195

Courtyard Green, 307

Cucumber Salad 562, 80

Danville Tan, 251

Decorators White, 51, 126, 294, 297

Dove White, 285

Elmira White, 68

Evening Dove, 34

Horizon, 77

Linen White, 206

Moroccan Red, 58–59

Mysterious AF-565, 80

November Rain, 230

Polo Blue, 110

River Reflections, 20

Sail Cloth, 68

Scarecrow, 284

South Beach 5043-50, 82

Super White, 141, 146

Tudor Brown, 160–161, 163

White Dove, 132

White Down 970, 94

Blue kitchens, 170–175, 176–177, 178–181

Blue paint colors. *See* Paint and stain colors

Bluestone
　countertop, 294
　flooring, 105, 109
Bohemian cottage
　wannabe, 10–15
Bowls, 15, 21, 37, 48, 193, 205
"Bravura" kitchens
　(bold vision with
　flair). *See* "Haute
　So Functional"
　kitchens; "Rebel"
　kitchens; "Rough
　Luxe" kitchens
Break-out sessions
　color consult, 78–83
　going green, 148–153
　island overview, 250–255
　kitchen planner, 36–41
Brown paint colors. *See*
　Paint and stain colors
Butcher block
　countertops/islands, 31,
　126, 181, 190, 191,
　193, 199, 214–215,
　216, 234, 243, 246,
　247, 249, 251,
　256, 293
　cutting boards, 37,
　168, 229

C

Cabinet/drawer hardware
　aged look, 274
　box latches, 196
　brass, 101, 102, 163
　buying tip, 180
　custom smooth steel,
　216, 217
　French-style, 72
　leather handles, 279
　mismatched, 15
　polished nickel, 147,
　278, 281
　reflecting stove knobs, 31
　simple, 57
　unobtrusive/
　inconspicuous, 16, 102
　updating, 56
　white-bronze, 294

Cabinets, 218–223. *See
　also* Armoires;
　Cabinets (colors and
　materials); China
　cabinets; Islands;
　Shelving (open)
above doorways, 274
appliances matching,
　42, 68. *See also
　specific appliances*
backless, on marble, 216
as baking stations,
　304, 305
changing feel of
　kitchen, 220
chicken-wire grilles,
　13, 15, 288
choosing, 40, 218–222
custom, flexibility of, 34
custom-made Japanese-
　inspired, 164–165, 167
display/storage above,
　37, 245
exhaust hood
　camouflaged as, 165
farmhouse-style, 108
framed painting
　hiding, 107
French-style, 227,
　228, 242–251
glass-front, 30, 66, 69,
　78, 82, 83, 122, 172,
　199, 208–209, 217,
　234–235, 278, 298
glass-front with
　curtains, 284, 285
gray painted, 34
hidden behind touch-
　latch panels, 105
hiding small appliances,
　74, 136, 149, 223
icebox look, 276–277
layout, 40
leaded glass fronts,
　234–235
lesson on, 218–223
lighting under, 126
metal, advantages, 65
minimizing, 263, 267
mirror-backed, 287

mirror-front, 13, 15, 222
Nantucket-style, 177
new old-look, 248–249
new Victorian, 270–287
optimizing inside
　space, 61, 62, 63
outdoor kitchen, 25, 29
overhead, storage and, 274
as pantries, 20, 60, 63,
　146, 190
plate racks instead of.
　See Plate racks
pull-outs in, 165,
　278, 281
replacing or refacing/
　repainting, 56
resembling furniture,
　98, 101
salvaged, 195, 197
small spaces, 60–61, 62
turned posts/rope trim
　on, 236, 238, 239
turquoise painted,
　78–79
varying finishes on, 301
wood floor, ceiling
　and, 221
Cabinets (colors
　and materials)
blending with decor,
　90–91, 95
brown painted,
　160–161, 163
butternut wood,
　270–275
cobalt blue, 170–175
color palettes, 78–83,
　100, 230, 238, 274, 275
dark lower/light
　upper, 163
distressed wood, 11, 15
oak, 71, 103, 300–301
powder-coated stainless
　steel, 65, 66–67, 69
reclaimed poplar, 23
recycled, 150
smoky gray blue, 177
stainless-steel, 25, 27,
　29, 65, 66, 69, 136, 216

walnut, 16–17, 18,
　19, 165, 166–167,
　276–277
white, 37, 48, 49, 58–
　59, 90–91, 113, 122–
　123, 126, 127, 135,
　138, 142–147, 180,
　199, 217, 234–235,
　287, 294, 316
CaesarStone, 52–53, 56,
　57, 158, 177, 277,
　278, 302
Canned goods as art,
　208–213
Ceilings
beadboard, 133, 143,
　147, 181, 192, 244
beamed, 22, 40,
　104–105, 227, 249,
　270–271, 285
brick-covered, 240–241
coffered, 128–129, 210,
　212, 213, 273
curvilinear/arched,
　160–161, 162, 163,
　195, 308–309
double-height, 137, 139
extra tall, making
　intimate, 82, 234–
　235, 239
low, enhancing, 40
theatrical design on, 83
tin tiles on, 234–235
vaulted/cathedral,
　68, 142–143, 145,
　160–161, 240–241,
　290, 291
wood, 221
Chairs. *See also* Stools
antique with drawer, 295
banquettes instead of, 75
Belgian dining, 296
black wicker, 212
to calm patterned
　floor, 297
club, 202, 203
cushions, 28, 195,
　230, 231, 249
Danish, 192

dark, good-looking, 144, 147
dark brown woven, 213
desk, 37, 145, 203, 207
English ladderback, 144
European antique, 110–111
French metal, 194–195
Italian fabric-covered, 74
leather, 10–11, 64–65, 69, 109
lesson on seating, 312–317
Louis XVI repro, 32, 36
matching to barstools, 275, 314
outdoor furniture, 27, 28, 232
plywood, 77
red painted, 58–59
red Windsor, 285
slipcovered, 32, 203, 204
upholstery matching lampshades, 49, 50, 51
walnut Nakashima, 164–165, 166, 169
wingback, 111
Chef's kitchen, 200–205
China cabinets
elevated, for easy access, 262
Martha Stewart brand, 35
woven wire grille for, 15
Christopher Peacock Paint
Mercury CPP1 18, 82
Satsuma, 82
Scullery White, 280
Collections
atop cabinets, 160, 162
candlesticks, 13
Chinese porcelain, 35, 173
pitchers, 15, 123, 194–195, 196, 197
plates, 15, 35, 199, 296
pottery, 192, 242–245, 246, 247, 268
prints, 101

shelves/cabinets for, 13, 111, 192, 199, 228, 230, 242–245, 246, 268, 296
Colors. See also Cabinets (colors and materials); Paint and stain colors; specific paint company names
accessories adding, 193
consult session, 78–83
contrasting light and dark, 18, 21
"Composed" kitchens (balance, rhythm, subtle elegance). See "Addicted to Alabaster" kitchens; "Plain Spoken" kitchens; "Shopkeeper" kitchens
Concrete
backsplashes looking like, 16–17, 18–19, 21
color mixed with, 28
countertops, 81, 84, 255, 260
raw-look wall, 130
tiles and flooring, 26, 81, 129, 131, 157, 232
Cooktops. See also Ranges
benefits of, 284
blending in, 91, 95
doubling as countertop, 61, 63
downdraft, 53, 56, 57, 243, 280
electric, 53, 56, 57, 61, 63, 84, 280
gas, 84, 87, 91, 193, 283
gas vs. induction vs. electric, 84
induction, 84, 87, 205
in islands, 53, 57, 193, 205, 245, 280, 283
in outdoor grill, 27, 29
ovens in separate room from, 93

Viking, 245
without knobs, 53, 57
Cooktops (brands)
Bulthaup, 87
Fischer & Paykel, 63, 193
Jenn-Air, 53, 56, 57
Miele, 87, 283
Thermador, 87
Viking, 91, 95
Countertops, 256–261. See also Granite countertops; Limestone countertops; Marble countertops
balancing pattern with backsplash, 182
basalt, 25
blending into living room, 253, 254
butcher-block, 31, 126, 181, 190, 191, 193, 199, 214–215, 216, 234, 243, 246, 247, 249, 251, 256, 293
CaesarStone, 52–53, 56, 57, 158, 177, 277, 278, 302
choosing, 40, 57, 197, 267, 275. See also maintenance considerations
color cue from, 253
concrete, 81, 84, 255, 260
contrasting light and dark, 18, 21, 283
cooktops doubling as, 61, 63
eco-friendly, 150
edge types (ogee, double-ogee, rounded, square), 256
extra thick, 106, 142–143, 245, 258, 260, 304
galvanized metal, 232
glass, 259
Italian bluestone, 294
lava stone, 261
lesson on, 256–261

L-shaped, 24–25
maintenance considerations, 209, 257, 261
oak, 252, 255
onyx, 258
Pietra Cardosa, 143, 145
Pietra del Cardoso, 214, 216
from recycled materials, 261
serving spoons on, 205
sinks and, 113, 168
slate, 158, 257
slatelike, 143, 261
in small spaces, 60–61
soapstone, 129, 184, 209, 233, 257, 264, 267, 283
space needed, 201, 278, 280
Squak Mountain Stone, 261
stainless-steel, 91, 92, 166, 168, 254, 259
stools with. See Stools
wall ovens and, 40
wall-mounted faucets and, 112
walnut, 18
zinc, 23

D

Dining-room kitchen, 102–103
Dishwashers. See also Dishwashers (brands)
concealed behind panels, 138, 167, 218, 236, 248, 251
drawers, 12, 15, 118, 119, 167, 251
heating units in, 119
in islands, 66, 105, 126, 263
longer wash times, 119
models and sizes, 118–119, 140, 280

multiple, 37, 62, 92, 118, 126, 132, 148, 176, 210, 236, 280, 293
in other rooms, 62, 135
quiet, 62, 119
stainless-steel, 40, 118, 119
storage near, 303
top features of, 119
Dishwashers (brands)
Bosch, 118, 126, 248, 251, 272
Dacor, 119
Fischer & Paykel, 118, 167
GE, 119, 140
Jenn-Air, 56, 119
KitchenAid, 12
Miele, 62, 118, 132, 138, 174, 293
Viking, 48, 119
Donald Kaufman Color, DKC-3, 138
Drawers. *See also* Cabinet/ drawer hardware; Cabinets
adjustable pegs in, 57
as cabinet door, 31
cabinets looking like, 294
dishwasher, 12, 15, 118, 119, 167, 251
embossed labels on, 279
instead of cabinets, 68, 274
microwave, 89, 251
for one-stop table setting, 188
organizing/customizing, 137, 139, 223, 281, 304
pot, 67, 136
pull-out, 223
refrigerator/freezer, 45, 46, 75, 83, 174, 177, 237, 251, 293
silverware, 35, 63, 281
simple, 297
solid walnut, 19
spice, 63

warming ovens, 87, 89, 148, 176, 251
Drying racks, 115, 117, 203

E
Eco in Black Forest, 150
Eco-friendly tips and products, 148–153, 159, 261

F
Farrow & Ball paints
Hardwick White, 34
Lamp Room Gray, 253
Pigeon, 108
Skylight, 113
Teresa's Green 236, 80, 221
Fashionable kitchens. *See* "Haute So Functional" kitchens
Faucets, 112–117. *See also* Faucets (brands)
arched/gooseneck, 21, 63, 115, 116, 140, 151, 168, 169, 179, 181
articulated (multijointed), 55, 115
brass finish, 115, 243
bridge, 73, 112, 151, 199, 310
bronze, 113
copper, 114
gallery of, 115
hands-free, 279
industrial sink sprayers, 30, 35, 92, 95, 114, 129, 131, 136, 137, 176, 191, 302
lesson on sinks and, 112–117
nickel, 73, 126, 133, 162, 295
placement and functionality, 112
pot, over sink, 198
pot, over stove, 71, 75, 115, 136, 140, 210, 228, 238

prep-sink, 66, 93
single-lever, 115, 183
sink without, 55
sterling-plated, 310
triflow filtered water, 63, 115, 251, 295
utilitarian sprayer, 35
varying between islands, 210
wall-mounted, 108, 112, 196
wing-like silhouette, 98

Faucets (brands)
American Standard, 117
Barber Wilsons, 138
Brizo, 66, 115
Danze, 30, 140
Delta, 279
Dornbracht, 93, 102, 116, 174, 179, 181, 302, 303
Elkay, 35
Franke, 113, 168, 169, 191, 295
Graff, 25
Grohe, 162, 210
Hansgrohe, 18, 21
Harrington Brass Works, 115, 228, 283
Kallista, 310
Kohler, 55, 113, 115, 151, 210
KWC, 98, 246, 248
Perrin & Rowe, 71, 73, 75, 112, 115, 236
Rohl, 63
Schon, 140
T&S Brass, 136, 137, 139
Waterworks, 114, 126, 131, 132
Westbrass, 176
Fireplaces
dramatic stone, 264
French cooking, mimicking look of, 229
outdoor kitchen, 28, 29
small elevated, 71, 73

Tuscan grill inset, 124, 125, 127
wood-fired, 125
Flooring, 154–159
choosing, 40, 154–159, 305
concrete, 128–129, 131
lesson on, 154–159
linoleum, 159
rugs, 105, 109, 132, 157, 240, 267
sanded/sealed glue as, 92
slightly distressed, 132–133
stone. *See* Flooring (tile and stone)
wood. *See* Flooring (wood)
Flooring (tile and stone)
black-and-white checkerboard, 154
bluestone, 105, 109
brick, 158, 233
caring for, 154
chemicals and, 154
creative designs, 157
geometric flower pattern in hexagonal tile, 157, 292–293, 295, 296
limestone, 134–135, 156, 249, 305
low-maintenance appeal of, 305
marble, 110
mosaic tile, 216, 217
sealing, 154
terra cotta, 124, 127, 155, 240–241, 246
travertine tile, 226–227
unglazed white, 138
Flooring (wood)
ash (colorful stained), 157
bamboo, 150, 152
blue painted, 177
blue painted stripes, 32, 34, 35
crest in, 62, 63

dark, with pale wood above, 221
dark, in white kitchen, 144, 146, 147, 235
eco-friendly, 152
elm (light or antique), 18, 21, 53
graywashed ash, 68
green and gray stained, 251
green painted, 307
laminate, 152
maintaining, 159
oak, 71, 235, 255, 272, 308–309
pine, 155, 162, 192, 266, 267, 284
sanding, effects of, 155
stains and finishes, 157, 159, 251, 310
walnut, 10–11, 164, 212, 230, 280
white painted, 50, 51, 207
wood cabinets, ceiling and, 221
Flowers (bouquets), 147, 163, 175, 204, 297
Fountain wall, 27
French style. See "Belle de Campagne" kitchens

G

Garden-party outdoor kitchen, 24–29
Geothermal energy, 149, 150
Glidden paints
White on White, 204
Wood Smoke, 204
Granite backsplashes, 67, 166, 271
Granite countertops
Absolute Black, 116, 299
basalt vs., 25
Bianco Tuscano, 228
CaesarStone vs., 302
clean lines, 64–65
Costa Esmeralda, 251
curved, 227
Galaxy, 257

Indian Premium black, 209
Jurassic Green, 67, 69
look-alike, 150
marble vs., 172, 180, 228, 257
Pine Valley green, 164, 166, 167
pros and cons, 67, 81, 228, 257, 259, 302
Typhoon Green, 271, 275
Gray paint colors. See Paint and stain colors
Green, going. See Eco-friendly tips and products
Green paint colors. See Paint and stain colors
Grills
built-in, 176
outdoor, 27, 29
Tuscan, fireplace inset, 124, 125, 127
Grout
with brick walls, 299, 310
color considerations, 183
glass and, 99, 181
invisible, in mosaic backsplash, 185
subway-tile backsplash, 182
types and characteristics, 158

H

Hardware. See Cabinet/drawer hardware
"Haute So Functional" kitchens
about: definition of, 48
Bright Star (bold with cutting-edge appliances), 52–57
Close Encounters (chic small space), 60–63
English Pop (straitlaced white to stylish), 58–59

Farm Nouveau (Provence inspired), 70–75
Gulf Course (beach house with views), 64–69
Pizzazz (color and joy), 48–51
True Original (old-fashioned to snappy), 76–77
Hoods
beadboard-covered, 143
brass and stainless, 59
cabinet panels blending in, 165
cartouche on, 83
as focal points, 59, 68, 84, 86, 176, 299, 311
galvanized, patinated, 38
going without, 56
limestone/limestone finish, 79, 84
low-profile, 87
matte graphite finish, 198
professional features on, 139
raising, on cooktops, 245
sheetrock-clad, 141
stainless-steel, 68, 72, 132–133, 136, 170–171, 176, 181
tile on, 123, 238
wood-clad, 271, 275
zinc, 38, 240

I

Ice-cream parlor feel, 194–197
Insider intel, 40–41, 152
Islands, 250–255. See also Countertops; Limestone countertops; Marble countertops
basket drawers under, 237

cabinets/drawers in, 16–17, 18, 19, 66, 105, 136, 149, 165, 199, 200–201, 220, 221, 250–255, 272, 283
candy-store counter as, 24–25
color cue, 253
conveniences in/on, 251
cooktops in, 53, 57, 193, 205, 245, 280, 283
dishwashers in, 66, 105, 126, 263
doubling as tables, 29, 36, 38, 39
French-style, 232, 233, 234–235, 236, 240–241, 242–243, 245, 250
going without, 11, 32
hardworking, 71, 75
lazy Susan at end of, 252
lighting on, 290
lighting over, 18, 48, 58–59, 71, 77, 101, 126, 179, 199, 250, 272, 287, 288, 289, 291
L-shaped, 16–17, 18
multiple, 190, 191, 210, 251, 254, 263, 287, 300–301, 305
niches in, 229, 270–271
outdoor, 24–25
oval, 96–97, 98
overview break-out session, 250–255
range in, 299. See also cooktops in
refrigerator drawers in, 174, 177
seating at, 16–17, 24–25, 36, 71, 74, 77, 100, 142–143, 162, 171, 200–201, 210, 245, 299, 312–317

shelving in, 85, 250, 266, 270–271, 272, 293

sinks in, 65, 66, 68, 114, 126, 129, 168, 210, 251, 280

size of, 40, 53, 66, 74, 136, 139, 143, 162, 190, 201, 205, 227, 276

in small spaces, 215

sofa up against, 104–105

turned legs on, 211

on wheels, 255, 297

wine storage in, 173

wood, 83

J

Japanese-style kitchen, 164–169

K

Knives and knife storage, 37, 61, 117, 126, 137, 196, 213, 251

L

Lava stone countertop, 261

Lighting, 286–291

brands of. See Lighting (brands/suppliers)

bulbs, 287

chandeliers. See Lighting (chandeliers)

on islands, 290

over islands, 18, 48, 58–59, 71, 77, 101, 126, 179, 199, 250, 272, 287, 288, 289, 291

lampshades matching chairs, 50, 51

lanterns. See Lighting (lanterns)

lesson on, 286–291

outdoor kitchen, 26, 29

pendants. See Lighting (pendants)

recesses. See Lighting (recessed)

sconces. See Lighting (sconces)

standard ceiling fixtures, 48

track, 287, 290

under-cabinet, 126

under-counter, 287, 290

Lighting (brands/suppliers)

Allan Knight and Associates, 212

Ann-Morris Antiques, 36, 133, 135, 162, 240, 243, 302, 307, 309

Arteriors Home, 21

Baker Furniture, 289

Baker Signature Lighting, 111

BoBo Intriguing Objects, 250

Bourgeois Bohème, 58

Charles Edwards, 199

Circa Home Living, 291

Circa Lighting, 147, 275

Coe Studios, 25

CX Design, 64

David Iatesta, 145

Demolition Depot & Irreplaceable Artifacts, 124

Dennis & Leen, 290

Dessin Fournir, 286

Fourteenth Colony Lighting, 231, 289

Holophane, 36, 135, 139, 162

Hudson Valley Lighting, 18

Ikea, 127, 150

Jamie Young Company, 15

John Beck Paper & Steel, 289

Kichler Lighting, 177, 289

Lampworks, 217

Licht im Raum, 54, 57

Lowe's, 31

Motif Designs, 289

Niermann Weeks, 131

Obsolete, 129

O'Lampia, 126

Pacific City, 262

Pagani, 289

Portfolio, 30

PW Vintage Lighting, 139

Rachel Ashwell, 130

Rejuvenation, 49, 179, 181, 262, 268, 285, 289, 297

Remains, 77, 289

Restoration Hardware, 139, 305

Rhone, 262, 268

Rose Tarlow Melrose House, 101

Sea Gull Lighting, 177

Serena & Lily, 69

Tom Dixon, 287

trans.LUXE, 50

Troy, 29

Tuvalu Home, 95

Urban Archeology, 21, 135, 137, 190, 210

Urban Electric Company, 289

Vaughan, 35, 226–227, 287

Visual Comfort, 71, 147, 202, 288, 289

Willis, 285

Lighting (chandeliers)

amidst hanging pot rack, 111

from antique bronze sconces, 96–97, 99

antler, 22

beachy, 69

bead and tassel, 147

burnished iron, 101

crystal, 119, 130, 145

ladylike, contrasting rough walls with, 130, 131

massive iron, 235

outdoor kitchen, 26

over island, 250

post-modern/pre-Edison combo, 212, 213

rope (1940s-style), 76–77

simple Louis XIV, 296

stainless-steel, 54

wood and iron, 291

Lighting (lanterns)

Asian fish-trap, 252

burnished iron, 286

centerpiece, 21

exotic look, 35

French-style, 231, 249

oversized black, 291

red toile, 226

sconces, 31

silver-leaf, 33

Lighting (pendants)

brass, 126, 272

buying en masse, 139

choosing, 291

double, brass, 126

double row of, 177

French-style, 129

gallery of, 289

hanging from dark chains, 163

industrial metal, 58–59

industrial-look, 135, 190, 197

mismatched, 11, 15, 287, 288

Murano glass, 64–65

Old-English mood, 302, 305

outdoor kitchen, 177

(not) over island, 272

over island, 18, 77, 287, 291

oversized lanterns, 291

in pot rack, 305

retro, 127

simple white opaque, 127

traditional minimalist, 133

types and models, 21

upholstered shades, 50, 51

vintage-look, 11, 15, 36, 77, 124, 129, 135, 139, 217, 285, 297, 307

Lighting (recessed)
alternatives/
complements to,
49, 77, 126, 181,
190, 272, 287, 290.
See also Lighting
(pendants); Lighting
(sconces)
bulbs for, 287
in cabinets, 13
concrete ceilings and, 290
square-shaped, 74
Lighting (sconces).
See also Lighting
(lanterns)
chandelier from,
96–97, 99
double candlestick, 290
flower bouquet, 95
industrial/boathouse-
style, 137, 139
old-fashioned charm,
179, 181
outdoor kitchen, 25, 29
17th-century Italian, 106
unkitchen-y, 94, 95
Limestone
characteristics of,
134–135
flooring, 134–135, 156,
249, 305
hood, 84
hood (faux limestone), 79
Iscan Blue, 134–135
in linoleum, 159
mantel, 229
pinned, 84
stove surround, 251
travertine, 94
Limestone countertops, 108
antique, from France, 12
Beauharnais, 249
CaesarStone and, 302
characteristics of, 257
French, 240–241, 257
Gascogne Blue, 77
Greek/Baltic vs.
French, 257
Lagos Azul, 108, 310
marble vs., 108

Petit Granit, 31
Velvet Taupe
Antique, 113

M

Marble
backsplashes, 72, 98–
99, 138, 141, 183
benefits of, 63
countertops. *See*
Marble countertops
flooring, 110
ice-cream counter,
194–195, 196
kitchen featuring,
214–217
limestone vs., 108
open-backed cabinets
on, 216
sink, 114
stainless-steel sink
set in, 206
wall niche, 214–216
wall tile, 49, 51, 115,
186, 214–216
Marble countertops
baking and, 251, 252,
263, 304, 305
Black Portoro, 197
CaesarStone look-alike,
277, 278, 302
Calacatta, 83, 220, 313
Calacatta Gold, 72,
142, 161, 214–215,
216, 228, 234–235,
236, 239
Calcutta Gold, 108
Calcutta Gold vs.
Carrara, 106
Carrara, 36, 48–49,
103, 123, 133, 136,
137, 140–141, 170–
172, 173, 174, 175,
186, 188–189, 190,
253, 257, 269
Danby, 186, 240
dealing with water
marks, 63
extra thick, 106, 142–
143, 246, 304

granite vs., 172, 180,
228, 257
islands, 16–17, 18,
24–25, 97, 106, 123,
136, 142–143, 171,
252, 261, 264,
269, 286
Nero Marquina, 293
removing stains from, 261
salvaged, 152
scratches and stains,
246, 261, 302
simplicity of, 198
Thassos, 131
Verde Guatemala,
60–61, 63
Vermont Quarries, 246
White Manhattan
Calacatta, 180
wood and, 18, 21, 126,
145, 193
Martin-Senour Paints
Belgian Endive, 100
Soapstone, 100
Spartan Stone, 100
Microwaves, 56, 66, 69,
89, 215, 223, 246, 251
Mirrors
cabinet backs, 287
cabinet fronts, 13, 15, 222
expanding space, 38
reflecting window
views, 96–97, 101

N

Napkins, 41, 197, 204,
213, 275
"New Victorian" kitchens
about: definition of, 262
Bridging the Centuries
(new with old),
262–267
Engrained Beauty
(paneled elegance),
270–275
New Found Glory
(Virginian beauty),
282–285

Old School
(elegant schoolboy
memories), 276–281
Southern Hospitality
(Old South look),
268–269

O

Object lessons
chill (refrigerators,
freezers, and
coolers), 42–47
chop & roll (countertops),
256–261
glow (lighting), 286–291
H_2O (faucets and
sinks), 112–117
heat (cooktops, ranges
hoods), 84–89
splash (backsplashes),
182–187
store your stuff, 218–223
take a seat (chairs and
stools), 312–317
tread (flooring), 154–159
Old Fashioned Milk Paint
Company, Bayberry
Green, 266
Onyx countertop, 258
Onyx tile, 185
Outdoor kitchens, 24–29,
176–177
Ovens. *See* Drawers,
warming ovens;
Ranges

P

Paint and stain colors. *See
also specific paint
company names*
blues, 34, 80, 110, 174,
177, 238, 246
browns, beiges, and
tans, 100, 163, 204,
238, 251, 273,
275, 284
grays, 74, 100, 108, 138,
230, 253, 269
greens, 80, 82, 148,
221, 230, 266, 307

mixed into concrete, 28
reds, 58–59
stained and unstained
  wood, 56, 168, 274
whites, 14, 20, 34, 51,
  68, 77, 94, 100, 113,
  126, 132, 141, 146,
  180, 186, 192, 204,
  212, 272, 280, 285
yellows, 28, 138
Paneled kitchens, 104–
  109, 270–275
Pantries
  armoires as, 39, 145
  bins in, 279, 304
  butler's, 37, 270, 273,
    275, 294, 297, 298
  cabinets as, 20, 60, 63,
    146, 190
  color palettes, 108,
    138, 275
  command central,
    92–93
  dishwashers in, 135
  dual sinks in, 92
  farmhouse-style, 108
  ladders in, 265, 267
  lighting in, 95
  mudroom doubling as,
    246, 247
  pull-out, 60, 63, 164,
    223, 237
  refrigerators in,
    105, 135
  shelving in, 265, 298
  showing off china, 273
  three separate, 138
Pendant lighting. See
  Lighting (pendants)
Pietra Cardosa countertops,
  143, 145
Pietra del Cardoso
  countertops, 214, 216
"Plain Spoken" kitchens
  about: definition of, 160
  Aqua Fresca (outdoor
    kitchen), 176–177
  Rhapsody in Blue
    (intense blue hue),
    170–175

Ship Shape (nautical
  style), 160–163
Wabi-Sabi (Japanese
  style), 164–169
Wall Art (accent wall
  scene-stealer),
  178–181
Planning kitchens, 36–41
Plate racks, 83, 144, 198,
  199, 303
Plates and dinnerware. See
  also Collections
  contrasting against
    shelves/cabinets, 51
  French dessert plates, 297
  handcrafted, 169
  multitask, 95
  plain white, 101, 102–103
  storing. See Cabinet
    references; Plate racks;
    Shelving (open)
Porcelain collectibles, 35,
  173, 175, 267
Porcelain sinks, 73, 179
Porcelain tiles, 157
Pot faucets. See Faucets, pot
Pot racks, 22, 60–61, 111,
  242–243, 253,
  263, 305
Potted plant holder,
  hanging, 26
Pratt & Lambert paints
  Chalk Gray, 74
  Glacier Sand, 186
  Pacific, 307
Prints over sink, 98, 101

R

Ralph Lauren Paint,
  Pocket Watch
  White, 180
Range hoods. See Hoods
Ranges, 84–89. See also
  Ranges (brands)
  alcoves/niches, 14, 22,
    106, 107, 136, 187,
    214–215, 216, 231,
    251, 290
  with backsplash, 101

dual-fuel, 36, 84, 87,
  146, 160, 171,
  200–201, 228
in islands, 299
knife block next to, 213
ledge behind, 107
lesson on, 84–89
open shelves by, 85,
  107, 123
salamander broiler
  with, 85
six-burner, 14, 68, 85,
  123, 174, 238
stainless-steel, 33, 68,
  79, 86, 87, 101,
  106, 136, 146,
  170–171, 181
unobtrusive, 95
Ranges (brands)
  Aga, 87
  Bertazzoni, 87
  Blue Star, 85, 238
  Dacor, 87
  Garland, 181
  GE, 140
  Kenmore, 87
  La Cornue, 33, 86
  Lacanche, 163, 184, 299
  Smeg, 87
  Thermador, 111, 196
  Viking, 14, 18, 22, 68,
    86, 95, 106, 129, 146,
    160, 171, 174, 198,
    200–201, 214–215
  Wolf, 36, 79, 84, 123, 136,
    210, 228, 265, 300
"Rebel" kitchens
  about: definition of, 90
  Double Take (dining-
    room kitchen),
    102–103
  Fantasy Follows
    Function (paneled
    "non-kitchen"),
    104–109
  Grand Manner (glamour
    and grace), 96–101
  Hidden Gem (artfully
    disguised kitchen),
    90–95

Read All About
  It (library-style
  kitchen), 110–111
Recessed lighting. See
  Lighting (recessed)
Recycled products, 150, 152,
  153, 159, 261, 280
Recycling bins, 63, 149, 251
Red paint colors, 58–59
Refrigerators/freezers,
  42–47. See also
  Refrigerators/freezers
  (brands); Wine
  cellars/coolers
  drawers, 45, 46, 75, 83,
    174, 177, 237,
    251, 293
  glass doors on, 42
  ice maker separate
    from, 46
  lesson on, 42–47
  like period cabinetry, 299
  matching cabinets, 43,
    64, 147, 171
  pass-through, 295
  sizes of, 42
  stainless-steel, 40, 44,
    274, 277, 295
  undercounter, 46
  zinc-clad, 23
Refrigerators/freezers
  (brands)
  Bosch, 45
  Liebherr, 45, 47
  Miele, 45
  Smeg, 43
  Sub Zero, 18, 37,
    44, 45, 72, 75, 82,
    83, 92, 128–129,
    170–171, 174, 177,
    237, 265, 274, 293,
    300–301, 302, 303,
    308–309
  Traulsen, 42, 43, 293,
    294, 295
  Whirlpool, 45

"Revival" kitchens (rooted in history). *See* "Belle de Campagne" kitchens; "New Victorian" kitchens; "Scullery" kitchens

"Rough Luxe" kitchens
  about: definition of, 10
  Barn Raising (new old-barn look), 30–35
  Different Strokes (mottled backsplashes and wood grains), 16–21
  Garden Party (outdoor kitchen), 24–29
  Old News (ancient-timbered farmhouse), 22–23
  Raw Ingredients (bohemian cottage wannabe), 10–15

S

Scandinavian look, 198–199

Schoolboy memories, 276–281

Sconces. *See* Lighting (sconces)

"Scullery" kitchens
  about: definition of, 292
  American Splendor (modern 19th-century beauty), 298–299
  English Complexion (English countryside feel), 300–305
  History Lesson (retro-renovation), 306–307
  Repeat Performance (old-world country style), 292–297
  Small Talk (big kitchen in small space), 308–311

Seating lesson, 312–317. *See also* Chairs; Stools

Shelving (open)
  bar area, 22, 33, 41

baskets on, 161

benefits of, 195

for collections. *See* Collections

elegant exposed kitchen, 188–193

holding two rooms together, 219

in islands, 85, 250, 266, 270–271, 272, 293

19th-century aura, 307

in pantries, 108, 265

pitchers on, 194–195, 196, 197

polished nickel frame, 144

by range, 85, 107, 123

small spaces and, 221

steel, 194–195, 200, 214–215, 217

styling items on, 141

white, 38, 49, 51, 81, 102–103, 129, 140, 141, 188–189, 192, 200–201, 206, 209

wood, 53, 111

Sherwin-Williams paints
  Bewitching Blue SW 6960, 80
  Pure White, 212

"Shopkeeper" kitchens
  about: definition of, 188
  The Chef ecommends (chef's haven), 200–205
  Northern Light (Scandinavian look), 198–199
  Parlor Game (ice-cream parlor feel), 194–197
  Shelf Life (open-shelf beauty), 188–193
  Small Miracle (gorgeous tiny space), 206–207
  Stone Cold Gorgeous (marble, mosaics, and more), 214–217
  Taking Stock (canned goods as art), 208–213

Sink mats, 157

Sink sprayers, industrial, 30, 35, 92, 95, 114, 129, 131, 136, 137, 176, 191, 302

Sinks, 112–117. *See also Faucets references*; Sinks (brands)
  apron-front, 113
  bar, 66, 210
  black, 216
  cabinets camouflaging, 90, 91
  in chest of drawers, 97
  copper, 25, 29, 113, 114, 236, 273
  countertops and, 113, 168
  deciding on one or two, 278
  extra-long, 12, 92
  farmhouse-style, 12, 35, 73, 127, 131, 180, 210, 216, 246, 303
  faucet-free prep, 55
  gallery of, 117
  German silver, 112, 243, 246, 247
  glass-topped, 117
  hammered nickel, 126
  in islands, 65, 66, 68, 114, 126, 129, 168, 210, 251, 280
  lesson on faucets and, 112–117
  lighting over, 29, 95, 137
  marble, 114
  modular, 117
  mosaic stainless, 117
  nickel silver. *See* German silver
  outdoor kitchen, 29
  placement of, 68, 106
  porcelain, 73, 179
  prep, 55, 93, 251
  prints over, 98, 101
  S-curve in, 117
  setting into countertops, 21

  stainless-steel, 108, 113, 116, 117, 137, 140, 161, 168, 174, 191, 206, 210, 211, 248, 278
  undermounted, 98, 102, 108, 113, 116, 137, 140, 146, 161, 180, 206, 303
  windows above, 29, 34

Sinks (brands)
  American Standard, 117
  Blanco, 102, 140, 166
  Elkay, 64, 116, 117, 162, 174
  Franke, 108, 113, 117, 136, 137, 176, 191, 210, 248, 283, 303
  German Silver Sink Company, 112, 117, 247
  Ikea, 31
  Julien, 117
  Kallista, 129, 310
  Kohler, 73, 117, 151, 203, 210, 251, 278
  Linkasink, 29, 117, 246
  Mythos, 117
  Native Trails, 25, 236
  Shaws Original fireclay, 12
  Waterworks, 14, 114, 115, 126, 127, 131, 132, 146
  Zeus, 113

Slate countertops, 158, 257

Slatelike countertops, 143, 261

Small spaces, 60–63, 206–207, 308–311

Soapstone countertops, 129, 184, 209, 233, 257, 264, 267, 283

Solar energy, 150

Southern charm, 268–269, 282–285

Spice storage, 63, 139

Spoons. *See* Utensil storage

Squak Mountain Stone, 261

Stainless steel
absence of, 218
backsplashes, 68, 182, 220
benefits of, 259
cabinet pulls, 57, 141
cabinets, 25, 27, 29, 65,
66, 69, 136, 216
chandelier, 55
countertop compost
bin, 151
countertops, 91, 92,
166, 168, 254, 259
dish drainer, 303
dishwashers, 40, 118, 119
downside of, 40, 179
hoods, 68, 72, 132–133,
136, 170–171,
176, 181
lighting, 289
maintaining
countertops, 259
outdoor kitchens
and, 25, 28, 29
paint colors with, 68, 82
ranges, 33, 68, 79, 86,
87, 101, 106, 136,
146, 170–171, 181
refrigerators, 40, 44,
274, 277, 295
salamander broiler, 85
shelving, 194–195, 200
sinks, 108, 113, 116,
117, 137, 140, 161,
168, 174, 191, 206,
210, 211, 248, 278
stools, 288
tray for cooking oils/
herbs, 129
utensils, 205
warming harshness of,
68, 129, 135, 171
wine cabinet, 47
Stone. See specific stone types
Stools
aluminum, 254, 315
backs for, 317
bar, 22, 24–25, 41,
77, 210, 270–271,
313, 315–317

bistro-style, 178–179
brushed-aluminum, 52
chairs instead of, 202
choosing, 317
dark, in white
kitchen, 317
English refectory–
style, 277, 281
farmhouse/basic,
74, 142–143
French-inspired,
226–227, 231
gallery of, 315
with goat's feet, 317
height of, 57
leather-covered, 54,
77, 210, 277, 281
leg room for, 316
lesson on seating,
312–317
making kitchen
snappy, 313
matching chairs
to, 275, 314
modern, 269, 288,
303, 305, 315
popularity of, 312
retro, 54, 190
screw-top, 41
Shinto, 75
simple, 316
space required per
stool, 313, 316
springs as, 313
stainless-steel, 288
for two, 315
upholstered, 49, 50,
181, 313, 316
vintage, 299
Windsor chair,
132–133, 312
Storage, 218–223. See also
Baskets; Cabinets
references; Drawers;
Knives and knife
storage; Shelving
(open); Spice storage;
Utensil storage

T
Tables (kitchen and dining)
antique, 59
banquette at, 212
butcher-block, 181
counter-height, 54,
57. See also islands
doubling as
Danish white, 192
dark, good-looking,
144, 147
dining-table-in-kitchen
considerations, 32, 65
Eero Saarinen, 50
as entertainment focal
point, 20
European antique,
110–111
family-focus, 32,
90–91, 130
French farmhouse, 32,
125, 144, 194–195,
197, 230, 266
glass-top satin nickel,
64–65
islands doubling as, 29,
36, 38, 39. See
also Islands
Italian Renaissance–
style, 296
lighting over.
See Lighting
(chandeliers);
Lighting (pendants)
in living room, 90–91, 94
long, 90–91, 94, 103, 212
marble, 97, 261, 264
oak, 103
outdoor furniture, 26, 232
reclaimed wood, 54
rustic stone, 77
setting, 204, 281
tavern, with blue
painted legs, 285
teak, 95
travertine, 94
walnut, 10–11, 164–
165, 166, 169
zinc-topped, 26, 230, 231

Tan paint colors. See Paint
and stain colors
Tile. See also Backsplashes
(tile); Flooring (tile
and stone); Tile (wall)
blue, 83
choosing, 40
concrete, 81
French-style, 81, 83
grout color, 183
multicolored, 81
shelves, 246
white, 127
wood-look porcelain,
35, 157
Tile (wall). See also
Backsplashes (tile)
blue glass, 179, 181
blue-and-white scenic,
234–235, 237,
238, 239
ceramic white, 127
floor- or counter-to-
ceiling, 123, 144,
183, 242–243, 247,
295–296
Gothic, 41
green glass, 305
handmade star and
cross, 188
hand-painted, 228,
237, 238
marble, 49, 51, 115,
186, 214–216
mural, 228
pale chartreuse, 38
subway-tile, 135, 136,
183, 194–195,
242–243, 247, 294,
295–296
white hand-poured, 189
Towel racks, 281, 295, 300
Tray storage, 251, 292
Trays, behind dishes, 51, 196
Triangle, work (cooking),
113, 149, 162

U

Utensil storage, 2, 37, 60, 117, 123, 193, 196, 197, 198, 205, 206, 223. *See also* Drawers; Knives and knife storage

V

Victorian kitchens. *See* "New Victorian" kitchens

W

Walnut
cabinets, 16–17, 18, 19, 165, 166–167, 276–277
flooring, 10–11, 164, 212, 230, 280
inside cabinets, 19, 21
paneling, 105, 106, 109
tables and chairs, 10–11, 164–165, 166, 169
warmth and texture of, 168
White kitchens. *See* "Addicted to Alabaster" kitchens; Cabinets, white
White paint colors. *See* Paint and stain colors
Window seat, 266
Window treatments
adding texture with, 163
going without, 138, 143, 246
lace, 12
shades, 69, 77, 163, 180, 213, 240–241
valances, 283
Windows
adding, 75, 91
awning, 30–31, 34
bay, 97, 100
casement, 83
desk by, 203
double-height ceiling and, 137, 139, 145

graphic patterns at, 181
inside cupboard, 306
interior wall of, 37
low-E, 148
mirrors reflecting, 96–97, 101
in outdoor kitchen wall, 29
Palladian, 212, 269
peekaboo interior, 284
pots hanging in front of, 191
repositioning, 140
seating by, 10–11, 19, 20, 37, 167
wall of, without cabinets, 293
Wine cellars/coolers, 37, 41, 47, 173
Wine racks, 22, 46, 47, 51, 55, 56, 57

Y

Yellow paint colors, 28, 138

Z

Zinc
appliances clad with, 23
countertops, 23
hoods, 38, 240
tabletops, 26, 230, 231

INDEX OF DESIGNERS AND ARCHITECTS

A

Abbott, Dana, 253
Adler, Jonathan, 48–51
Allman, Michele, 226–231
Angle, Alexandra, 221

B

Baird, Penny Drue, 82
Bakes, Robert, 16–18,
    19, 21, 40
Barrett, Judith, 134–139
Bell, Jason, 82, 154
Bell, Robin, 256
Berger, Jonathan, 222
Berman, Michael, 159
Bernhard, Dianne,
    176–177
Bilhuber, Jeffrey, 306–307
Bird, Sandra, 38, 41, 113
Bond, Lindsey, 140–141
Boorstein, James, 155, 159
Booth, Ray, 252
Bowers, Shannon, 81
Brinson, Jill Sharp, 261
Brooks, Ursula, 43
Brown, Alton, 218
Brown, Betsy, 102–103
Browne, Rosemary, 271

C

Cargill, Katrin, 198–199
Cheng, Fu-Tung, 220
Cohen, Lisa, 234–239
Colicchio, Tom, 40
Cummings, Eleanor, 22–23

D

De Giulio, Mick, 42, 46,
    84, 142–147
Decesare, Caroline, 208–213
Del Piero, Michael, 261
Deniot, Jean-Louis, 159
Derrick, Kimball, 312,
    313, 316, 317
Derse, Athalie, 257
Dhong, Benjamin, 220
Diamond, William, 261
Dixon, Barry, 252
Dixon, Stanley, 253
Donovan, T. Keller, 250,
    259, 291, 312
Dossetter, Susan, 43, 44, 86
Dunham, Peter, 58–59
Duté, Michael, 83

E

Einhorn, Sharone, 118
Eisner, Chad, 38, 186
Ellsley, Beverly, 187
Ewart, Krista, 43

F

Fazio, Alexandra, 16–20
Fee, Kathryn, 170–175
Fernandez, Waldo, 257
Ferrier, Susan, 251, 316
Fishel, Peter, 42, 85, 116,
    156, 255
Fouquet, Kim, 41, 64–69
Fulk, Ken, 288, 313

G

Gambrel, Steven, 76–77,
    298–299
Garten, Ina, 37,
    200–203, 290
Giogaia, Louis, 86
Glasser, Carol, 198–199
Gorrivan, Philip, 116
Gottschall, Jamie, 252

H

Hamel, Thomas, 287
Hanes, Smith, 250
Hayne, Hillary, 10–15
Hefner, William, 70–75
Hoefer, Myra, 317
Hoffman, Marty, 154, 158
Holland, Sandi, 160–163
Hudson, R. Roman, 85, 112

J

Jayne, Thomas, 282–285
Jeffers, Jay, 218

K

Kamens, Adam, 259
Kaufman, Donald, 79
Kedigian, Garrow, 219
Kennedy, Mary Richardson,
    148–151
Kettles, Craig, 262–267
Kincaid, Cathy, 240–241
King, Jonathan, 5, 188–193
Koepke, Sandy, 24–28
Kramer, Brenda Kelly, 152

L

Lalli, Carole, 122–127
Larette, Jean, 317
Larkins, Ty, 268–269
Leslie, Mark, 96–101
Lewis, Jeff, 52–57
Lyon, Dana, 232–233

M

MacIsaac, Heather
    Smith, 220
Mann, David, 254
Marshall, Mallory, 254
Martin, Erin, 83, 84,
    255, 258
McCarthy, Lisa, 170–175
McDowell, Kelley, 291
Mendelson, Gideon, 82
Miller, Anne, 287
Mitchell, David, 155, 183
Moore, Joeb, 36–37
Musser, Hilary, 242–247

N

Neunsinger, Amy, 128–131
Norris, Richard, 96–101

O

O'Brien, Thomas,
    251, 289, 305
Oetgen, John, 38
O'Neill, Ellen, 206–207

P

Patterson, McKee, 270–275
Peacock, Christopher, 40,
82, 223, 276–281, 297
Pearson, Anik, 260
Pennoyer, Peter, 282–285
Penry, Casey, 286, 287,
290, 291
Perchuk, Florence, 257, 261
Pohl, Ray, 160–163
Pounds, Melanie, 40, 184
Proctor, Bill, 256
Pursley, Ken, 104–109,
221, 290

Q

Quinn, Matthew, 40

R

Radin, James, 132–133
Redd, Miles, 41, 82
Roberts, Markham, 314
Rodgers, Marguerite,
164–169
Roop, Frank, 187
Rottman, Christina, 78–79
Ruhland, Dan, 158

S

Saladino, John, 286
Sallick, Barbara, 182, 183,
186, 187
Scarborough, Terry, 40
Scheerer, Tom, 316
Schindler, Joan, 194–197,
292–297
Schnell, Paige, 186
Schrage, Diana, 112, 113
Schumacher, Craig, 39
Segalman, Eileen, 118
Segura, Jacqueline
Derrey, 155
Selke, Annie, 40
Slatkin, Harry, 214–217
Smith, Michael S., 114,
129, 183, 308–311
Smith, Windsor, 110–111
Sommers, Ruthie, 313
Stilin, Robert, 200–203
Stokes, Stephanie, 60–63
Stott, James, 188–193
Strum, Adam, 47
Stuart, Madeline, 86, 118,
254, 259

T

Tiddens, Katherine, 152
Trifiro, Dionne, 300–305
Tucker, Suzanne, 248–249

V

Valencich, Erinn, 152
Vallone, Berkley, 208–213
Veltman, Ruard, 90–95

W

Wade, Patrick, 46, 257
Watson, Marshall, 152,
178–181
Weiner, Stephen, 119
Westbrook, Barbara, 219
Wilson, Robin, 148–149, 150
Wolf, Ann, 182, 221
Wolf, Vicente, 152
Wong, Eldon, 51, 113, 259

Y

Yager, Megan Rice, 30–35

HEARSTBOOKS

An Imprint of Sterling Publishing
1166 Avenue of the Americas
New York, NY 10036

ISBN 978-1-58816-900-6

    Library of Congress Cataloging-in-Publication Data
Cregan, Lisa.
  House Beautiful kitchens / Lisa Cregan.
      p. cm.
  Includes index.
  ISBN 978-1-58816-900-6 (print format) – ISBN 978-1-58816-957-0 (ebook)
  1. Kitchens. 2. Interior decoration. I. House beautiful. II. Title.
  NK2117.K5C74 2012
  747.7'97–dc23
          2011032366

Distributed in Canada by Sterling Publishing
c/o Canadian Manda Group, 664 Annette Street
Toronto, Ontario, Canada M6S 2C8

Distributed in the United Kingdom by GMC Distribution Services
Castle Place, 166 High Street, Lewes, East Sussex, England BN7 1XU

Distributed in Australia by Capricorn Link (Australia) Pty. Ltd.
P.O. Box 704, Windsor, NSW 2756, Australia

For information about custom editions, special sales, and premium and corporate purchases,
please contact Sterling Special Sales at 800-805-5489 or specialsales@sterlingpublishing.com.

Manufactured in China

10 9 8 7 6 5 4 3

www.sterlingpublishing.com

EVERYONE WANTS TO BE IN THE KITCHEN.